The Academic Skills Handbook

Sara Miller McCune founded SAGE Publishing in 1965 to support the dissemination of usable knowledge and educate a global community. SAGE publishes more than 1000 journals and over 800 new books each year, spanning a wide range of subject areas. Our growing selection of library products includes archives, data, case studies and video. SAGE remains majority owned by our founder and after her lifetime will become owned by a charitable trust that secures the company's continued independence.

Los Angeles | London | New Delhi | Singapore | Washington DC | Melbourne

SAGE Study Skills

The Academic Skills Handbook

Diana Hopkins & Tom Reid

Your Guide to Success
in Writing, Thinking and
Communicating at University

Los Angeles | London | New Delhi
Singapore | Washington DC | Melbourne

Los Angeles | London | New Delhi
Singapore | Washington DC | Melbourne

SAGE Publications Ltd
1 Oliver's Yard
55 City Road
London EC1Y 1SP

SAGE Publications Inc.
2455 Teller Road
Thousand Oaks, California 91320

SAGE Publications India Pvt Ltd
B 1/I 1 Mohan Cooperative Industrial Area
Mathura Road
New Delhi 110 044

SAGE Publications Asia-Pacific Pte Ltd
3 Church Street
#10–04 Samsung Hub
Singapore 049483

Editor: Mila Steele
Assistant editor/Editorial assistant: John
    Nightingale/Shelley De Jong
Assistant editor, digital: Chloe Statham
Production editor: Nicola Carrier
Copyeditor: Andy Baxter
Proofreader: Derek Markham
Indexer: Silvia Benvenuto
Marketing manager: Catherine Slinn
Cover design: Shaun Mercier
Typeset by: C&M Digitals (P) Ltd, Chennai, India
Printed in the UK

Library of Congress Control Number: 2018935291

British Library Cataloguing in Publication data

A catalogue record for this book is available from
the British Library

ISBN 978-1-4739-9714-1
ISBN 978-1-4739-9715-8 (pbk)

At SAGE we take sustainability seriously. Most of our products are printed in the UK using responsibly sourced
papers and boards. When we print overseas we ensure sustainable papers are used as measured by the PREPS
grading system. We undertake an annual audit to monitor our sustainability.

CONTENTS

ACKNOWLEDGEMENTS

Our thanks go firstly to our Commissioning Editor, Mila Steele, whose vision and constant support got this book off the ground. Thanks also to our Assistant Editor John Nightingale, who has worked patiently with us and whose positivity and enthusiasm has kept us going, and to Nicola Carrier for all her work on the production side. Many thanks also to all at SAGE Publishing who have contributed along the way, and to the readers involved on commenting on early drafts. And of course we would like to acknowledge the generosity and help provided by our contributors, listed below, all of whom have allowed us to use their work as models and/or tasks in this book. Specifically, thanks to:

John-Mark Allen
Abigail Burns
Dan Challinor
Gabriella Chapman
Claire Garnett
Rose Gerrard
Sophie Hedges
Yishu Hu
Laura Kurz
Sarah Lewis
Owain Matthews
George Millsopp
Alexander Nettle
Laura Nettle
Toby Fenton-O'Creevy
Gaby Oliver
Katharina Richard
Amelia Shuttle
Alec Stokes
Jonny Wordsworth
Rebecca Young

And finally, a thank you to our families, Laura, Alexander, and Ned, Jeni and Erin, for their support, understanding and encouragement at every stage in this long journey.

INTRODUCTION

Welcome to *The Academic Skills Handbook.*

Congratulations!

You have succeeded in the first steps towards your future. You have gained a place at university and the world of knowledge awaits your arrival.

Now let the learning begin!

UNDERSTANDING ACADEMIC CULTURE

Going to university can be an amazing and life-changing experience, and present a mind-boggling array of possibilities for intellectual development, self-improvement, new friendships and more. But it can also be a culture shock and you may find yourself on a steep learning curve when it comes to your studies. But like any move to a new culture, you need to plan and prepare carefully to ensure you get the most out of your visit.

This involves becoming familiar with and then mastering the academic rules, conventions, practices and behaviours of your hosts, so that slowly you learn how to apply these effectively in your academic work, integrate and flourish in the new culture, and succeed in your university studies.

This is where *The Academic Skills Handbook* comes in. Our book will equip you with all the essential academic skills you will need to excel in your academic aspirations.

WHAT IS *THE ACADEMIC SKILLS HANDBOOK?*

The *Academic Skills Handbook* is a one-stop shop for all your academic skills needs. It is a highly practical and hands-on toolkit to help you learn, build and extend your skills in all areas of your study, from essay and scientific writing, presentations, note-taking and seminars, to research reading and critical thinking.

Who is the book for?

The Academic Skills Handbook is for:

- **New Undergraduates** – our book will help you step up from A level to university level study.

- **New Postgraduates**, returning to higher education – for those students moving directly from undergraduate level study or re-entering higher education after a break, our book will help you re-orientate and refresh your skills, and build your confidence.
- **Continuing Undergraduates and Postgraduates** – our book will help you develop and extend your academic skills, troubleshoot issues you have encountered in your studies, and improve your performance in course work, assignments and assessments.

What is covered in the book?

The Academic Skills Handbook encompasses three areas of expertise.

1. Assignment Process and Key Features

   This area includes: step-by-step action plans on how to get started on your first assignments; analysis of structural features; and reading, critical thinking and analysis.

2. Core Skills

   There are five core skills at the heart of effective communication in all genres of writing and speaking:

   - Accuracy
   - Style
   - Clarity
   - Concision
   - Being informed.

These five core skills inform the content of *The Academic Skills Handbook*, with dedicated chapters to help you apply them with confidence and expertise.

3. Samples Library

   You will have access to real-world examples of students' written work across a variety of disciplines; from standard and reflective essays, to lab reports, and longer works such as literature reports and dissertations. The samples library provides models of good academic practice to help inform your academic writing development.

The Academic Skills Handbook – areas of expertise

The three areas of expertise combine to maximise your skills development (Figures I.1 and I.2).

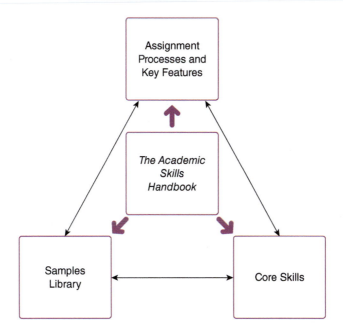

Figure I.1 Areas of expertise covered in *The Academic Skills Handbook*

How is the book organised?

For ease of navigation, the book is divided into three Parts with dedicated chapters.

Part 1: Writing Skills, Chapters 1–8

We begin with an easy to use and highly practical step-by-step guide on how to get started on your first essay and lab report. We unpack the key stages; from assignment analysis, planning, structuring and preparation through to incorporating your research, drafting and completion. We also include analysis of key structural features and academic conventions, and provide an annotated sample of each type of assignment.

Part 2: Reading and Critical Analysis Skills, Chapters 9–10

We provide help and advice on how to organise your reading and research skills. We show you how to plan, manage and use your reading to maximise the effectiveness of your assignments. We provide guidance on how to include evaluation and criticality in your work to help you achieve a good outcome.

Part 3: Presentations, Speaking and Listening Skills, Chapters 11–14

Of course, it's not all about the writing. In this book you will find helpful ideas about how to build your confidence in your presentation skills. We lead you

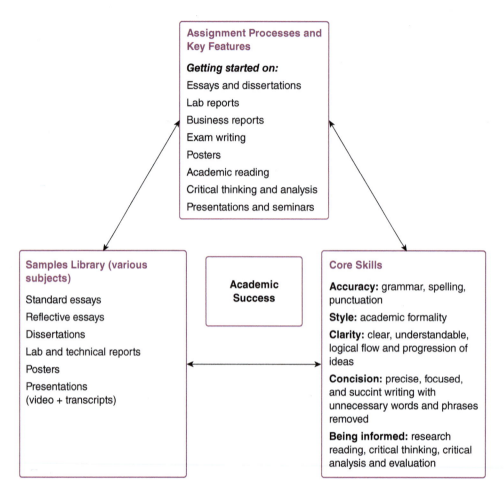

Figure I.2 Combined areas of expertise

through the steps you should take to create a presentation you are proud of, and we raise your awareness of the sorts of tasks you may find in a seminar or workshop. We also provide tips on how to ensure you get the most out of your lectures, including tips on preparation, note-taking and reflection.

Organisation of chapters

Each chapter has a similar format which includes:

- Dashboards

  o The chapter begins with 'Your chapter dashboard'. The dashboard provides a snapshot of the chapter topic and aims. The dashboard also includes the chapter diagnostic (see below).

- The Diagnostic
  - The chapter diagnostics are designed to help you identify your strengths and weaknesses in specific skills areas, and which parts of the chapter you should focus on. You can then navigate your way through the book according to your needs.

- Input and practice tasks
  - The chapter provides comprehensive input on key skills areas and guidance on what is expected and how to improve. Extracts of students' work are used to inform and illustrate key points, alongside a number of practical, hands-on tasks to help you practise some of the skills covered and check your understanding.

- Takeaways
  - Each chapter ends with a 'takeaway' which includes a useful checklist to help you 'takeaway' the key skills you have learnt and apply them in your academic studies.

The Academic Skills Handbook also includes a detailed online Answer Key to help you check your responses and learn from the tasks, and additional samples and examples with further useful support.

HOW TO USE THIS BOOK

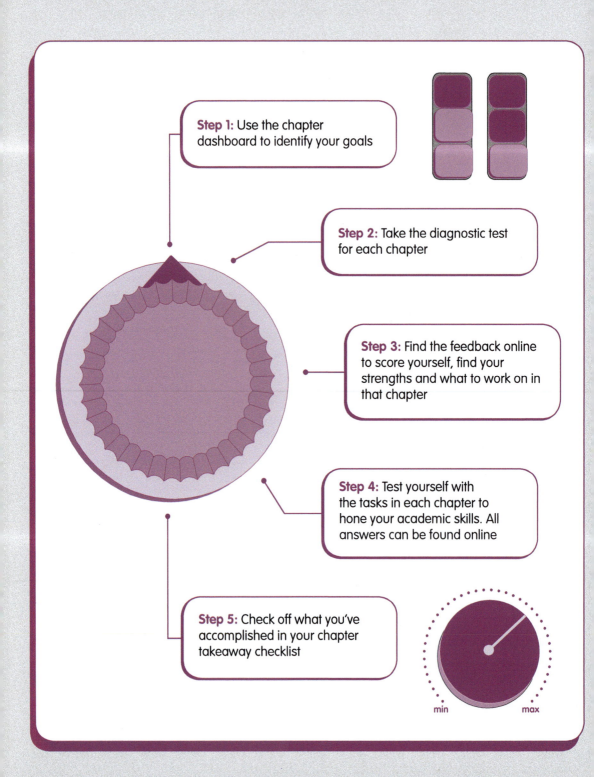

Step 1: Use the chapter dashboard to identify your goals

Step 2: Take the diagnostic test for each chapter

Step 3: Find the feedback online to score yourself, find your strengths and what to work on in that chapter

Step 4: Test yourself with the tasks in each chapter to hone your academic skills. All answers can be found online

Step 5: Check off what you've accomplished in your chapter takeaway checklist

min   max

ONLINE RESOURCES

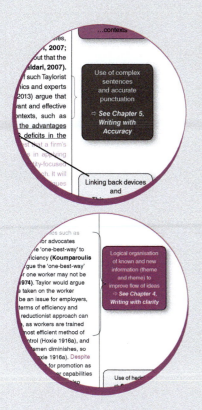

Writing Sample Library

Annotated examples of real writing from real students, full of notes and tips from the authors to help you anticipate what your tutor will look for. Here you can find sample essays for every subject area, a lab report, reflective essay, a dissertation and a sample poster.

Diagnostic Toolkit

Score yourself from the diagnostic test in each chapter of the book, so you can identify your strengths and weaknesses and can plan your own, personal plan to build up your academic skills.
Find the answers to all guided tasks in the book too!

YOUR PROGRESS

Everything is online at:
https://study.sagepub.com/hopkinsandreid

PART 1
WRITING SKILLS

The big picture

Academic writing is at the heart of all scholarly activity. During your studies, you will be required to complete a range of written assignments and examinations in a variety of genres and formats; from essays and reports to critical reviews, case studies, technical reports and reflective writing.

Academic writing can be challenging because you will be expected to use a range of academic conventions that may be unfamiliar and difficult to apply in practice. These may include adopting an unfamiliar formal style and incorporating a critical and evaluative approach in written tasks and assignments. It is vital therefore that you acquire, develop and extend your academic writing skills to maximise your success in your studies.

Skills you'll learn

This Part will provide you with a practical, easy-to-use skills toolkit to help you get started, plan and write successful academic assignments. By following this step-by-step approach, you will be able to:

- establish a solid foundation on which to build your academic expertise.
- learn from real students' work, short tasks and activities.
- develop, practise and apply the five principles of good writing in your academic work: being accurate, being clear, being concise, being appropriate and being informed.

YOUR PROGRESS

CHAPTER ONE

Getting Started on Your Essay

YOUR PROGRESS

CHAPTER DASHBOARD

Your objectives list:

 Identify and address what your tutor expects from your essay assignments

 Follow a step-by-step process to successfully start, plan, structure and complete your essay

 Incorporate all core elements of a standard university essay

min   max

'It ain't whatcha write, it's the way atcha write it.'

– Jack Kerouac

My three essay writing goals:

1 ....

2 ....

3 ....

What your tutor is looking for

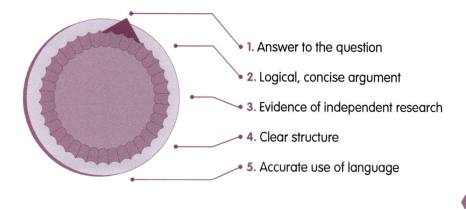

1. Answer to the question
2. Logical, concise argument
3. Evidence of independent research
4. Clear structure
5. Accurate use of language

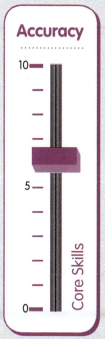

Accuracy

10
5
0

Core Skills

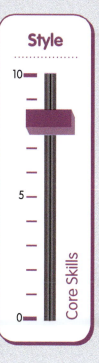

Style

10
5
0

Core Skills

Clarity

10
5
0

Core Skills

Being concise

10
5
0

Core Skills

Being informed

10
5
0

Core Skills

WATCH OUT FOR:

Ensure that you answer **all** parts of the assignment question

Diagnostic
How confident are you about your academic writing ability?

On a scale of 1–5 , where 1 = little or no confidence and 5 = very confident, score the following statements about your academic writing ability.

1. I have a good knowledge and understanding of the types of written assignments I will be required to do at university

2. I know what university tutors are looking for in written assignments

3. I am familiar with university marking criteria and can address these areas in my writing

4. I can differentiate between A level/tertiary level and university assessment levels and criteria

5. I can start an assignment

6. I have a good knowledge of how to achieve a high mark at university for my written assignments

7. I can write an essay

8. I can analyse and deconstruct an assignment question

9. I can structure an essay

10. I can write an effective introduction and know what elements it should contain

11. I know what a thesis statement is

12. I can write a thesis statement

13. I can produce a logical and coherent flow of ideas in my writing

14. I can write accurately using correct grammar and punctuation

15. I can cite sources in my essay and reference accurately

16. I can develop a thorough, coherent and reasoned argument in my essay

17. I can incorporate sources in my writing to support my argument or position

18. I can use an appropriate style

19. I can write effective conclusions and know which elements to include

20. I can edit and proofread my work effectively

My score

For feedback on your score, go online at:
https://study.sagepub.com/hopkinsandreid

THE ACADEMIC ESSAY

An academic essay is a piece of formal writing designed to demonstrate to your tutors that you have understood, questioned and evaluated a topic in depth. In general, academic essays follow certain conventions and share common structural features that will need to be incorporated into your work.

Writing an essay is a process with clear and logical steps. Knowing how to begin is the first step and there are then a number of further steps you can follow to enable you to complete your essay successfully and make the whole process more efficient and less daunting.

This chapter will provide you with an easy to follow step-by-step process to help you get started, plan and structure your essay, incorporate key structural features and academic conventions, and edit and proofread your draft. These steps will ensure you meet the expectations of your tutor, and build your essay writing skills.

The complete essay

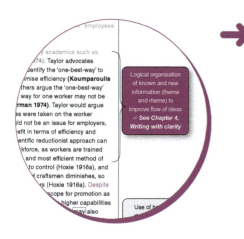

Go online **https://study.sagepub.com/ hopkinsandreid** to see an example of a complete essay, with annotations to help you identify and understand the features that contribute to successful writing. There are information boxes (purple) that focus on points relating to structure.

There are also (grey) information boxes that focus on communication features (language), etc. These boxes also refer you to the relevant chapters for more information on the particular feature of the essay/writing.

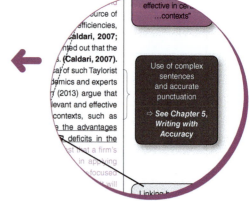

Essay types

During your studies, you may encounter different types of essays. These can be divided into:

a. 'Show what you know'-type essays. For example:

- Argument/Discussion Essay
  - ○ Requires you to investigate a topic, collect and evaluate evidence and present a reasoned and supported position.
- Problem–Solution Essay
  - ○ A type of argument essay that identifies a problem and proposes one or more solutions, supported by your investigation and research.
- Cause and Effect Essay
  - ○ Focuses on reasons why something happens (cause) and what happens as a result (effect).
- Reflective Essay
  - ○ Requires the writer to reflect and examine his or her own personal attitudes, experiences, thoughts and feelings about a specific topic or activity, and how this has impacted on their learning and/or life.

YOUR TURN

Task 1

Indicate whether these essay titles are (a) 'show what you know'-type questions or (b) 'show what you think'-type questions.

1. To what extent do you consider the legacy of the Olympics justifies the expense of staging such an event?   a / b

2. How is *Homo sapiens* adapted to environmental variation?   a / b

3. How can Archaeology be used to identify and explain the characteristics of the state? What are the key arguments used to explain increasing social complexity during primary state formation and in your view, which are the most convincing?   a / b

4. Critically assess the impact of the *Challenger* disaster on the effectiveness of engineering policy in the USA.   a / b

5. What is the role of slow- and fast-twitch muscle fibres in exercise?   a / b

 Answers online at: https://study.sagepub.com/hopkinsandreid

b. 'Show what you think'-type essays. For example:

- Definition or Factual Essay
    - ○ Explores and explains what a specific term means. Terms can be concrete (e.g. nuclear fusion, greenhouse effect) or abstract (e.g. trust, caution, fear).
- Review Essay
    - ○ Asks you to summarise and critically evaluate one or more texts (e.g. a journal article, case study, chapter of a book).

Essay structure

Academic essays tend to adopt a standardised structural format. This includes a short introduction which establishes the context and reason(s) for writing the essay, main body paragraphs which develop key themes and topics around the writer's position or argument (thesis), which link together to produce a coherent and logical progression

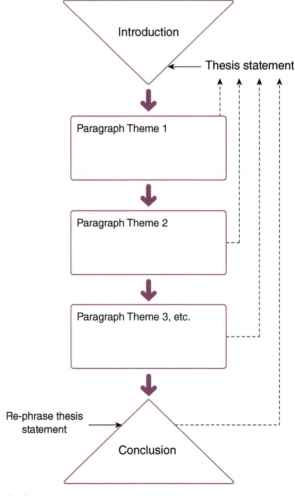

Figure 1.1 The fishbone essay plan

of ideas. This is followed by a short conclusion which summarises the content of the essay, and presents concluding arguments and any implications for the future.

There are, of course exceptions to the rule, but in general most essays follow this basic pattern.

The fishbone essay plan (Figure 1.1) illustrates the standard structure of an essay. Note how the main topic of each paragraph links directly to the thesis statement (more on this later).

Introductions, thesis and purpose statements
The introduction

Your introduction is very important as it establishes the context, topic and focus of your response to the question. A good introduction should present an interesting, clear, succinct and logical reason(s) for writing the assignment that will encourage your readers to continue to read and engage with your line of reasoning.

An introduction usually includes the following key elements:

- An attention-grabbing statement
  - For example, identification of a problem, a controversial issue or point of view, or the relevance of the topic today.

- Definitions and explanations of key terms and ideas
  - You should have identified these in your title analysis.

- Background and scene-setting
  - Provides an overview and context for the topic. You might also briefly describe and summarise the conditions that have led to a problem.

- Identifying the focus
  - Narrows the context to the focus area, relevant title and thesis statement. You might include some of the key writers, critics, theorists and experts connected to the research and discussions.

YOUR TURN

Task 2

Label the introduction below with the following key elements by writing the element number in the boxes provided:

1. Attention-grabbing statement.
2. Background and scene-setting.
3. Identifying the focus and key writers.
4. The thesis statement.
5. The purpose statement.

(Continued)

(Continued)

Title: 'Taylorism and the Scientific Management model is still relevant today'. In what ways do you agree or disagree with this statement?

Introduction

It is argued that for large-scale business enterprises, one of the great strengths of the Scientific Management model (the Taylor Approach) is that it rationalises and standardises production methods which leads to significant improvements in efficiency and productivity, and maximises profits for an organisation. The Taylor approach incorporates division of labour, predetermined methods of work, repetition of simple movement, minimum training requirements, financial incentives and time optimisation. While the system has great capacity to be a source of economic success for some employers due to these technical efficiencies, a number of critics (including Marshall, 1919, cited by Caldari, 2007; Smith, 1988; Greeves, 1998; and Baker, 2004) have pointed out that the model can lead to serious disadvantages for employees. (Caldari, 2007). Hoxie (1916a) and Braverman (1974) have been critical of such Taylorist labour principles. Despite these criticisms, some academics and experts such as Locke (1982) and Huczynski and Buchanan (2013) argue that scientific management approaches continue to be relevant and effective in certain business, industrial and manufacturing contexts, such as high volume production. This essay will demonstrate the advantages of Taylorism for employers, whilst also identifying key deficits in the theory from the perspective of the workforce. It will suggest that a firm's operating context is an important determinant of success in applying Scientific Management principles to work design, with quantity-focused manufacturing industries best placed to benefit from the approach. It will account for the structures, labour methods and motivation techniques promoted by Taylor through analysis of specific examples of its application, whilst examining numerous theories to support the thesis and explain the continuing relevance of the methodology.

 Answers online at: https://study.sagepub.com/hopkinsandreid

Introductions should also include one or both of the following.

Thesis statement

A thesis statement is a short and simple, one or two-sentence summary of the position or argument that you are going to develop in your assignment.

It is used in 'show what you *think*'-type essays (i.e. argument or discussion essays) to establish your position as soon as possible, so that the reader can follow your line of reasoning throughout the essay.

The thesis statement also tests your ideas by distilling them into a snapshot sentence. If your thesis statement is confusing, then it is likely your essay will become the same.

It also provides a clear direction and purpose for your assignment, and helps to organise and develop a clear and logical structure, and build a convincing argument.

Example: *This essay will argue that there is a measurable correlation between increasing levels of childhood obesity and the number of targeted marketing campaigns launched by leading confectionary companies in the last ten years.*

In this example, you can see that the writer's position is clearly established.

Purpose statement

A purpose statement is different from a thesis statement in that it describes what you are going to do in your assignment. It acts like a short, summarised roadmap to help the reader navigate the various stages of your essay. It is used primarily in 'show what you *know*'-type essays. But it can also be used to complement the thesis statement in 'show what you *think*'-type assignments (i.e. factual or comparative essays).

Example: *First the essay will examine the key factors involved, then it will … and finally …*

TIP

Purpose statement

While the thesis statement is a vital element in argument and discussion essays, the purpose statement can be helpful but may not be essential. **BUT**, for other essay topics and types (such as factual or comparative essays), a purpose statement may be sufficient as you are not required to take a position but explore key ideas, practices and so on.

YOUR TURN

Task 3

Are the following thesis statements good or poor?

1. This essay will look at the key elements of the bilateral agreement, consider the advantages and disadvantages of decisions taken, and explore the flaws in the decision-making process that led to breaches in the agreed terms. good / poor

2. There are three important aspects to the rise of fascism in 20th century Germany. good / poor

3. Although people may believe that modern democratic societies have achieved gender equality, the paper will show that this is in fact not the case, and that persistent and continuing inequality may be related to women's biology. good / poor

(Continued)

(Continued)

4. First I will look at the traits that *Homo sapiens* have evolved in order to be able   good / poor
   to adapt to diverse environments. I will then look at how humans can adapt to
   temperature, solar radiation and altitude, both in terms of temporary responses
   and acclimatisation, looking at biological and behavioural adaptations.

 Answers online at: https://study.sagepub.com/hopkinsandreid

Body paragraphs

Body paragraphs should also follow certain academic conventions.

Each paragraph should:

- begin with a topic sentence – a one sentence summary of the theme of the
  paragraph
- focus on one theme only
- connect directly to your thesis statement
- use supporting evidence to persuade the reader that you have a strong and
  convincing case (see Chapter 10, Critical thinking and analysis)
- include link and signpost words to help the reader navigate your ideas
- include information at the end of the paragraph that provides a link to the
  next paragraph (see Chapter 4, Writing with clarity).

TIP

Body paragraph

If a paragraph topic does not connect to the thesis, then it is irrelevant and should be
adapted or removed.

 **YOUR TURN**

Task 4

Examine the following sample on p.15 using these pointers:

1. Highlight the topic sentence.
2. Underline link and signpost words.
3. Analyse the impact of the use of sources on the reader.
4. Does the writer provide a link to the next paragraph?

Sample

Taylorism has been widely critiqued by academics such as Hoxie (1916a), and Braverman (1974). Taylor advocates time-and-motion studies, which identify the 'one-best-way' to undertake a job in order to maximise efficiency (Koumparoulis & Solomos, 2012). However, others argue the 'one-best-way' concept is flawed, as the best way for one worker may not be so for another worker (Braverman, 1974). Taylor would argue that if time-and-motion studies were taken on the worker performing the task, this would not be an issue for employers, and that they would then benefit in terms of efficiency and productivity.

However, this scientific reductionist approach results in a deskilling of the workforce, as workers are trained to execute the easiest, quickest and most efficient method of work. This makes workers easier to control (Hoxie 1916a), and the need for more expensive skilled craftsmen diminishes, so clear cost benefit accrues to employers (Hoxie, 1916a). Despite this apparent benefit, it may limit worker scope for promotion as there are fewer opportunities to demonstrate higher capabilities (Marshall, 1919, cited by Caldari, 2007). De-skilling may also lead to job specialisation, which 'deprives workers of engagement, initiative and inventive genius' (Hoxie, 1916a: p. 65), and this causes creativity and flexible-working issues.

Thus, while rigid structures promoted by Taylor provide short-term technical efficiencies, it may cause long-term inefficiencies as a firm's flexibility becomes increasingly limited (Marshall, 1919, cited by Caldari, 2007). Taylor would argue that efficiency benefits are more important than being flexible and having the capacity to deal with uncertain events, which by definition cannot be planned for. However, in industries prone to rapid change such as design and technology firms that operate in creative environments, Taylorism may be less applicable.

Taylor's view of labour as a tool that 'could be engineered to achieve efficiency' (Koumparoulis & Solomos, 2012: p. 150), has been challenged by Lawrence (2010) and Marshall (1919, cited by Caldari, 2007) who contend that while Taylorism may offer certain benefits to employers, it may not lead to a dynamic, flexible and creative workforce, which are now considered essential job skills for many 21st century business organisations.

   Answers online at: https://study.sagepub.com/hopkinsandreid

The conclusion

Your conclusion is very important as it presents the final words of your essay. It should leave the reader satisfied that you have provided a thorough, well-researched and reasoned response to the assignment question.

Your conclusion should include:

- a re-formulated thesis statement – the same thesis but using different words and/or phrases

- a brief summary of what was covered in your essay
- any implications, limitations, future investigations that may be needed
- a final indication to the reader that the essay is finished, the purpose of the essay has been achieved, and that the question has been answered.

Your conclusion should *not*:

- contain any new information, new sources, new arguments or new evidence
- end with a quote – the essay is your work so you should have the final word.

Language of the conclusion

The conclusion will include a mix of tenses. In the summary of what was done, the past tense will be used, and the discussion of the results may mix past and present. There will be further use of 'hedging' language to consider future implications, studies or actions.

YOUR TURN

Task 5

The following conclusion has been jumbled up. What is the correct order? Re-order the paragraphs by inserting 1, 2 or 3 in the boxes below.

Section 1

Consequently, future business enterprises may need to think carefully when considering the possible adoption of a scientific management approach, as there may be more suitable models available.

Section 2

By considering the structures, labour methods and motivation techniques pro moted by Taylorism, it is clear that in industries where products are fairly standard, employers can benefit via increased productivity and efficiency, as shown by the UK Civil Service. However, workers are inevitably disadvantaged with promotion and creativity opportunities limited due to the rigid structure Taylor advocates.

Section 3

It is these issues that mean Taylorism is most suited to manufacturing environments, and less applicable to creative sectors. However, the criticisms of Taylorism do not underpin the validity of its principles in all business environments. The essay has shown that Taylor 'was able to create a system founded on issues present in his lifetime, that could transcend time and in some circumstances be beneficial to all generations, be it past, present or future' (Koumparoulis & Solomos, 2012: p. 155), as shown by McDonaldization. However, shortcomings with regard to employee performance and achievements have also been highlighted (Hoxie, 1916a; Braverman, 1974; Marshall, 1919, cited by Caldari, 2007).

The correct order is 2, 3, 1.

The conclusion should now look like Figure 1.2.

TIP

Your conclusion should move from the specific to the general as shown by the arrows

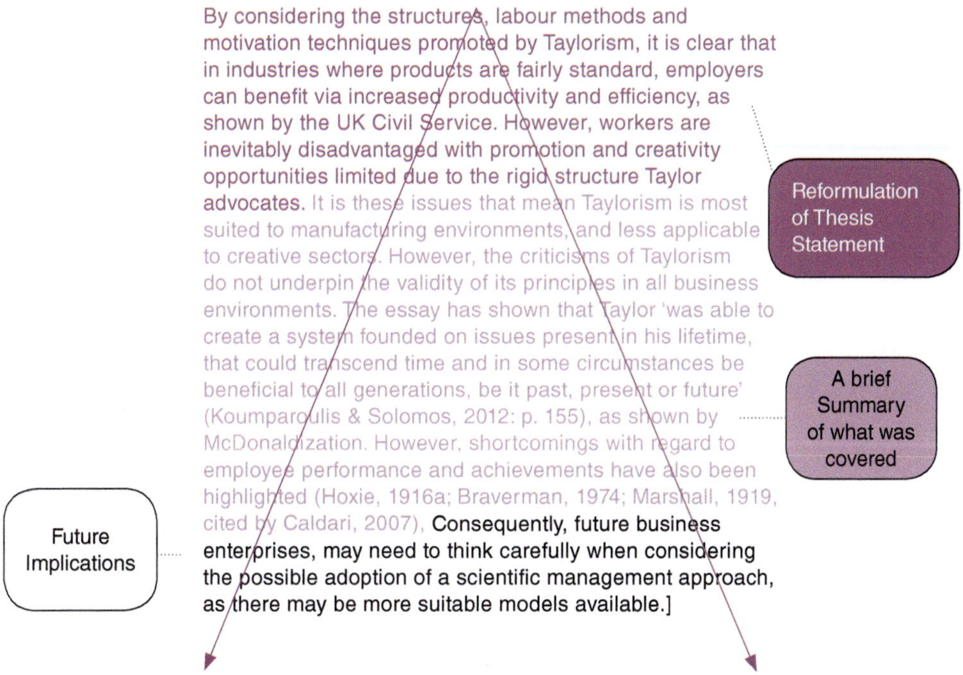

By considering the structures, labour methods and motivation techniques promoted by Taylorism, it is clear that in industries where products are fairly standard, employers can benefit via increased productivity and efficiency, as shown by the UK Civil Service. However, workers are inevitably disadvantaged with promotion and creativity opportunities limited due to the rigid structure Taylor advocates. It is these issues that mean Taylorism is most suited to manufacturing environments, and less applicable to creative sectors. However, the criticisms of Taylorism do not underpin the validity of its principles in all business environments. The essay has shown that Taylor 'was able to create a system founded on issues present in his lifetime, that could transcend time and in some circumstances be beneficial to all generations, be it past, present or future' (Koumparoulis & Solomos, 2012: p. 155), as shown by McDonaldization. However, shortcomings with regard to employee performance and achievements have also been highlighted (Hoxie, 1916a; Braverman, 1974; Marshall, 1919, cited by Caldari, 2007), Consequently, future business enterprises, may need to think carefully when considering the possible adoption of a scientific management approach, as there may be more suitable models available.]

Reformulation of Thesis Statement

A brief Summary of what was covered

Future Implications

Figure 1.2 Annotated example conclusion

WRITING YOUR ESSAY

Understanding the task – what does your tutor want you to do?

Before you begin your assignment, it is vital that you understand exactly what your tutor wants you to do and to clearly identify the key elements of the task. This requires careful scrutiny of the assignment instructions and guidelines, and analysis of the assignment title or question.

Spending time on this stage will ensure that you address and answer all parts of the question in your response, and help you make a confident and logical start on your assignment.

Analysing assignment instructions

Your tutor will normally provide you with clear guidelines and instruction on what you will be required to do in your assignment. These are usually found in your course handbook. Instructions may include:

- assignment type (essay, report, critical review, etc.)
- word count
- deadlines
- format and style guidelines
- marking criteria
- which referencing system to use
- additional information, instructions and guidance from your tutor.

Marking criteria

When your tutor marks and grades your work, it is most likely that she will follow standardised marking criteria to help her select the most suitable level (see Table 1.1). Some tutors, however prefer to use their own, so you will need to confirm this when you begin your studies.

Common areas that tutors focus on include: structure, accuracy, answering all parts of the question, depth of research and investigative work, critical analysis and originality. Each area may be marked as a proportion of the overall total. Critical analysis and evaluation is usually considered the most important area, and the distribution of marks may reflect this.

University versus A level/tertiary level

It is very important to understand that university study requires a higher level of critical understanding of the topic, and a more in-depth analysis of assignment tasks. You will be required to raise your knowledge and skills base, and demonstrate this in your writing (see also Chapter 10, Critical thinking and analysis).

It is vital, therefore that before you begin any assignment you have a clear understanding of what your tutor wants you to do, and focus on developing vital academic skills to help you meet and hopefully exceed your tutor's expectations.

Table 1.1 is an example of typical marking criteria used by tutors at UK universities. Please note the weightings for different aspects of the essay.

Table 1.1 Typical essay marking criteria

Grade	80–100 Excellent/ Outstanding	70–79 Excellent	60–69 Good Pass	50–59 Pass	40–49 Low Pass	35–39 Borderline Fail	0–34 Fail
Structure 10%	Develops convincing and logical argument based on excellent linking of all elements of the essay. Excellent thesis statement	Develops logical argument. Links aims, objectives, investigation, findings and conclusion	Generally very good. Some minor inconsistencies	Good, but lacks flow and progression of ideas and conclusion is limited	Poor links between paragraphs. Lacks logical flow with no clear introduction thesis statement and conclusion	Key themes and arguments are unclear. Poor or missing thesis statement. Weak overall conclusion	Disorganised. Random structure. Lacks direction and purpose
Use of English 10%	Excellent. No errors present	Very good. Clear and concise use of English	Good use of English and accurate use of technical terminology	Mostly clear with some minor grammatical or spelling errors	Some points unclear. Some persistent extensive grammar and spelling issues	Many points unclear. Extensive grammar and spelling issues. Some misuse of technical terminology	Very difficult to understand. Poor use of English throughout
Research and investigation 20%	Scrupulous and conscientious exploration of key ideas. Evidence of extensive and relevant reading beyond course work	Thorough investigation of key ideas. Evidence of relevant reading beyond course work	Very good exploration of up-to-date literature	Good use of relevant books and articles	Sufficient use of relevant source material but little or no evidence of reading beyond course work	Limited use of relevant literature. Some irrelevant or missing material	Inadequate and irrelevant sources used

(Continued)

Table 1.1 (Continued)

Grade	80–100 Excellent/ Outstanding	70–79 Excellent	60–69 Good Pass	50–59 Pass	40–49 Low Pass	35–39 Borderline Fail	0–34 Fail
Understanding of the subject 25%	Evidence of sophisticated understanding of complex ideas. Evidence of thinking beyond course work. Original and creative interpretation of key concepts and arguments	Very clear and detailed understanding of key concepts and arguments. Evidence of interesting and original interpretation of key ideas	Key ideas, issues, and arguments clearly identified and explored	Identifies and explores most ideas, issues, and arguments. Provides clear explanation	Some important points are missing and explanations and interpretation unclear at times	Some misunderstanding of key concepts, and inclusion of irrelevant materials	Little or no understanding of basic concepts
Critical analysis 25%	Demonstrates exceptional analytical ability. Evidence of a higher level critical and evaluative approach using a range of sources to build an evidence-based critical response	Excellent analytical ability with evidence of a strong critical and analytical approach using a good range of sources to synthesise ideas and build a convincing argument and conclusion	Good use of examples and theory with evidence of some critical analysis and evaluation. Provides a logical and evidence-based conclusion	Limited analysis of key ideas. Lack of in-depth exploration of theories and minimal use of supporting evidence	Very limited analysis, or evaluation. Examples are mostly descriptive and lack sufficient detail	Descriptive, generalised information with little analysis or evaluation. Subjective and unsupported assertions and conclusions	No critical analysis present
Referencing 10%	Perfect	Very good	Correctly cited and listed	Some minor flaws and omissions	Adequate but more extensive flaws and omissions	Poor and incomplete	None

Analysing the title/question

The next stage of the process is to deconstruct the assignment question to more fully understand what it is your tutor is asking you to do, and ensure that you answer all parts of the question. Assignment analysis can also help you organise and rationalise the topic in your mind, and help you devise a logical and workable plan.

Analysis of an assignment question involves identifying four core elements:

- the Subject
- the Focus
- the Scope (or limits)
- the Instruction Words.

The subject

This is the general subject area of the essay topic. For example, 'Human Resource Management' in Management or 'Democracy' in Politics.

The focus

This is the narrower and more specific topic area within the wider subject context. For example, *recruitment* in human resource management or the *parliamentary system* in a democratic country.

The scope (or limits)

This indicates how far you should go within the focus area of the assignment question, and sets the parameters or limits.

For example, 'Discuss the use of pesticides in British farming in the *1970s*.'

Examine the following examples: 'Analyse the use of Skype interviews in the recruitment process.'

Focus: Recruitment process

Scope: Skype interviews

'Discuss the role of the House of Lords within the UK parliamentary system.'

Focus: Parliamentary system

Scope: House of Lords

Generating questions

You are ready now to generate some questions, based on your title analysis.

Your list of questions can range from 'simple definition and explanation'-types to more complex and analytical. Devising a list of questions is important as they will help you to:

- focus and target your research reading
- formulate a basic essay plan
- develop your thesis statement.

TIP

Generating questions

- At this stage, you may be able to draw on prior knowledge and experience to answer some of your questions. But even with little or no knowledge of the topic, your list will provide you with the keys to open the doors to your research.
- You may also have a first response to the question, and have formulated an initial view or position. But as your research and investigations continue, you should maintain an open mind and be prepared to change your views, and the direction of your assignment.

YOUR TURN

Task 8

Write down 6–8 questions you can ask about essay question 5 from Task 6 (use your title analysis to help you).

> 'Taylorism and the Scientific Management model are still relevant today.' In what ways do you agree or disagree with this statement?

Questions:

1 ....

2 ....

3 ....

4 ....

5 ....

6 ....

7 ....

8 ....

Your list should look something like this:

What is Taylorism and the Scientific Management model?

Who was Taylor?

When was the Scientific Management model first used?

How was it used?

Where was it used?

What was the impact of its introduction?

What are the strengths of Taylorism?

What are the weaknesses of Taylorism?

Who supports Taylorism? How? Why?

Who criticises Taylorism? How? Why?

Is it still relevant and practised today? If so, where, why. If not, why not?

Notice how the questions move from simple definition questions, to more complex and involved.

PLANNING, STRUCTURING AND RESEARCHING

Making a provisional plan

Use your questions to start working on a provisional essay plan

You can use the **fishbone essay plan template** (Figure 1.1) to help you design and structure your essay, and fit your list of questions into appropriate sections. You can do this before you begin your research reading.

TIP

Essays

Your choice of structure and content depends on your thesis statement, and the position you are presenting in the essay.

Task 9

You can download your fishbone essay plan template from the online resources on the website. Slot the questions from the list you made in Task 8 into the plan.

➡️ **You can download your fishbone essay plan template from the website.**

Researching the topic

Now you are ready to look for answers to your questions.

Use the **10-step** process in Figure 1.4 to help you (see also Chapter 9, Reading skills).

TIP

Wikipedia

During this initial orientation stage you could use online resources such as Wikipedia to provide you with some basic background information. **But be careful**: online sources can be unreliable and inaccurate. You should aim to use only credible academic sources in your essay.

TIP

Starting your writing

- If you find it hard to know how to start the actual writing, you can, if you prefer, start with a section of your essay you feel most confident about, *even if* it is not the first section of the essay. This will help 'kick start' your writing. You can then edit it later to fit with the other sections.

COMPLETING YOUR ESSAY

Editing and proofreading

When writing your assignment, it is important to ensure you factor in sufficient time for editing and proofreading your work. You should aim to devise an editing system that works for you. Here are some recommendations.

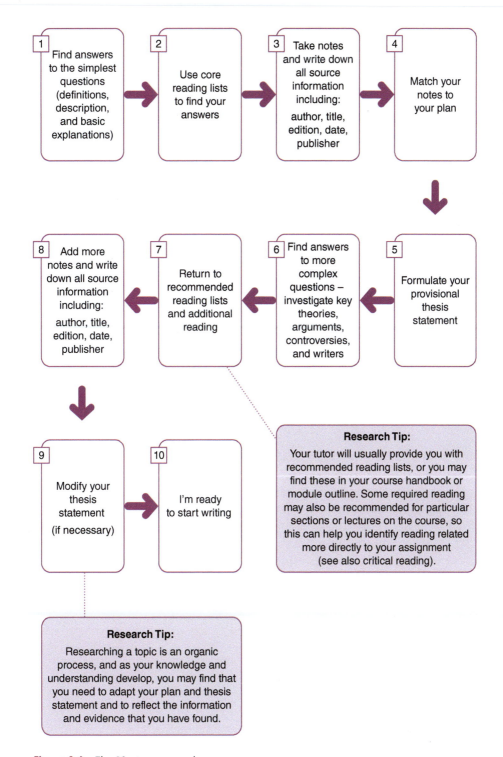

Figure 1.4   The 10-step research process

When you have completed your first draft, you need to:

- Let your essay rest for some time (perhaps 2–3 days), and don't be tempted to look at it. This will create some distance between the process and challenges of writing and the work itself, and when you return, you will be able to view it with a refreshed and critical eye.
- Review your essay in **bite-sized chunks**. This involves focusing on different elements of the assignment. You should aim to spend no longer than 20–30 minutes reviewing each element, and ensure that you have regular breaks.

Table 1.2 provides a list of bite-sized review items and questions you should ask yourself about this area of your assignment, and links to sections of the book that will help you improve your draft.

Making revisions, improvements and enhancements

Task 10

Using the editing checklist (Table 1.2), identify <u>five</u> problems in the following paragraph and make some revisions.

> The ideal future workplace should be seeking for even more effective ways to maximise workers emotions and happiness to produce the best results. Thus when designing my ideal future workplace I will be using a hedonistic approach which provides a platform to build the rest of my workplace. Fisher states that 'happiness at work is likely to be the glue that retains and motivates the high-quality employees of the future'. Creating a workplace around this philosophy, as shown in the following sections, brings large reaching benefits for the organisation and employees. These will range from enhanced creativity and productivity amongst employees, better well-being and a reduced chance of stress and burnout as well as talent retention.

1 ....

2 ....

3 ....

4 ....

5 ....

 Answers online at: https://study.sagepub.com/hopkinsandreid

Table 1.2 Editing checklist

Review item	Questions	Improve your draft (Follow links below)	
Content and argument	Have I answered the question?	pp. 18–23	☐
	Does every paragraph address my thesis statement?	pp. 18–23	☐
	Is my critical analysis sufficiently in-depth?	pp. 236–243	☐
	Have I provided sufficient explanation?	p 11	☐
	Are my conclusions justified?	pp 15–17	☐
Research material	Are there sufficient sources, examples, evidence to support the points I make?	pp. 228–229	☐
	Do all my citations and quotes relate directly to the topic/thesis statement?	pp. 14–16, 26–28	☐ ☐
	Have I paraphrased sufficiently and is the meaning the same?	pp. 223–228	☐
	Is the main line of argument clear?	pp. 10–11, 240–243	
Structure and cohesion	Does my introduction and conclusion include all key elements?	pp 11–17	☐
	Do my ideas connect together?	pp. 100–124	☐
	Do my paragraphs connect together?	pp. 100–124	☐
	Are ideas presented in the correct order?	pp. 101–103	☐
	Are my sentences too repetitive?	pp. 157–158	☐
Style	Have I used a formal academic style throughout?	pp. 165–170	☐
	Have I used the first person? (If so, does my tutor say this is OK?)	pp. 176–177	☐
	Have I used any informal words or phrases, slang, text-speak?	pp. 100–124 p. 167	☐
Clarity	Is my use of language clear and easy to read?	pp. 99–109	☐
	Are any of my sentences too long and complex?	pp. 109–111	☐
	Are my explanations of technical language easy to understand?		☐
Language and grammar	Is my punctuation and spelling accurate?	pp. 122–139	☐
	Have I used tenses accurately and appropriately?	p. 16	☐
Referencing and citation	Are my in-text citations accurate, consistent?	pp. 187–195	☐
	Are my uses of reporting verbs appropriate and varied?	p. 238	☐
	Is my reference list accurate, is it formatted correctly, and does it include all sources used in my assignment?	pp. 195–198	☐

TROUBLESHOOTING (COMMON EDITING PROBLEMS)

My essay is too short

Ask yourself:

- Are my introductions and conclusions too short?
- Do I need to add more information to make my explanations and arguments understandable to the reader?
- Is there anything I can add to improve or develop my line of reasoning?
- Have I included enough sources?

BUT BEWARE: Don't add waffle; add content.

My essay is too long

Ask yourself:

- Are my introduction and conclusion too long?
- Have I included quotes and the reference list in my word count? (They usually don't count!)
- Is there anything I can remove as repeated or irrelevant information?
- Can I remove unnecessary descriptions or vocabulary, or reduce the size of my sentences?

BUT BEWARE: Don't lose the meaning.

YOUR CHAPTER TAKEAWAY

Essay Writing Process Checklist

✓(tick when completed)

Have I ...

○ analysed/deconstructed the assignment title?

○ made a list of questions (from simple to complex)?

○ made a provisional plan using the fishbone essay template (with questions slotted into the appropriate sections)?

○ researched each question one by one (collected information/arguments/evidence/examples/data, etc.)?

○ taken notes and written down all source information: author(s), edition, title (or web address), date of publication (or access date if online), page number(s), publisher, place of publication?

○ slotted research material into your provisional plan?

○ formulated an introduction and provisional thesis statement?

○ started writing up paragraphs?

○ written more questions and carried out further research?

○ revised my thesis statement and developed paragraphs using my sources (critical analysis and evaluation)?

○ written a conclusion and completed a first draft?

○ let my assignment rest?

○ reviewed, revised, re-edited and re-drafted?

○ handed in?

My one takeaway

....

....

YOUR PROGRESS

CHAPTER TWO

Getting Started on Your Lab Report

YOUR PROGRESS

CHAPTER DASHBOARD

Your objectives list:

 Follow a step-by-step process to help you get started, plan, structure and successfully complete your lab report

 Identify what different sections to include in a lab report

 Clarify the language of the different sections

min   max

'Doing an experiment is not more important than writing.'

– Edwin Boring

My three lab report goals:

1 ....

2 ....

3 ....

What your tutor is looking for

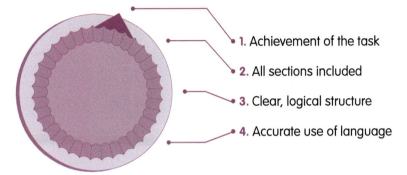

1. Achievement of the task
2. All sections included
3. Clear, logical structure
4. Accurate use of language

Accuracy

10
5
0

Core Skills

Style

10
5
0

Core Skills

Clarity

10
5
0

Core Skills

Being concise

10
5
0

Core Skills

Being informed

10
5
0

Core Skills

WATCH OUT FOR:

Ensure that your final lab report includes enough information to enable another person to carry out the experiments

Diagnostic
How confident are you in your writing skills for a lab report?

On a scale of 1–5 , where 1 = little or no confidence and 5 = very confident, score the following statements about your academic writing ability.

1. I have a good knowledge and understanding of the types of written assignments I will be required to do at university

2. I know what university tutors are looking for in lab reports

3. I am familiar with university marking criteria and can address these areas in my writing

4. I can differentiate between A level/tertiary level and university assessment levels and criteria

5. I can start a lab report

6. I have a good knowledge of how to achieve a high mark at university for my lab reports

7. I can write a lab report

8. I can analyse and deconstruct an assignment question

9. I can structure a lab report

10. I know what sections are needed in a lab report

11. I know what information each section should contain	
12. I can produce a logical and coherent flow of ideas in my writing	
13. I can write accurately using correct grammar and punctuation	
14. I can cite sources in my lab report and reference accurately	
15. I can develop a thorough, coherent and reasoned discussion section	
16. I can write effective conclusions and know which elements to include	
17. I can incorporate sources in my writing to support my points	
18. I know what tenses to use in each different section	
19. I can use an appropriate style	
20. I can edit and proofread my work effectively	

My score

For feedback on your score, go online at:
https://study.sagepub.com/hopkinsandreid

Academic writing is not all about the essay. There are many other types of writing that you may be required to do as part of your degree. For science, engineering and social science students, one of these is the laboratory (or 'lab') report, sometimes called a technical report.

A lab report is a document that provides a record of an experiment in sufficient detail for someone else to be able to reproduce it. In other words, it is a document that states what was done *and what was found,* and then discusses *what this means* and *why it is important.* Through analysis of data or findings, and a discussion of their significance, you can draw conclusions and make recommendations.

This chapter will provide you with an easy to follow step-by-step process to help you get started, plan and structure your lab report, incorporate key structural features and academic conventions, and edit and proofread your draft. These steps will ensure you meet the expectations of your tutor, and build your lab report writing skills.

UNDERSTANDING THE TASK

Analysing assignment instructions and marking criteria

Assignment instructions are usually found in course or lab handbooks. Information may include:

- assignment type (whole lab report, one section, two sections, whole lab report without abstract, etc.)
- word count
- deadlines
- format and style guidelines
- marking criteria
- which referencing system to use
- models to guide you
- additional information, instructions and guidance from your tutor.

Table 2.1 is an example of the sort of marking criteria used for a lab report by tutors at UK universities.

Table 2.1 Typical lab report marking criteria

	F	P	S	G	VG	Ex	O
Presentation of content	0–19	20–39	40–49	50–59	60–69	70–79	80–100
Is the report written in a clear, accurate and appropriate scientific style?	☐	☐	☐	☐	☐	☐	☐
Is there a clearly written abstract which includes the main findings?	☐	☐	☐	☐	☐	☐	☐

	F	P	S	G	VG	Ex	O
Presentation of content	0–19	20–39	40–49	50–59	60–69	70–79	80–100
Is there a clearly written introduction that includes theory?	☐	☐	☐	☐	☐	☐	☐
Is the method section easy to follow and in the appropriate style?	☐	☐	☐	☐	☐	☐	☐
Is there a clearly written results section that includes appropriate figures and tables?	☐	☐	☐	☐	☐	☐	☐
Is the significance of the results discussed sufficiently in the discussion section?	☐	☐	☐	☐	☐	☐	☐
Is there a clearly written conclusion?	☐	☐	☐	☐	☐	☐	☐
Are all tables and figures numbered and labelled appropriately and referred to in the text?	☐	☐	☐	☐	☐	☐	☐
To what extent have external sources been used and referred to accurately?	☐	☐	☐	☐	☐	☐	☐
Technical content	F	P	S	G	VG	Ex	O
Has the relevance of the experiment been demonstrated?	☐	☐	☐	☐	☐	☐	☐
Have the test method and sources of errors been discussed?	☐	☐	☐	☐	☐	☐	☐
Have the calculations been made clear?	☐	☐	☐	☐	☐	☐	☐
Have the results been analysed and the significance discussed?	☐	☐	☐	☐	☐	☐	☐
Total mark							

Key: F = Fail; P = Poor; S = Satisfactory; G= Good; VG = Very Good; Ex = Excellent; O = Outstanding

Please note the weightings are *not* equal for different aspects of the work

PLANNING, STRUCTURING AND RESEARCHING YOUR REPORT

Lab report structure: What goes where?

A lab report comprises certain **obligatory** sections and some **optional** sections.

TIP

Sections

Some departments require slightly different section names and contents. You should check with your tutor before starting to write.

Obligatory sections

These are the sections that you would expect in every lab report. However, sometimes, two or even three of these sections may be fused to form one section. For example, it is not unusual to have a section titled 'Results and Discussion'. Remember to check with your tutor for exact instructions.

Obligatory sections listed in order

Title and abstract (or summary)
Introduction
Method/experimental/procedure
Results
Discussion
Conclusion
References.

Optional sections

These are sections that you may be required to include, but they are unusual in a shorter lab report. They may include:

Theory/theoretical background
Acknowledgements
Appendices.

Researching the topic

You will be writing your lab report after you have completed the laboratory experiment. Before the lab work you should:

- Read about the theories that underpin your experiment(s), taking notes and recording the source of the information. Your sources may be books, articles, lecture notes, etc. (See Chapter 8 for how to cite sources.)
- Prepare your logbook or report forms so that you are ready to record the results clearly and accurately. A dedicated logbook is best for this.
- Ensure your tables are systematic and clear, as you may be required to show your logbook/results.
- Prepare your record forms so that results are recorded as 'raw' data in the first instance. If they need to be scaled in some way, have a separate column for this, to follow the raw data.

The lab report: Section by section

Each section has a purpose. Before you start writing, make sure you know what each section is for. Note also that in UK universities you are usually required to avoid using personal language such as 'I' and 'we'. Instead, use the third person (sometimes this means using the passive voice).

Title: What to write at the top of your lab report

The title is a brief summary of the contents of the lab report. It should be short and clear. The reader wants to know quickly what the report is about.

Abstract: What it is, and what to include

The abstract summarises the whole report. It is usually a single paragraph, not more than 200 words long (but this can vary, so you need to check). It should answer the following questions:

1. What was done? (Describe the purpose, what theories were relevant, and a summary of the experiment.)
2. What were the results? (Highlight the important findings, and include quantitative results if appropriate.)
3. What is the significance of the results? (Analyse what these results indicate, and how they relate to the theory.)
4. What conclusions can be drawn? (State if your aims have been achieved, and summarise what has been learnt from the experiment.)

 **YOUR TURN**

Task 1

Does this sample answer the four questions? Which parts answer which questions?

> The 'energy gap' theory of thermal excitation of a silicon semiconductor in which the resistance decreases with increasing temperature was tested by measuring variation of resistance with temperature of a thermistor made of a fairly pure sample of silicon. The trend of readings fitted that expected by the theory both in and out of the intrinsic region. A value for the energy gap of 1.05 ± 0.02 eV was calculated, which is consistent with the expected value of 1.0–1.1 eV.

1 ....

2 ....

3 ....

4 ....

 Answers online at: https://study.sagepub.com/hopkinsandreid

TIP

Abstract

Although the abstract is the first section of the lab report (after the title), it should be written last. This is because it is a mini version of the whole report. You can only write it when you know what the whole report includes.

Introduction: What is it for, and what to include?

The introduction tells the reader:

- why the work was carried out (the objectives or aims)
- what has been done before, and the important background information needed to understand the experiment
- about key theory, assumptions and equations.

The introduction does NOT:

- include the calculations needed to process raw data. Put these in an Appendix.

If you are including **equations** relating to the theory, they need:

- to be indented
- to have a space above and below them
- to be numbered, with the numbering justified to the right (see Figure 2.2).

Introductions move from general information to specific information related to the experiment(s) and usually include the following elements:

- An introduction to the topic
  - For example, identification of a problem, description of a theory that needs to be tested, or description of skills that need developing.

- Definitions and explanations of key terms and theories
  - For example, terminology that is essential to the report.

- Background to the experiment
  - Here you provide details of the theory that relates to the experiment or background to the problems under investigation. You may need to refer to the literature to show what has gone before and what is known.

- Aims of the experiment
  - You should ensure you highlight the purpose of the experiment by stating clearly the objectives you want to fulfil.

Figure 2.1 illustrates the key elements in a lab report introduction.

Semi-conductors act as non-metals at low temperatures, with high resistivity. However, when the temperature is increased, the energy levels of the electrons in the valence band also increase, allowing the electrons to move more freely. This results in conduction and a decreased resistivity, and these are characteristics of metals. The energy difference between the top of the valence band and the energy required for an electron to move freely is called the 'energy gap'. The energy gap theory of semi-conductor resistance states that charge carriers in the semi-conductor can be in one of two energy states, separated by an energy gap Eg (Holgate, 2009). The aim of the experiment is to test the validity of the 'energy gap' theory of semi-conductor resistance by using a thermistor (a specialised temperature-sensitive resistor) made of silicon.

Introduction to the topic

General background information/ theory

The specific aim of the experiment

The test of this theory depends on accurate measurements of resistance and temperature. Random error can be reduced by taking readings over a range of temperature and then using graphical analysis to test the relationship (and thereby find R and the energy gap).

Definition of key term

The resistance of the thermistor is obtained by measuring both current and voltage across the thermistor. However, in order to eliminate any possible systematic error in the measurement of resistance, a potential divider (with a known resistor) can be used. A thermocouple is used to measure voltage, as it will give a more accurate measurement than a liquid-glass thermometer, which can be fragile at high temperatures.

Specific details necessary to understand the experiment

Figure 2.1   Key elements in a lab report introduction moving from general to specific information

To simplify the theoretical model to a beam cantilever problem, several assumptions had to be made. Firstly, the frame that the beam was attached to was assumed to be fixed, and the weight attached to the beam was applied at a single point, acting vertically downwards. Secondly, any lateral forces or movement were discounted to allow the problem to be reduced to two dimensions. Given these assumptions, the deflection of the beam can be taken to be:

Space above the equation

Symbols defined using 'where' ...

$$\delta_x = \frac{Fx^2}{6EI} \ (3L-x),$$ *Comma after the equation*   (1)

where δx is the beam's deflection, F is the applied load, x is the distance between the fixed point at the beam's end and the deflection measuring point, E is the Young's modulus of the beam, I is the second moment of area of the beam, and L the distance between the fixed point of the beam and the load application. I can be calculated from the beam dimensions as follows:

$$I = \frac{bh^3}{12},$$ (2)

Space below the equation

Number at the right

where b is the width of the beam and h the thickness. By measuring the applied load, F, and the deflection, Young's modulus, E, can then be calculated for the beam.

Figure 2.2   Layout and language conventions when using equations

Using equations to show theory

In a science or engineering lab report or technical report introduction you may need to show theory through equations. There are certain layout conventions you need to follow when using equations. Figure 2.2 highlights the conventions.

The language of the introduction

The introduction includes information about *theory*, *concepts* and *aims*. This means we need to make appropriate tense choices to reflect this.

Task 2

Underline the verbs in the following sample from an introduction.

> Semi-conductors act as non-metals at low temperatures, with high resistivity. However, when the temperature is increased, the energy levels of the electrons in the valence band also increase, allowing the electrons to move more freely. This results in conduction and a decreased resistivity, and these are characteristics of metals. The energy difference between the top of the valence band and the energy required for an electron to move freely is called the 'energy gap'. The energy gap theory of semi-conductor resistance states that charge carriers in the semi-conductor can be in one of two energy states, separated by an energy gap E_g (Holgate, 2009). The aim of the experiment is to test the validity of the 'energy gap' theory of semi-conductor resistance by using a thermistor (a specialised temperature-sensitive resistor) made of silicon. The test of this theory depends on accurate measurements of resistance and temperature. Random error can be reduced by taking readings over a range of temperature and then using graphical analysis to test the relationship (and thereby find R_0 and the energy gap). The resistance of the thermistor is obtained by measuring both current and voltage across the thermistor. However, in order to eliminate any possible systematic error in the measurement of resistance, a potential divider (with a known resistor) can be used. A thermocouple is used to measure voltage, as it will give a more accurate measurement than a liquid-glass thermometer, which can be fragile at high temperatures.

What tenses are used and why?

....

....

....

Answers online at: https://study.sagepub.com/hopkinsandreid

The Introduction mainly uses *present* and *future* forms (see the Answer Key). This is because theory remains true (present) and objectives may test predictions (future). Of course, other tenses may be evident in an introduction too, but make sure you use present tenses to talk about current theories and factual information.

Method/experimental/procedure: What is it for, and what to include?

The method section (also sometimes called experimental or procedure) describes *what was done* in the experiment.

TIP

Method

Think of the method as an ordered description of the steps that were taken to carry out the experiment.

You need to give sufficient detail so that your reader is able to:

- reproduce the experiment
- assess the appropriacy of the conclusions you later draw.

You should:

- include a clear description of any apparatus or equipment used (including diagrams, images or drawings)
- describe how you set this equipment up
- describe how your measurements were taken
- describe how you reduced the possibility of errors
- describe the steps that were taken to carry out the experiment in a logical order (i.e. the order you carried them out).

The language of the method section

Do *not* write the method in the form of instructions. Your lab handbook will probably do this, but your report should be a chronology of what *was done*.

Avoid using personal pronouns (I, we, me, us, they, etc.), and instead use an objective, impersonal style. (But check this with your tutor, as some departments use different rules of style.)

YOUR TURN

Task 3

Look at the underlined verbs in this extract from the method section of a physics lab report. What tense is used and how does the writer create an objective, impersonal style?

> A first reading <u>was taken</u> at the point where the image on the screen <u>was considered</u> to be sharpest. Then upper and lower bound readings <u>were taken</u> around this point by adjusting the lens position until the image <u>became</u> unambiguously out of focus in either direction. These bounded readings <u>were used</u> to estimate the error in the focal length of the lens.

....

....

....

➡️ **Answers online at: https://study.sagepub.com/hopkinsandreid**

Describing equipment and apparatus

Sometimes you will need to describe apparatus or equipment. You may need to accompany this description with a diagram or drawing (which needs to be referred to in the text). When describing equipment we use the *present tense* (because it is considered to be permanent).

The example below shows how the present tense is used (in a passive form).

An optical wedge <u>is positioned</u> between the test-flash beam and the artificial pupil. At the beginning of the experiment the optical wedge <u>is set</u> to its highest setting. It <u>can be rotated</u> via a knob to adjust the intensity of the test flash.

Results: What to include and what not to include

In the results section you should present your experimental findings in the form of data and text. Your key results need to be clearly presented and described.

--- TIP ---

Results

Another person should be able to understand the results so that it is possible for them to draw their own conclusions, or use them for a different interpretation.

You should:

- label the origins of any theoretical results being used, e.g. tables of results can be used to present the theoretical values alongside the experimental results
- present the results of any calculations
- place details of the calculations in the Appendix, along with the raw data
- include any formulae you have used to derive final results from the raw measured data (or refer to them by the equation number used in the introduction/theory section)
- include tables and/or figures; these need to complement and clarify the information in the text, and be clearly referred to in the text, e.g. as in Figure 2.3
- never simply 'dump' tables and figures into your lab report without directing the reader to them in your writing.

Use of figures and tables

Your results section is highly likely to include tables and/or figures. There are some rules and conventions that you need to follow when incorporating these into your lab report.

YOUR TURN

Task 4

Find at least seven problems with the table below.

	Rider position	Correction
Mirror:	50cm	0.0cm
Pointer A:	47.445cm	+2.6cm
Pointer B:	46.5cm	+3.50cm

Table three – Calibration data

1 ....

2 ....

3 ....

4 ....

5 ....

6 ....

7 ....

→ **Answers online at: https://study.sagepub.com/hopkinsandreid**

Key points when including figures and tables

The problems with the table in Task 4 are highlighted in the corrected version below. The corrected version of the table demonstrates the conventions you need to follow when including tables in your lab report. Notice how captions for tables are positioned *above* the table, and for figures captions are positioned *below* the figure.

Numbered table. Caption above

Table 3.   Calibration data for mirror and pointers

	Rider position (cm)	Correction (cm)
Mirror:	50.0	0.0
Pointer A:	47.4	+2.6
Pointer B:	46.5	+3.5

Column titles in bold, with units

Row titles in bold

Figures in columns are aligned, there is consistency of decimal point places and consistency of font

You should *always* refer your reader to the tables and figures using expressions such as: 'Table 1 shows …', 'the results are given in Figure 1'. This is demonstrated in the example below notice that there is a caption, it is below the figure, and the written text directs the reader to the figure.

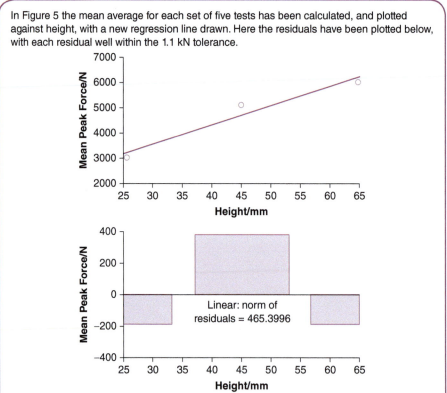

In Figure 5 the mean average for each set of five tests has been calculated, and plotted against height, with a new regression line drawn. Here the residuals have been plotted below, with each residual well within the 1.1 kN tolerance.

Linear: norm of residuals = 465.3996

Figure 5. A linear regression line drawn to fit the mean peak force for each height, projected against the size of each residual

---

TIP

Tables and figures

Note the use of capital 'F' to refer to the figure. Always use capital T for Table and F for Figure in your text when you refer to them by number.

The language of the results section

When describing how you gathered your results use past forms, but when referring to the tables and figures and the information they represent, you should use the present tense. The tenses have been underlined in the following sample, with grey indicating present forms and purple indicating past forms.

Figure 3 shows the line gradients for each AOC. These represent the Belt Tension Ratio (BTR). The differential of ln (BTR) with respect to AOC represents the coefficient of friction between belt and pulley. This can be determined graphically by finding the gradient of a linear best fit line plotted against data points calculated from experimental data (see Figure 4). The value obtained can then be used to calculate a theoretical estimate for the BTR; Figure 5 shows this prediction plotted against the actual data recorded. At AOC 270°, the input power supplied by the motor, and the output power developed by the belt drive were calculated using data supplied by the motor multimeter and belt drive tachometer. These power values were then used to calculate the motor efficiency at each level of torque recorded (see Figure 6).

Notice how all figures are referred to in the text.

Discussion: What it is and what to include

The discussion section is where you analyse the results your experiment has yielded. This section is key to the success of your lab report.

You should:

- discuss the *significance* of the results
- discuss your *interpretation* of them
- discuss what they do or do not *demonstrate* (and why)
- explain what can be deduced from your results
- discuss possible *limitations* and *errors* with the experimental procedure or data analysis
- describe possible causes of the errors
- make suggestions for improvements, if possible
- make recommendations for further experiments, if appropriate.

YOUR TURN

Task 5

Label the following sample from the discussion for the following features:

1 Significance of the results and what they demonstrate.
2 Further clarification of significance and limitation.
3 Development of discussion of errors.
4 Explanation of cause of errors.

> The value of 1.05 ± 0.02 eV is consistent with the quoted value for a silicon energy gap of 1.0–1.1 eV [1], and the results from this experiment lie within this range at the one-sigma level. Whilst this supports the validity of the theory, it does not constitute an accurate determination of the energy gap value for silicon as the silicon used was not a pure sample. Other errors to be considered include errors in the readings of the voltages across the potential divider. The method used for recording these measurements involved trying to read off a continually changing scale at the right moment. It is therefore likely that the reaction time of the person taking the readings affected the result. This is likely to be the main source of systematic error.

 Answers online at: https://study.sagepub.com/hopkinsandreid

TIP

Discussion

Use this checklist after writing your discussion. Does it:

- Compare the calculations expected in theory and the actual measurements taken?
- Provide suggestions for the causes of any discrepancies between theoretical and experimental measurements?
- Discuss sources of errors?
- Suggest how to improve the experiment?
- Discuss the significance of the results? For example, do they confirm your hypothesis or the objective of the experiment?

The language of the discussion

In this section you are discussing the outcome of the experiment, and this will demand mainly present forms. However, when discussing possible errors with equipment or methods, you may need to describe what was done (using a past form). The tenses in the following extract are underlined, with present tenses in grey and past tenses in purple.

Notice the use of 'hedging' with words like 'could', to show possibility rather than certainty (see also Chapter 7, Writing in academic style). This is useful language for discussing possible sources of errors.

The temperature of the ice-water bath in this experiment was assumed to be 0°C, but was not actually measured. As the table used for converting measured voltages to temperatures for the thermocouple [1] was calibrated for cold junctions at 0°C this could introduce some serious error, especially if the temperature were to drift over the course of the experiment. As the variation of voltage with temperature is non-linear even simple zero-error here could affect the trend in the final results. The experiment could be improved by monitoring the temperature of the ice-water bath throughout.

Conclusion: What is it, and what to include?

Your conclusion shows the reader what you have learnt by doing the experiment(s). This is the section of the lab report where you discuss your objectives and whether or not they were met. In the conclusion you should:

- summarise the experiment *briefly*
- state what has been achieved
- state what the significant results are
- comment on how your objectives have or have not been met
- NOT include anything new in the conclusion.

Notice that a conclusion section differs from the discussion by including information that has already been discussed in all the previous sections. It is there to draw your writing to a close. The conclusion will move from the specific to the general (in other words, it is the opposite shape to the introduction).

Figure 2.4 gives an example.

Comparison with expected values

Restatement of theory

Summary of experiment aim

Summary of results

Resistance in a silicon thermistor was measured over a range of temperatures in order to test the energy gap theory. Voltage readings were taken across a potential divider and a value for the energy gap of 1.05±0.02 eV was calculated. This value is consistent with the expected value of 1.0–1.1 eV. Although the method did not eliminate the possibility of systematic errors, it was appropriate for testing the theory of thermal excitation in a semiconductor, and the results confirmed that resistance in a semiconductor decreases with increasing temperature.

Figure 2.4   Conclusion – example of what to include

The language of the conclusion

The conclusion will include a mix of tenses. In the summary of what was done, the past tense will be used, and the discussion of the results may mix past and present. There will be further use of 'hedging' language to consider implications and any sources of error.

References

This section is simply a list of each source referred to in the lab report. There are different referencing systems. You will need to check with your tutor to find out what system they would like you to use. The most important thing is to be consistent and not mix conventions from two (or three) different referencing systems.

- Numeric referencing system: the references are listed in the order the source was cited.
- APA and Harvard referencing systems: the references are listed in alphabetical order.

For more details on how to write your reference list go to Chapter 8, Referencing with accuracy.

YOUR TURN

Task 6

Decide which section of the report the following samples are most likely to be taken from.

Sample A

The results obtained are not as expected; the value of E obtained falls outside the range originally specified of 190–210 GPa by a significant margin. Random error within the measurements of deflection and applied load can be discounted. However, the critical dimensions of the beam were only measured once. Thus, it is possible that one of the measurements of the beam was taken incorrectly due to human error.

Sample B

The dimensions for the beam were measured with a combination of vernier callipers and a ruler; the width, length and thickness, as well as the distance for which the deflection was to be measured from were all recorded, together with the uncertainties of the measuring equipment. Next, both the dial gauge and potentiometer were calibrated to zero whilst the beam remained unloaded within the frame.

Sample C

The aim of the experiment is to determine the deflection in a cantilever beam when a load is applied to the centre. The experimental value E can be determined by comparing the theory of a simple steel beam equation to the measurements made, using both theory and statistical methods to identify sources of error within the data and to reduce uncertainty.

Sample D

Figure 1 shows that the data taken from the potentiometer clearly does not follow a linear relationship. Also apparent is that despite using the maximum estimate of E as 210 GPa, the estimate line does not match the dial gauge data very closely.

Sample E

An experimental value of E was found through the use of least squares analysis. At 231 GPa, it falls outside of the range supplied for the steel the sample was made from. This presents two conclusions; either an error in measuring the critical dimensions in the beam occurred, or the range supplied is simply wrong. However, the data matches the linear trend predicted by the theory, so is at least qualitatively correct.

Sample F

In this experiment a small steel beam was placed on an aluminium extrusion frame and mass was applied incrementally to one end, whilst the other end remained fixed. The deflection of the beam was measured with both a dial gauge and a potentiometer. The experimental data was then compared with a theoretical model to provide an experimental value of Young's modulus for the beam. Least squares analysis of the data, combined with the calculation of standard error, produced a value of 231 GPa as the Young's modulus (E) of the steel beam, with a standard error of 1.06 GPa. These results are outside of the range supplied for the sample; E should fall within 190–210 GPa. Nevertheless, the standard error is very low, suggesting that there is either a systematic error remaining that has not been identified, or one of the control measurements is incorrect.

 Answers online at: https://study.sagepub.com/hopkinsandreid

Other points about lab reports

Although all lab reports include the same basic structure, there may be some small variations in the labels for the different sections, and different university departments may have slightly different requirements.

Title

You may have to provide your own title. If so, make sure that it provides a clear focus on the contents of the report.

Abstract

In some departments the abstract may be divided into paragraphs or bullet points with sub-headings summarising the aims, methods, results and conclusions of the experiment.

Sometimes, the abstract is called 'Summary' (e.g. in Mechanical Engineering).

Method

For some subjects, such as social science and psychology the method section may be divided into sub-sections with the following possible headings:

Participants: Here you describe who the subjects are for the experiment.

Materials: Here you provide information on the equipment and/or test materials used.

Design: Here you outline the test design that is being used. You should include information about the independent and dependent variables that are being measured.

Procedure: This is where you describe the steps that were taken (what was done).

Results and discussion

Sometimes the results and discussion sections are combined. You should check with your department and tutor.

Optional sections

Theory/theoretical background: When the theory that underpins the experiment(s) you are writing about is very long, you may be asked to include it in a separate section (rather than within the introduction). If so, this section will follow the introduction.

Acknowledgements: If someone has helped you, you may feel they deserve a mention in an acknowledgements section. This section comes *after* the references section.

Appendices: Use appendices for *extra* information that will support your report but that is *not essential* for the reader to read. Examples: complex mathematical derivations, specifications, detailed lists of equipment, etc.

- All appendices should have a title and must be referred to in the body of the main report (e.g. 'see Appendix A').
- Appendices are placed after the list of references (or after the acknowledgements).

COMPLETING YOUR LAB REPORT

Editing and proofreading

When you have completed your first draft, you need to do a number of things.

Firstly, have a break. Don't look at your work for at least a day. This will create some distance between the process and challenges of writing and the work itself, and when you return, you will be able to view it with a refreshed and critical eye.

Review your lab report in bite-sized chunks. This involves focusing on each section separately. For each section ask yourself the following questions.

Content

- Have I included the relevant information?
- Have I included anything that is not relevant (and can therefore be deleted)?

Research material

- Are there sufficient, sources, examples and evidence to give the background theory?
- Have I paraphrased the original source sufficiently and is the meaning the same?

Structure and cohesion

- Do my ideas connect together?
- Do my paragraphs connect together logically?
- Are ideas presented in the right order?
- Have I produced an effective introduction and conclusion?
- Have I put the sections in the correct order?
- Is there any unnecessary repetition in the different sections?

Style

- Have I used a formal academic style throughout my lab report?
- Have I used the first person (I, we)?
- Have I used any informal words or phrases, or slang expressions?
- Have I over-used any words or phrases?

Clarity

- Is my use of language clear and easy to read?
- Is there anything confusing or difficult to follow?
- Are any of my sentences too long?
- Are my explanations of technical language easy to understand?

Language and grammar

- Is my punctuation and spelling accurate?
- Have I used accurate tenses and sentence structures?

Referencing and citations

- Are my in-text citations accurate, consistent and appropriate?
- Is my reference list accurate, is it formatted correctly, and does it include all sources used in my essay?

Making revisions, improvements and enhancements

 **YOUR TURN**

Task 7

Using the editing checklist (Table 1.2), identify problems in the following paragraph from a method section of a lab report and make some revisions.

> We took the first reading at the point where the image on the screen was sharpest. After this, upper and lower bound readings were taken around this point by adjusting the lens position so until the image just becomes unambiguously out of focus in either direction. The error in the focal length of the lens was estimated using these bounded readings. It is also noted that the distance from the mirror to the lens should make no difference, as if the lens is at the focal point it should refract the diverging rays into a set of parallel rays.

....

....

....

 Answers online at: https://study.sagepub.com/hopkinsandreid

TROUBLESHOOTING: COMMON EDITING PROBLEMS

My lab report is too short

Ask yourself:

- Are my introduction and conclusion too short?
- Do I need to add more information to make my explanations and arguments understandable to the reader?
- Is there anything I can add to improve or develop the clarity of my report (e.g. more detailed data analysis, more depth to my discussion)?
- Have I included enough sources?

BUT BEWARE: Don't add waffle; add content.

My lab report is too long

Ask yourself:

- Are my introduction and conclusion too long?
- Have I included quotes and the reference list in my word count? (They usually don't count!)
- Is there anything I can remove as repeated or irrelevant information?
- Can I remove unnecessary descriptions or vocabulary, or reduce the size of my sentences?

BUT BEWARE: Don't lose the meaning.

The complete lab report

Identifies the problem under investigation Summary of background information and the objective which you hope to achieve. Include references to previous published studies where necessary (e.g. if you are trying to build on replicate someone results).

elas
character

The objective to determine an through a simple by comparing the measurements mad identify sources of e

To simplify the theor several assumptions beam was attached weight attached to vertically downw discounted to Given these be:

Go online **https://study.sagepub.com/hopkins andreid** to see an example of a complete lab report, with annotations to help you identify and understand the features that contribute to successful writing. The boxes refer you to the relevant chapters for more information on the particular feature of the lab report/writing.

YOUR CHAPTER TAKEAWAY

Lab Writing Process Checklist

✓ (tick when completed)

Have I ...

○ ordered the sections correctly?

○ made each section clear and appropriate?

○ used scientific language?

○ understood the instructions and followed them accurately?

○ included the necessary theory and shown the relevance of the expriment(s) in my introduction?

○ referred to an appropriate number of good-quality sources?

○ used the correct referencing system and cited my sources accurately and been consistent in style?

○ written the correct amount of words for each section (and not exceeded the wordcount)?

○ discussed the significance of the results in the discussion section?

○ labelled my tables and figures correctly?

○ mentioned my tables and figures in the written text?

Your one takeaway

....

....

YOUR PROGRESS

CHAPTER THREE

Writing Exams, Reflective Essays, Dissertations and Posters

YOUR PROGRESS

CHAPTER DASHBOARD

Your objectives list:

 Develop skills and confidence in exam writing

 Identify the key features of different types of academic writing

 Build strategies for getting started on different types of written assignments

min   max

'Writing is easy. All you have to do is cross out the wrong words.'

– Mark Twain

My three other assignment goals:

1. ....

2. ....

3. ....

What your tutor is looking for

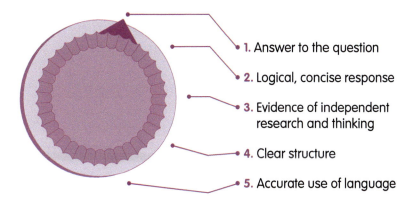

1. Answer to the question
2. Logical, concise response
3. Evidence of independent research and thinking
4. Clear structure
5. Accurate use of language

Accuracy

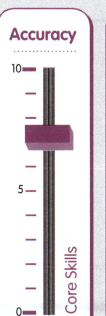

10
5
0

Core Skills

Style

10
5
0

Core Skills

Clarity

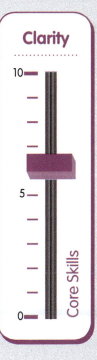

10
5
0

Core Skills

Being concise

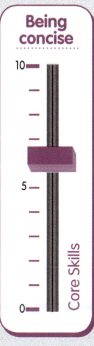

10
5
0

Core Skills

Being informed

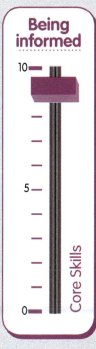

10
5
0

Core Skills

WATCH OUT FOR:

Make sure you understand academic conventions for different types of writing, and use an appropriate style

Diagnostic

How confident are you about different types of academic writing?

On a scale of 1-5, where 1 = not confident and 5 = very confident, rate your responses to the following statements.

Writing exams

I know how to write effective exam answers ☐

I know how to revise efficiently and effectively ☐

I know how to focus my response ☐

I know how to answer all parts of exam questions ☐

I know how to manage my time during exams ☐

Writing reflective essays

I know how to write a reflective essay ☐

I know what reflection means ☐

I know how to get started on a reflective essay ☐

I know what style should be used ☐

I know how to balance personal experiences with academic content ☐

Writing dissertations

I know what sections are included in a dissertation ☐

I know how to get started on a dissertation ☐

I know how to find a gap in the literature ☐

I know how to write a research question ☐

I know how to write a literature review ☐

I know what a literature review should include ☐

Writing posters

I know how to write a poster for a presentation ☐

I know what a good poster presentation should look like ☐

I know what elements should and should not be included ☐

I know what information should be included ☐

I know how much information should be included ☐

I know how to make it visually attractive ☐

My score ⬭

For feedback on your score, go online at:
https://study.sagepub.com/hopkinsandreid

Although essay and lab reports are common assignments at university, you may be asked to write other types of texts such as exams, reflective essays, dissertations and posters. The rules of good academic writing apply no matter what the genre, but there are some key things you need to consider when preparing to do these other kinds of tasks. It is vital, therefore, that you are able to recognise the specific features and conventions used in different writing genres so that you can then apply them effectively in your own writing.

This chapter is divided into four sections, each focusing on a different genre of academic writing: writing exams, reflective essays, writing your dissertation and posters. Each section will identify and deconstruct the key features and conventions of writing in that context and provide you with strategies to help develop your skills and confidence, and complete tasks successfully.

WRITING EXAMS

Taking examinations can be stressful and challenging for everyone. The types of writing you will be required to do in exams can vary across disciplines; from short answer and multiple choice responses to longer essay-style questions. While each type has its own set of challenges, the following strategies will help you build confidence and succeed in all exam environments.

Before the exam

Follow our **3P** process for effective preparation before your exam.

Plan

- Devise a revision plan that works for you.
- Choose revision location(s) that work for you (e.g. do you like quiet or noisy study spaces?).
- Start revising early (not the night before!!) and stick to your revision plan.
- Build revision into your daily routine.
- Prioritise your study – identify strengths and gaps in your knowledge.

Prepare

- Target relevant content and revisit your notes (lectures/seminars/readings/ assignments).
- Attend revision sessions with your tutors (they will often give you clues to exam content/topics).

- Take notes of your notes:
  - scale down/simplify/shrink ... then ...
  - scale up/expand/add detail in your own re-phrased words.
- Use the Cornell note-taking template (see Figures 14.2 and 14.3) to revise 'trigger' words and phrases (memory cues).
- Revise in short bursts of intense study/note-taking – maximum 40 minutes per revision session.
- Revise with friends and classmates – test each other.
- Vary your revision methods (e.g. don't just write everything down – say it out loud – present ideas to friends. etc.). This will ensure your brain stays active.

Practise

- Make up some questions based on key exam topics and practise answering them a few days later, after you have revised.
- Use exam papers from previous years to practise writing up answers under exam conditions (or use the questions as revision prompts). You should be able to access these via your university library or department.
- Work with friends and classmates to test each other.

During the exam

Follow our **CONFIDENCE** process for exam writing success.

C is for Clear

- Your response should be simple, clear and easy to follow.
- Key ideas explained, analysed and evaluated.
- Relevant and most significant information presented: key theories, concepts, examples, authors.
- All content should relate directly to the question.

O is for Outline

- Before you write, make a short plan – what are you going to include and how are you going to structure your response?
- Note down key words/phrases/concepts, etc.
- Create headings.

You may feel like you don't have time to do this, but transferring key words from your head to paper will help focus your ideas and actually reduce stress and build your confidence.

N is for Names

- Include some key authors/critics in your response (if relevant). It is unlikely you will be asked to memorise quotes, but adding key writers will help to improve the quality of your answer.

F is for Focus

- Make sure that you answer all parts of the question and do not include irrelevant information.

I is for Informed

- Include critical analysis and evaluation in your response – avoid too much description.
- Demonstrate that you have read beyond your lecture notes and incorporate a range of evidence around the question topic: pros and cons, supporters and critics and so on.

D is for Detail

- Provide sufficient and relevant detail in your response so that it moves beyond a generalised and limited summary of ideas. Detail may include clear and concise explanations, examples, some data and statistics to support your ideas.

E is for Examples

- Include some examples to help explain your points, and enhance your answer. Examples might include real-world cases, research studies, data and statistics, etc.

N is for Neat

- Make sure your handwriting is legible, neat and tidy. You will be required to handwrite many of your exams. It is essential therefore that your handwriting is legible and tidy, so that your marker can read your response! This can be difficult when you have to write quickly and under time pressure.
- Practise your handwriting to improve legibility, speed and control. We don't hand write as much as we used to, so our writing muscles need to be trained and exercised.
- If your writing is poor, practise writing in capitals.
- If you make a mistake or alteration, cross it out with a single line – DON'T SCRIBBLE IT OUT.

C is for **Concise**

- Keep your sentences short and simple.
- Nail down key ideas as succinctly as you can and avoid/eliminate waffle.
- Use bullets and headings to streamline your answer and save time.

E is for **Evaluation**

- Ensure that you include some analysis and evaluation in your response, such as strengths and weaknesses, advantages and disadvantages, implications and your own views (if appropriate).

TIP

During the exam: don't forget to **PASS**

Prioritise your answers – choose the easiest first, as this will help build your confidence.

Analyse the question – break it down into four parts: Topic, Focus, Instruction Words, Scope/Limitations.

Structure your response – before you write, make a plan and write down key words/ideas, section headings, relevant writers and examples, etc.

Scrutinise your answers – leave enough time at the end of the exam to check and review your answers and make any changes as necessary.

After the exam

- Rest, relax and put it out of your mind – take a break.
- Don't revisit or dissect your answers – it's too stressful (and too late!).
- Move on to the next exam – or celebrate that it's the last one!

REFLECTIVE ESSAYS

As part of your course you may be asked to do some reflective writing. Being able to reflect is important because it enhances our learning. We learn by looking back on experiences and assessing the value of the way we did something (perhaps by comparing it with the way someone else did the same thing). The following quotation explains the importance of being a reflective practitioner.

Reflect, often. If we take time to notice what just happened, we learn how the system operates. Without reflection, we go blindly on our way, creating more unintended consequences, and failing to achieve anything useful. (Wheatley, 2002)

Wheatley, M. (2002) *It's an Interconnected World*. Available from: http://margaret wheatley.com/wp-content/uploads/2014/12/Its- An-Interconnected- World.pdf

What is reflective writing?

Reflection starts with you and your experiences. However, it is more than just description. To reflect successfully you need to:

- describe what happened/your experiences and what the outcomes were
- analyse why it happened and what contributed to the outcomes
- evaluate the significance of the experience in terms of learning.

YOUR TURN

Task 1

Compare the following three samples from a piece of reflective writing written by a pharmacy student. Which one is the most successful in terms of reflection and why?

Sample A

For our first placement I spent three days with a community pharmacist in situ, and shadowed her working day. On my first day I watched her carrying out her administrative work, and then make up some of the prescriptions. She worked in the pharmacy giving out the prescriptions as well. In the afternoon she did some work for the local General Practitioners' surgery, working with referred patients to discuss their medication and ways of administering it. Each of the following two days were exactly the same. I enjoyed my time with the pharmacist as it was informative and interesting and I learnt a lot.

Sample B

For our first placement I spent three days with a community pharmacist in situ, and shadowed her working day. Each day began with some administrative tasks, but once the pharmacy opened to the public her time was taken up with patients coming in to collect their prescriptions and with dispensing these. At first I was not aware of the skill with which she talked to the patients, but over the three days I realised that she was using her conversation with the patients to elicit information about them and was then able to advise them on health matters. For example, a woman came in to collect a prescription for her son's asthma, and through the careful use of questions the pharmacist was able to determine that the child lived in a house in which two adults smoked heavily. She used further questions that led to the woman expressing a wish to cut down on her smoking, and the pharmacist then directed her to a local smoking support group.

Sample C

For our first placement I spent three days with a community pharmacist in situ, and shadowed her working day. Each day began with some administrative tasks, but once the pharmacy opened to the public her time was taken up with patients coming in to collect their prescriptions and with dispensing these. At first I did not realise the skill with which she talked to the patients, but over the three days I realised that she was using her conversation with the patients to elicit information about them and was then able to advise them on health matters. For example, a woman came in to collect a prescription for her son's asthma, and through the careful use of questions the pharmacist was able to determine that the child lived in a house in which two adults smoked heavily. She used further questions that led to the woman expressing a wish to cut down on her smoking, and the pharmacist then directed her to a local smoking support group.

During my time in the pharmacy I was given the opportunity to dispense some of the medicines and to talk to the patients myself. At first I was not very good at this. I found it hard to think of things to say. However, through analysis of her techniques, I realised that if I started by asking questions about their day, and their plans, a more relaxed conversation began to flow. I learnt that by being friendly and warm, people are more likely to reveal concerns and worries that I could then advise on. I feel that my aware-ness of the day-to-day realities of being a pharmacist was raised significantly through this placement, and I have learnt more about the skills I need to develop. I now know that there is substantially more to the role than an extensive knowledge of drugs and medicines, and people skills are a crucial part of the job of a community pharmacist.

....

....

....

The third sample is the most successful as a reflective piece. The first sample includes description only. The second sample includes analysis and this is sup-ported by an example. The third sample takes the reflection a step further and includes evaluative comments about how the awareness has led to understanding of what needs to be done.

Figure 3.1 shows how reflective practice is not a linear process, but involves ques-tioning and assessment of outcomes in order to result in changes in behaviour (or confirmation of behaviour) in similar situations in the future.

A good piece of reflective writing will move from description to analysis and result in an evaluation of how to behave or respond in a similar situation at a future time.

Sample C from Task 1 is marked up in Figure 3.2 to show how it successfully moves beyond mere description.

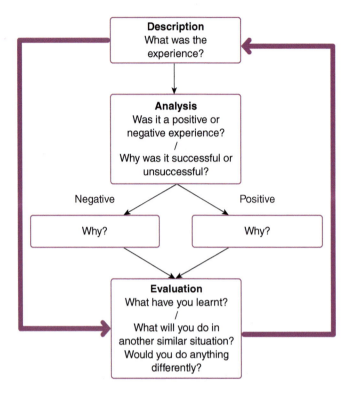

Figure 3.1 The reflective practice process

For our first placement I spent three days with a community pharmacist in situ, and shadowed her working day. Each day began with some administrative tasks, but once the pharmacy opened to the public her time was taken up with patients coming in to collect their prescriptions and with dispensing these. At first I did not realise the skill with which she talked to the patients, but over the three days I realised that she was using her conversation with the patients to elicit information about them and was then able to advise them on health matters. For example, a woman came in to collect a prescription for her son's asthma, and through the careful use of questions the pharmacist was able to determine that the child lived in a house in which two adults smoked heavily. She used further questions that led to the woman expressing a wish to cut down on her smoking, and the pharmacist then directed her to a local smoking support group.

Description of the day's activities

Analysis of what was done: why was it successful? Example to support the analysis

Description of the writer's own experience

During my time in the pharmacy I was given the opportunity to dispense some of the medicines and to talk to the patients myself. At first I was not very good at this. I found it hard to think of things to say. However, through analysis of her techniques, I realised that if I started by asking questions about their day, and their plans, a more relaxed conversation began to flow. I learnt that by being friendly and warm, people are more likely to reveal concerns and worries that I could then advise on. I feel that my awareness of the day-to-day realities of being a pharmacist was raised significantly through this placement, and I have learnt more about the skills I need to develop. I now know that there is substantially more to the role than an extensive knowledge of drugs and medicines, and people skills are a crucial part of the job of a community pharmacist.

Analysis of what was done: why was it successful?

Evaluation: what the writer has learnt and what the outcomes are

Figure 3.2 Marked up Sample C from Task 1

Different types of reflective writing

Although all reflective writing needs to include description, analysis and evaluation, different types of tasks may require slightly different ways to organise your information and ideas.

YOUR TURN

Task 2

Using the reflection template below, divide the following assignment titles into whether they demand reflection on a training experience, reflection on an activity or require a description of learning from a problem.

a. What have you learnt on your placement?
b. Describe a time when you were faced with a problem and explain what you did to solve it.
c. What did you gain from working in a group and how will you apply this knowledge in your future career?
d. Now that you have completed your ten hours teaching practice, what changes will you make to the way you approach lesson planning?
e. What challenges did you face in your laboratory work and how did you overcome them?
f. Using what you have learnt on this unit write an account of a time where your motivation has been enhanced by active employer policy, and reflect on how your experience does or does not support theories of motivation at work.

Task 2 reflection template

Reflection on training	Problem solving	Reflection on a specific activity or experience

Answers online at: https://study.sagepub.com/hopkinsandreid

Using sources in your reflective writing

Any kind of academic writing will draw on *evidence* to support the writer's stance and to demonstrate awareness of previous research or theories relating to the topic. In reflective writing a large part of the evidence will come from *you*. However, some assignments will require you to assess theories against your own experience and show your understanding in relation to personal knowledge.

The title in (f) above states clearly that the assignment requires reference to published sources.

YOUR TURN

Task 3

Look at the sample from an answer to the assignment title (f). How does the writer incorporate sources to build their arguments whilst also including their own experience and thoughts?

> Herzberg's two-factor theory states that employees will be motivated by the presence of both motivator factors and hygiene factors and that the absence of the latter, in particular, will lead to poor morale and effectiveness at work (Herzberg, 1959). According to Herzberg (1959), motivator factors include feeling that your work is acknowledged, and that there are opportunities for career progression, and hygiene factors include factors such as salary, relationships with managers and colleagues, and the work environment. Herzberg's theory fits with my own experience of working in a large company where there was a cultural shift in the time that I worked there. Initially, the environment was pleasant with a non-hierarchical model of management (Dieffenbach, 2013), and good relations between all employees. At this time, I felt happy to go to work, enjoyed being with my colleagues and despite the reasonably poor comparative salary, I considered the company a good employer. However, a change in management led to a greater divide between managers and workers, which in turn led to increased feelings of being unsupported in our work, and I began to feel unappreciated, and overworked. These negative feelings are described by McClelland (1961), who built on Herzberg's ideas and suggests that …
>
> I would argue with Mullins (2004) who suggested that motivation is a 'driving force', as this suggests effort and energy and I feel that my own experience indicates that is not the case for all situations. When my employer improved the working environment to include a seating area and plants, I did not feel any greater drive or energy to get on with my work, but there was a more positive, relaxed atmosphere amongst colleagues.

Notice how the sources are woven into the text and used to set ideas up against which we test our own experience.

TIP

Using sources

Ensure you are absolutely clear about the nature of your reflective writing task before you start. Does your tutor expect you to include sources, or is it simply an expression of your own learning from an experience?

How to organise your reflective writing

In order to ensure you include description, analysis and evaluation you can use the **CIDER** approach to organise your writing.

The **CIDER** approach

Include information on the following:

Context/situation.

Idea/action.

Development/outcome.

Evaluation.

Reflection.

However, your reflective writing may involve a *problem*. That requires the **SPIDER** approach.

The **SPIDER** approach

Include information on the following:

Situation/context.

Problem.

Idea/action.

Development/outcome.

Evaluation.

Reflection.

Task 4

Look at the sample answer to the following task:

> Problem solving: Reflect on an experience where you led and motivated a group (400–600 words)

How well does it follow the requirements of a reflective writing piece? Does it follow the SPIDER approach?

During my first year at university I volunteered at a care home for the elderly in Bath. Specifically, I visited the care home with my bandmates, and we played music from the fifties, sixties and seventies to the residents. Usually, this was straightforward, but on occasions some problems would arise with the residents which were related to the music we were playing. As a volunteer with little experience of working with the elderly, I was not very comfortable trying to take control in difficult situations. However, as the lead singer of the band, the residents generally tended to direct any requests, and on occasion, their frustrations, to me rather than the other members of the band (guitarist and percussion player).

On one visit, we arrived a bit later than usual due to transport problems. One resident, an elderly man in his eighties with dementia, called Graham, was showing signs of distress, shouting and appearing anxious. This upset some of the other residents who also began shouting. We started playing music as quickly as we could because we thought that might help calm the situation. Some of the carers were trying to help Graham but he started shouting that I should stop singing. I found this particular situation very challenging and I was not sure what to do: should I continue to sing in the hope that the music would calm him down, or do as he asked and stop singing? For a while, we carried on with the song, but as he became more agitated and louder, I decided to stop singing and went and sat with Graham to ask him what he wanted me to do. The result was instant – he stopped shouting, and he asked us to play his favourite Beatles song. Whilst I chatted to him, my bandmates talked individually to each other resident and collected requests which we then played. This worked well, with the residents enjoying being identified as the person who had requested each song we played.

On reflection, it seems clear that taking steps to relieve anxiety is the best approach when someone is displaying aggressive behaviour and I should have stopped singing immediately. In the end, by choosing to talk directly to Graham and allowing him some control over the decisions, I successfully defused the situation. I think that getting the whole band involved in talking to each resident and asking for requests allowed everyone to feel valued and have some control. After the incident, we discussed the situation with the staff, and they suggested that Graham's outburst may have been due to our late arrival. Any changes to the day's plans can cause anxiety, and we, unfortunately, played our part in the problem that arose on this occasion. I now realise that it may have been more sensible to find out why Graham was upset before we started playing. By speaking to him at the outset, we may have been able to alleviate the distress caused.

As a result of this experience, we changed the way we organised our visits to start with a quick chat with each individual resident, collecting song requests from them to inform our play list. I learnt that groups of people should be treated as individuals with differing needs, and you should listen to each individual and allow them to feel valued and in control of decisions. I believe this is a wise and appropriate approach to take when working with groups of people, whatever the situation, and hope to use the skills gained here in future contexts.

S ....

P ....

I ....

D ....

E ....

R ....

➡️ **Answers online at: https://study.sagepub.com/hopkinsandreid**

The language of reflective writing

Using personal pronouns

Although reflective writing is personal, it is still academic writing, and you need to follow the conventions discussed earlier in this section. However, there is one major difference from other types of academic writing: you are writing about yourself (and other people) and your own experiences, and you therefore need to use the personal pronouns *I*, and *we*.

TIP

Language

Although you are writing about yourself and including personal insights, remember to use formal academic style. Do not use contractions (e.g. *didn't* or *couldn't*), or informal vocabulary.

Avoiding being judgemental

Sometimes our reflection and learning may involve analysis and evaluation of other people's behaviour. It is important to remain non-judgemental and objective when writing about this.

Task 5

Compare the two versions below. How does writer B manage to avoid being judgemental?

Writer A

In our group one girl was really annoying. She wouldn't speak to the rest of us except when directly asked a question, and she didn't contribute any ideas.

Writer B

Not all people in the group contributed equally. One girl seemed very reticent and did not speak except when directly asked a question. It may have been more difficult for her than the rest of us, as she did not know any of us before we were put in this group, whereas the others in the group lived in the same building and were friends. We may have been quite intimidating, and I wonder if we did enough to include her. In future I will try to make sure that we start group work activities by getting to know each other first before starting the tasks.

 Answers online at: https://study.sagepub.com/hopkinsandreid

Task 6

Rewrite the following short sample to be less judgemental and to use more appropriate formal language.

Although I enjoyed working in the lab, the team leader was difficult to work with. He was very unfriendly, and never seemed happy with anything any of us did. He didn't seem to get that we were meant to be a team and didn't sit with us in coffee breaks. I have to admit that it was down to him and the fact that I didn't really know whether he thought my work was any good that I didn't enjoy the placement as much as I could have.

....

....

....

....

....

....

....

....

....

➡ **Answers online at: https://study.sagepub.com/hopkinsandreid**

Top tips for reflective writing

- Use personal pronouns (I and we).
- Ensure you move from description to analysis and make evaluative comments to show your learning.
- Ensure you are non-judgemental when discussing the behaviour and characteristics of others.
- When other people are part of your learning, consider the situation from their point of view – is it the same as yours?
- If possible, demonstrate the transferability of your learning.
- Where expected, ensure you refer to sources, theories and ideas from others to support (or refute) your own experience.

WRITING YOUR DISSERTATION

Most degree programmes include a requirement in your final year for you to carry out a research project of some kind, which you then need to write up in the form of a dissertation. The purpose of this dissertation is to allow you to investigate in depth an area of particular interest to you. This investigation is different from most of the work you have done on your degree because it is (in most cases) on a topic that you choose yourself, does not have any taught element, and involves a write-up that is longer than any previous assignment. An undergraduate dissertation is usually between 10,000 and 15,000 words long. You will have a 'supervisor' in your department who will advise you and support you at all stages of your assignment.

The process of writing up your project/research

Initially, the whole process of carrying out a research project may seem daunting. However, if you tackle the process following logical steps you will find that it can be an exciting and rewarding experience.

Step 1: Choosing your topic

Some students know right away what they want to investigate. Others may not have any idea at first. You need to settle on a topic that you will enjoy delving into. To get started, ask yourself the following questions:

a. Which topic on my degree so far have I enjoyed the most?
b. What aspect of this topic did I like and why?
c. What specific areas of focus would I like to know more about?

After answering these questions, you should have an idea of the general area you would like to investigate.

Step 2: Creating your research questions and devising a 'working title'

A working title is your initial title that will allow you to get started on the research process. It may change as you work through your reading and carry out your investigation, but it is a necessary starting point that allows you to narrow down the area of focus.

A different approach is to devise your research questions first and then create a working title. You need to know what it is you are trying to find out, so you should consider one or two concise questions that summarise what you are looking for answers to.

For example, if your general area of interest is *the changing role of women in sport*, and you were particularly interested in cricket, your research questions could be:

How easy is it for women to participate in cricket in the UK?

Has this changed over the past 20 years?

And your working title could be something like:

An investigation into the current state of women's cricket in the UK and how participation rates have changed over the past 20 years.

Step 3: Using your research questions to guide your research

Now that you have your research questions and a working title, you can start reading to provide the background knowledge necessary to help you devise your research plan. You should follow the advice for reading given in Chapter 9, starting with question generation, leading to finding relevant sources, taking clear notes, making annotations on your notes to show how they relate to the questions, and questioning what you read at every stage.

Your reading is necessary for two key reasons:

1. You need to ensure that you know what research has been done already into your topic. If your research questions have been comprehensively answered, you may need to alter your research questions to focus on a less well documented area. For example, if after reading, you discover that there is a great deal of research into women in sport, and how it has changed, but not much that specifically focuses on women's cricket, your focus is good. If, however, you find that there has been research that has asked exactly the same questions as you and used adult women cricketers in the studies, you could decide to narrow your focus down to cricket in schools.

2. You will need to write a literature review in your dissertation document, and this is where you demonstrate that you have knowledge of previous studies, key theories and current research into your field.

Step 4: Making a plan of action

Your reading will have helped you understand what is already known in your field and what is left to be found out. You may have adjusted your questions and working title in the light of your reading (or not!). Your questions should be addressing a gap in the knowledge (or aiming to replicate what is known to confirm its veracity).

Therefore, you need to make a plan of action so that you leave enough time to write up your dissertation. The first stage is the actual research or study. You need to know **when**, **where**, **how**, and **with what** or **whom** you will do your research, and **how** you will **collect** and **analyse** your **data**.

Once you have your data, you need to write up your dissertation.

Use the following rules to plan your writing up:

- Write about a page a day.
- Work backwards from at least two weeks before the submission date to calculate when you need to start your writing. (A page is about 500 words, so, for example, if your dissertation is 15,000 words long, you will need at least 30 days to do the writing.)
- Leave two or more weeks at the end for editing and proofreading.
- Ask a close friend to read it bit by bit and provide feedback on clarity, accuracy and appropriacy.

TIP

Dissertation planning

Use time-management tools to help you stay on track, e.g. a Gantt chart, or a planning app on your phone. It will probably take you three times longer than you expect to write up your dissertation! Be prepared, and plan!

Step 5: Writing up your dissertation

Your dissertation is a longer version of other reports or essays you have written, and the structure is similar to the fishbone structure shown in Chapter 1. It will have an introduction, body and conclusion. There are some sections that you need to include that you may not have included in other work, however. Your dissertation needs to include the following sections (Figure 3.3):

- Notice that the first thing your reader will read (after the title) is your abstract. However, you need to write this **last**. Your abstract is a summary of the whole project, and will include aims and objectives, methods, results and conclusions. You cannot write this until you have completed your write-up (see below for more information about writing an abstract).

Remember, you are telling a story, and it needs to flow logically from beginning to end. To help the reader, the chapters of your dissertation need to be numbered, as do the sections within the chapters. You may also have sub-sections, and these will need to be numbered too.

Your headings and sub-headings need to be consistent both in style and in grammar.

Your contents page will look something like Table 3.1 (although, of course, there will be variations depending on the subject and your discipline).

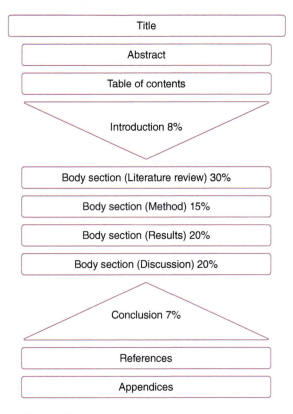

Figure 3.3 Dissertation sections

Table 3.1 Example contents page

Contents	Page
1. Introduction	3
1.1 Background to the study	3
1.2 The scope of the study	5
1.3 Aims and objectives	5
2. Literature review	
2.1 The local market	6
2.1.1 The local shop sector	6
2.1.2 Decline of the independent store	8
2.1.3 Rise of specific independent stores	9
2.2 The Economic Benefits of Local Shopping	9
2.2.1 The Local Multiplier Effect	10
2.2.2 Community benefits	11
2.3 Consumer behaviour	11
2.3.1 Current trends	12
2.3.2 Different kinds of consumer	12
2.3.3 Different kinds of product purchasing behaviour	13

(Continued)

Table 3.1 (Continued)

YOUR TURN

Task 7

How many inconsistencies can you find from this section of a dissertation contents page?

2.0 Introduction

   2.1 What is the problem

   3.2 Why coaching children is a special case

   4.3 Scope of project

   5.4 Aims and objectives

....

....

 Answers online at: https://study.sagepub.com/hopkinsandreid

TIP

Proofreading

Often students who get low marks hand in a write-up that is not fully completed. Check you have completed information where you wrote 'Figure xx', or 'see Chapter xx', or '(Brown, 2009, p. xx)'.

Writing an abstract

Your abstract is the last thing you should write, and it summarises the entire project. It therefore needs to be concise, clear and accurate. Usually, your abstract is not included in your word count.

In order to write your abstract, look at each section of your dissertation one-by-one and summarise the main points to:

- justify the research and give the objectives (introduction)
- identify the key points needed to provide background (from your introduction)
- describe the overall methods
- give the main results/findings
- discuss and show the significance of these results
- give your overall conclusions.

 **YOUR TURN**

Task 8

Does the following abstract cover all of the points above?

This project investigated how public perception of women in sports commentating has changed over the past fifty years. Fifty years ago women's sport was rarely in the public eye, and female commentators were non-existent. However, in the past twenty years this has changed, and there are now a small number of women commentators reporting across a range of sports. This investigation used questionnaires to assess the views of sports spectators on male and female commentators for a variety of sports, and used a small focus group discussion to triangulate. The findings suggest that there is still some negativity relating to women commentating, but this is very sports-dependent, with football and rugby having the most negativity and tennis and golf the least. Over 80% of respondents felt that female presenters commentating on male tennis matches was acceptable, but only 40% of respondents felt the same for rugby. The findings suggest that there

(Continued)

(Continued)

> is still bias relating to women in sports commentating, but that this is declining. This is probably due to an increase in prevalence of women in sports commentating, making it a less unusual phenomenon, alongside an increase in the visibility of women's sport in general. Further research is needed into why certain sports inspire more negativity around this topic than others.

- ☐ justify the research and give the objectives (introduction)

- ☐ identify the key points needed to provide background (from your introduction)

- ☐ describe the overall methods

- ☐ give the main results/findings

- ☐ discuss and show the significance of these results

- ☐ give your overall conclusions.

➡ Answers online at: https://study.sagepub.com/hopkinsandreid

A reader needs to be able to get an overview of the whole project from your abstract, so when you have written it, check that it does this.

Writing a literature review

Your literature review is the part of your report where you show what is already known about the area under investigation and demonstrate the need for your particular study. You should approach this just as you have the writing of an essay. It is **not** a description or list of everything you have read. Instead it is a synthesis of your reading, with evaluation and analysis. Use the guidelines for reading and writing your essay in Chapters 9 and 1 as a guide.

One significant difference between an essay and a report like a dissertation, aside from the length, is that you will be organising your ideas under headings and sub-headings. Ensure that you organise your reading and notes by the sections they are most relevant to (you will have identified your sections at the planning stage).

TIP

Literature review

Don't try to write it all in one go. Plan your sections and write them in small chunks.

Writing the other sections (see also Chapter 2, Getting started on your lab report)

Method

You need to tell the reader what was done. This means describing the research methods and explaining your choice. This will include information on the following:

- Are your methods qualitative or quantitative?
- Who (if any) are the participants?
- Are you analysing any documents, systems, organisations? If so what are they and why are you analysing them?
- What did you do first, second, etc.?
- What ethical considerations are there?

It is a common style convention to write what *was done* rather than what you did, and write it so that someone else would be able to replicate your study.

Results

Here you describe what you have found out. You need to identify the most significant patterns in your data, and use tables and figures to support your description. Your tables and figures are a visual representation of your findings, but remember to describe what they show in your writing.

Discussion

Here you show the significance of your results or findings. You analyse what they mean, and what the implications may be. Talk about any limitations to your study, and make suggestions for further studies to build on your findings.

Conclusion

This is a summary of your project, reminding the reader of the background to your study, your objectives, and showing how you met them. Do **not** include any new information that you have not discussed before.

References

As you have done in all your previous work at university, this is the list of all the sources you have cited in your dissertation. Ensure you are consistent and follow the conventions for the particular referencing system you are using (see Chapter 8, Referencing with accuracy).

Appendices

Include any extra information that your reader *may* like to read. It should not be essential for your reader to read them in order to understand your dissertation. Your appendices should be labelled (e.g. Appendix A, Appendix B, etc.). Examples of material for the appendices include detailed data tables (summarised in your results section), the complete version of a document you have used an extract from, etc.

POSTERS

Writing a poster

A poster is a visual way of communicating research. University programmes frequently ask students to submit posters as part of their assessed work. This provides excellent practice for any future situations where you have to communicate your ideas in a succinct and interesting way.

To make a successful poster you need to first consider what the purpose of the poster is. A poster is not a research paper printed on a large piece of paper. A good poster uses interesting and carefully thought-out ways to communicate ideas in a visual medium.

YOUR TURN

Task 9

Look at the unsuccessful poster in Figure 3.4. How many problems can you identify? This poster is very poor for the following reasons:

....

....

....

....

....

....

....

....

Answers online at: https://study.sagepub.com/hopkinsandreid

This report aims to assess the level and distribution of heavy metal contamination across a public park. The source of these metal arisings lies in the historic use of the site. The site has been used extensively in the past as a military training site, and more recently as a landfill site. Since 1990, however, the site has been used exclusively as a public area for recreation. A risk assessment was carried out in order to identify any high-risk areas of the park in terms of heavy metal contamination.

At contaminated sites, common heavy metals found in order of abundance are; lead, chromium, arsenic, zinc, cadmium, copper and mercury (USEPA, 1997). Prior knowledge of the historical use of the land in question can help guide compilation of a contaminated land register.

The unregulated nature of waste disposal at the time this land was used in this way, the historic use of the heath, specifically military use and landfilling, are all important points to consider when analysing the distribution of heavy metal contamination across the heath. Also useful in indicating general environmental conditions, are the pH and calcium content of the soil. Calcium is present as part of the calcium cycle and is important for plant growth, it also neutralizes acid or alkaline conditions (Growers Mineral Solutions, 2015).

An Investigation into the distribution of heavy metal contamination across a publicly used park

By Tom and Diana using Student As research.

Cadmium, copper and nickel can be seen in higher concentrations in the soil towards the centre and East of the park. This is a similar area to where the most recent 1966 and 1971 landfills were. Higher levels of these metals are are also reflected in the groundwater; borehole samples show a hotspot for all the metals, except Nickel, at a borehole on the northeast side of the park. The topography of the park is lower, therefore gravity may have driven heavy metals through the groundwater to this location. Areas of good soil quality appear at the north and centre of the park. Poorer quality is evident to the east, and in patches to the south of the park.

Current recreational use of the land is deemed appropriate. This investigation has been carried out using strict soil guideline values. It is unlikely that this land will be deemed a high risk due to contamination in the future even if policy was to change. More detailed risk assessments into specific areas of the park are advised. If a higher risk from contaminants is revealed, more complex remediation methods might be necessary such as pumps or subterranean plastic walls to stop any hydraulic connection between contaminated groundwater and clean sources. Research into the most appropriate remediation technologies may be required based on the geology, topology and nearby features of the land.

Soil, water and river sediment samples were collected over a one-day period in February, 2017, and were analysed by acid digestion followed by inductively coupled plasma-optical emission spectrometry (ICP–OES).

Additional characteristics of soil, water and sediment samples were also recorded in order to give an indication of the extent of soil degradation; calcium content, pH, moisture content, texture, odour, colour and biodiversity.

Our strategy involved collecting the following samples:

- 90 soil samples from across the park to gain an idea of the contamination levels within the topsoil.

- 10 duplicate soil sample locations to test for field sampling error.

- 6 borehole samples to test the groundwater.

- 4 upstream and 4 downstream river water samples at different locations on the River Plum to gain an understanding of surface water contamination.

- 4 upstream and 5 downstream river sediment samples to aid understanding of surface water contamination.

Soil was collected from across the park using an auger to carry out three-point composite sampling. The auger sampled topsoil to a depth of 10cm to ensure the effect of surface conditions was minimised.

Water was extracted from the boreholes across the park and from the River Plum using a bucket and a syringe. The pH was measured before samples of 9ml were added to test tubes containing 1ml of nitric acid to start the digestion process.

Sediment was taken from the bed of the river using a spade.

References

Natural Resources Conservation Service(1993), Soil Quality indicators: PH (Online). Available from: http//urbanext.illinois.edu/soil/sq_info/ph.pdf

Figure 3.4 Example of an unsuccessful poster

From this poor example of a poster, we can deduce some key pointers to making a successful poster. You need to always remember the purpose of a poster. It is **not** an academic paper printed out in a large font. It is **not** the text from a presentation. It is an alternative way to communicate your research or knowledge, using a visual grammar.

Usually, posters are designed to be used at 'poster presentations', where a number of posters are displayed on boards in a large open space, and the 'audience' walk around looking and taking an interest in posters that catch their eye. Frequently the creator of the poster will be standing nearby ready to answer any questions about the research. Therefore, there are specific goals that a poster needs to achieve.

The aim of a poster at a poster presentation

The first aim of a poster is to attract an audience. Once people have been attracted to the poster, they need to be able to read it and understand it quickly. This means that your poster needs to be:

- eye-catching
- attractive
- visible from five metres away
- easy to read (from a distance of two metres away)
- logically organised (and therefore easy to follow)
- clear and concise
- interesting.

You need to consider a layout that is logical and does not allow the reader to get lost. It should not be a maze that the reader needs to negotiate, so you need to consider using techniques such as numbering or arrows.

The layout of your poster can be portrait or landscape, and you can use a ready-made template such as through a single PowerPoint slide or other available software. Figure 3.5 shows possible choices for layout. Of course, there are many other designs, and these are only initial ideas.

A step-by-step approach to designing and writing your poster

The best way to make a poster is to follow a systematic process. This will involve following logical steps.

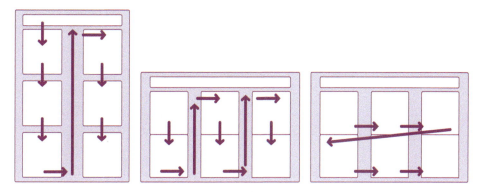

Figure 3.5 Layout choices

Task 10

Use the steps (a)–(j) to fill in the missing information in the flow chart in Figure 3.6 to create a logical order for going about designing and writing a poster (Step 1 is already filled in).

a. Write clear sub-headings for your sections.

b. Check your poster against the criteria given above to ensure it fulfils the aims of a poster and make final tweaks.

c. Write brief notes for each section.

d. Use your notes to write more detailed information for each section.

e. Arrange your brief notes on the page to get an initial idea of design.

f. Can any of the information be in a diagram or visual format?

g. Create your visuals.

h. Finalise your layout, and edit, edit, edit.

i. Go to Step 7.

j. Edit your writing to avoid blocks of text. Use bullet points and short statements instead.

(Continued)

(Continued)

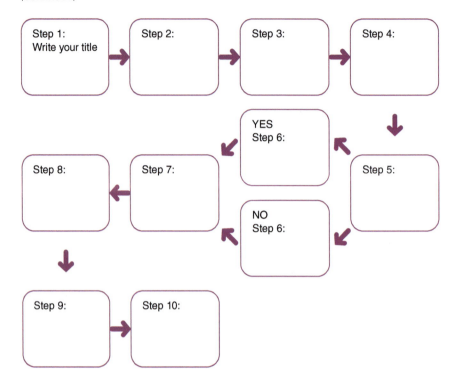

Figure 3.6 Fill in the missing steps in the flow chart

 Answers online at: https://study.sagepub.com/hopkinsandreid

TIP

Designing your poster

Write your initial notes on Post-it notes using different colours for each section. Then arrange them on a sheet of A4 to get an idea of design.

Other things to consider

The example of a successful poster in Figure 3.7 demonstrates the following points:

1. The sections are numbered to help the reader navigate the poster.
2. The use of complementary colours (as in original) can aid design.
3. The sections have sub-headings, and both academic and lay terminology to help any readers that are not from the field.

4. There is a diagram that helps support the message.
5. Results include a diagram to present data in a visual format.
6. Title is in a large font, and section headings are in a slightly larger font than the main text.
7. Language used is academic and formal, although bullet points can be used.
8. Sources that have been cited are included in the list of references.
9. There is no abstract. An abstract in an academic paper is a *summary* of the contents of the paper, and given that the contents of a poster is also a summary, an abstract is an unnecessary waste of precious space (although it is not actually *wrong* to include one).

Size and font

Design your poster to scale. You can use PowerPoint or other ready-made templates, but if you do, use the setting of about 300 dpi (dots per inch), and A1 size.

Use (around) 24 point font size for your body text (including captions to figures and tables). Your headings and sub-headings need to be slightly larger than this, and your title should be bigger still (see Table 3.2).

Table 3.2 Suggested font sizes for posters

Section	Font size
Title	72–120
Sub-title	48–80
Section headers	36–72
Body text	24–48

Final edits

Make sure your layout is clear and easy to follow. And make sure you proofread your text. You do not want to go to print with any errors!

TIP

Proofreading

Ask someone else to read your poster before you submit it for printing or for marking. They may pick up errors that you have not noticed!

I thought I heard my name: the Cocktail Party Phenomenon revisited
Name and contact details

1. Background and theory – What we know:

- The cocktail party phenomenon describes how people are only able to focus on one voice at once when there are multiple conversations going on around them.
- Moray (1959) tested this idea on 12 participants by playing a different monologue in each ear but they were told to concentrate only on one. Only 33% of participants noticed their name when it was mentioned in the background monologue.
- There were limitations with this research: the sample size was too small; the use of retrospective reports meant some participants may have forgotten what they heard; and the use of male voices only may have affected attention.

2. The experiment: What the second researchers then did:
Due to the limitations of Moray's research, Wood and Cowan (1995) tried to replicate the results using more up-to-date and rigorous methodology:

- They used 34 undergraduate students (male and female) who heard a female voice reading 300 words in the right ear (the main channel), which they then had to repeat and a male voice reading 300 words in the left ear which they were told they should ignore.
- Once the sounds stopped they were asked to complete a questionnaire which asked them if they heard anything unusual or if their name had been mentioned.

Left ear

Right ear

Instructions: Listen to the RIGHT ear.
Ignore the LEFT ear!

Main channel
Right ear: random words, and participant repeats out loud

Either
1. Control: random words, NO NAMES

Or
2. Random words, NAMES after 4 minutes

Or
3. Random words, NAMES after 5 minutes

References: Cherry, E. C. (1953). Some experiments on the recognition of speech, with one and two ears. Journal of the acoustical society of America, 25, 975–979.

Conway, Andrew R.A., Cowan, Nelson, and Bunting, Michael F. (2001). The cocktail party phenomenon revisited: The importance of working memory capacity. Psychonomic Bulletin & Review, 8(2), 331–335.

Wood, N and Cowan, (1995), The Cocktail Party phenomenon revisited: How frequent are attention shifts to one's name in an irrelevant auditory channel? Journal of experimental psychology: Learning Memory and Cognition, 21(1), 225–260.

3. The results: What did they find out?

Heard their name in Left ear (W. & C.)	Heard their name in Left ear (Moray)	Noticed that it was a male voice
50%	40%	35%

Participants said attention only shifted to channel they were supposed to be ignoring when they lost their concentration.

4. What does this mean? Implications for the real world:

- Some people may be able to notice relevant information in background 'noise' without losing attention on the main focus. However, most research now suggests that it is a negative characteristic, indicating that people are unable to block out distracting information, thereby affecting their focus on the significant information. For example, students who are better at filtering out background noise may be more efficient at concentrating on a task.
- This could suggest those with hearing impairments may be less likely to be able to distinguish between relevant and irrelevant conversations in situations such as a room full of people conversing.

5. What Next?
More research to find ways to help the 33% of people who are disadvantaged by this phenomenon would be useful.

Figure 3.7 A successful poster

YOUR CHAPTER TAKEAWAY

Exam writing Checklist
✓ (tick when completed)

Have I ...

○ created a revision plan and engaged in active note-taking?

○ varied my revision methods to improve active study?

○ identified and included key ideas, theories, writers and examples?

Reflective writing Checklist

○ included a clear description of the context (what, why, when, where)?

○ analysed what happened/who did what/why it happened, etc.?

○ evaluated the things that went well and things that did not go well?

○ related my experience to literature if that is required?

Writing your dissertation Checklist

○ written clear and focused research questions?

○ included a detailed and accurately numbered contents list? (Check this at the end.)

○ organised my literature review logically and included examples and evaluation of information?

○ cited all sources and included an accurate reference list?

Poster Checklist

○ planned the content?

○ made the order of information clear to the reader?

○ chosen visual ways to give information?

○ used headings and sub-headings to make it clear?

Your one takeaway

....

....

YOUR PROGRESS

CHAPTER FOUR

Writing with Clarity

CHAPTER DASHBOARD

Your objectives list:

 Express ideas clearly in writing

Produce writing that is interesting and easy to follow

Develop strategies to improve the clarity of my writing

min   max

'When the meaning is unclear, there is no meaning.'

– Marty Rubin

My three goals for writing clearly:

1 ....

2 ....

3 ....

What your tutor is looking for

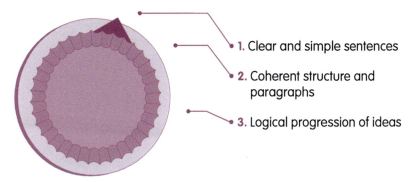

1. Clear and simple sentences

2. Coherent structure and paragraphs

3. Logical progression of ideas

Accuracy

10

5

0

Core Skills

Style

10

5

0

Core Skills

Clarity

10

5

0

Core Skills

Being concise

10

5

0

Core Skills

Being informed

10

5

0

Core Skills

WATCH OUT FOR:

Read your work out loud – if it sounds confusing, it **is** confusing

Diagnostic
How would you rate the clarity of your writing?

Find and underline anything you think is unclear. Then label what you underlined with the following:

a. Poor organisation of ideas.

b. Poor flow of meaning from one sentence to the next.

c. Problem with links between sentences.

d. Difficulty understanding individual sentences.

e. Ambiguous meaning.

Infants of about 7 months (crawling age) are placed on a surface covered in a regular, chequered patterned material. First devised by Gibson and Walk (1960), this is a famous study known as the 'visual cliff'. This material drapes over the edge of the surface and next to it is a sheet of transparent, safety glass. Mothers beckoned their children towards them across the glass and over the 'cliff'. This study is limited as it cannot be used for infants who have not started crawling yet. This experiment focused on depth perception. Campos et al. (1981) divided pre-locomotor infants into two groups, with no locomotor experience and with 40 hours of experience in a baby walker. The heart rate dropped in the first group, whilst the heart rate increased in the second group when presented with the 'visual cliff'. The heart rate increase is the mature response to steep drops. The studies by Gibson and Walk (1960) and Campos et al. (1981) and others indicate that infants can distinguish different depths before learning to crawl though don't understand what the depth cues mean until about 7 months.

How many problems did you find?

For feedback on your score, go online at:
https://study.sagepub.com/hopkinsandreid

n spoken communication, it is easy to get your message across clearly without much planning. If the person you are speaking to does not understand you, they can tell you, or ask questions, or demonstrate with body language their confusion, and you can then put it right.

With written communication, it is not so easy. If your reader finds your message hard to follow, there is a danger they will become irritated or confused and decide not to continue. This is not the effect you want to be having on your tutor.

This chapter will provide you with a range of skills to help you focus your ideas and improve the clarity of your writing. This will enable the reader (your tutor) to understand what they are reading easily and quickly. By developing these skills you will greatly improve your prospects of a high mark (see Figure 4.1).

ORGANISING IDEAS

What tutors say:

'Good writing puts me in a good mood which is a good idea when I'm marking your work.'

'If I have to work hard to understand a student's ideas, I consider it bad writing.'

Figure 4.1   Writing with clarity – tutor quotes

To achieve clarity, essays and other academic writing need to:

- be well organised, so that ideas progress logically
- guide the reader through the use of signpost words and phrases
- make links forwards and backwards throughout the text
- focus on the main message.

A key feature of clear writing is that it demonstrates a logical progression of ideas, and is both *coherent* and *cohesive*.

Progression of ideas

Coherence

For ideas to progress, your text needs to be coherent and cohesive. Coherence refers to:

- the way a text makes sense to the reader through the organisation of its content
- the relevance and clarity of its concepts and ideas.

A paragraph has coherence if it contains a series of sentences that develop a single, main idea.

Cohesion

Cohesion refers to:

- the linking of ideas from one sentence to another.

Task 1

Is this paragraph coherent? Is it cohesive?

> Flamingos are a type of wading bird. Wading birds are usually found near water such as lakes or oceans. Oceans take up 71% of the earth's surface, whose layers are made up of rock formed from ancient cooled volcanic lava. Lava is still flowing out of a recently-erupted volcano in Hawaii.

....

....

....

The paragraph is an example of writing that *is* cohesive, but *lacks* coherence.

It sticks together with backward references, but it does not give a clear message. There is no clear, single topic for the paragraph.

The working backwards test

Task 2

Read the *last sentence* in the *introductory paragraph* of a magazine article. What information do you expect to have come *before* it? How do you know?

> Today, we have huge numbers of musical instruments, some new and some still recognisable from those first ancient percussion instruments.

This is the preceding sentence.

> Much later, about 5,000 years ago, stringed instruments such as harps and lyres were played.

Now what do you think came before this one?

> In prehistoric societies, about 40,000 years ago, humans made drum-like instruments out of sticks, logs and rocks and flute-like instruments out of animal bone.

And here is the whole paragraph:

> People have always had music in their lives. In prehistoric societies, about 40,000 years ago, humans made drum-like instruments out of sticks, logs and rocks and flute-like instruments out of animal bone. Much later, about 5,000 years ago, stringed instruments such as harps and lyres were played. Today, we have huge numbers of musical instruments, some new and some still recognisable from those first ancient percussion instruments.

What language allowed you to predict backwards?

....

....

You were able to predict what had come before the final sentence because of:

- vocabulary:
  - o repetition of key words, e.g. *instruments*
  - o words relating to musical instruments (lexical chains): *musical instruments, stringed instruments, harps, lyres, flute-like, drum-like, percussion*

- grammatical features of text such as:
  - o referencing devices, e.g. *this, those, we*
  - o linking devices, e.g. *such as*
  - o deixis (words or phrases that cannot be understood without more information about the context), e.g. *much later, today, those.*

TIP

Cohesion

Read the last sentence of your paragraphs to see if you have included clues to what has come before. If not, you need to check that your paragraph is clear. Remember that each paragraph should develop a single theme or idea.

Focus on flow

We usually:

- begin our sentences with *known information*
- and end them with *new information.*

Look at the example texts below and the way the information flows.

Sample 1: Topic reiteration

Here, the known information is repeated in beginning position of each clause.

Though **monitoring** offers a simple solution to eliminate worker shirking and [**monitoring**] is likely to be implemented to some extent in most firms, **it** does not seem to impose a coherent, cost-effective design to stimulate employees.

Sample 2: Zig zag

Here the new information becomes the *known* information in the next clause to give a zig zag pattern (Figure 4.2).

Race car development is complex. **This complexity** arises from the implementation of the solution, **where** often several design considerations have to be balanced to produce the best result. **These results** can be affected by **relatively small effects**. For example, **the drop in acceleration for a fraction of a second produced by a gear change** could win or lose a race.

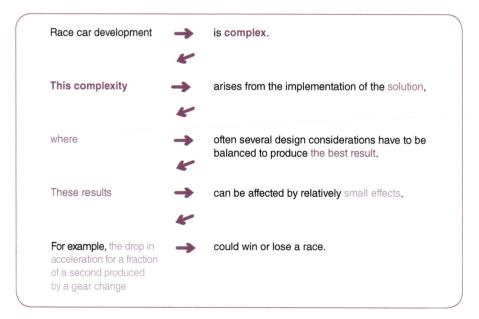

Figure 4.2 Example of zig zag flow

TIP

Flow

Write your sentences out in separate lines and underline the beginnings of each sentence (and clause, if you can – see Chapter 5). Has the information in each beginning been mentioned before? If not, the flow *may* not be clear. Ask someone to read it as a check.

YOUR TURN

Task 3

Choose the best following sentence (a) or (b).

1. Multi-criteria analysis was carried out to identify the most preferential location for a ten-hectare school.

   a. Criteria of importance included human health, cost, and environmental risk.
   b. Human health, cost, and environmental risk were the important criteria used.

2. The aim of the experiment is to test the validity of the 'energy gap' theory of semiconductor resistance.

   a. Charge carriers in the semiconductor can be in one of two energy states, separated by an energy gap E_g, according to this theory.
   b. This theory states that charge carriers in the semiconductor can be in one of two energy states, separated by an energy gap E_g.

3. Economic changes may also signify increasing social complexity, especially the emergence of full time craftsmen.

   a. Craft specialisation can be seen from concentrations of artefacts relating to different crafts.
   b. Concentrations of artefacts relating to different crafts show craft specialisation.

4. If the Government had taken a less neoliberal approach, it is likely to have been more successful in safeguarding thousands of jobs.

   a. Different nation states react unilaterally to safeguard/stimulate their economy over time, so this re-enforces how much of a threat neoliberalism poses to workers in a globalising world.
   b. This re-enforces how much of a threat neoliberalism poses to workers in a globalising world, where different nation states react unilaterally to safeguard/stimulate their economy over time.

 Answers online at: https://study.sagepub.com/hopkinsandreid

Linking back and forward

As we saw in the text about musical instruments, we use words like *it, them, they, this, these*, to link back and forwards in a text without repeating the same words. Using words like this is called **referencing**.

YOUR TURN

Task 4

Identify what the underlined pronouns are referring to in the following extract.

By far the most common social organisation in the world today is <u>that</u> of the state; the first example of this type of society emerged in Mesopotamia, around 5,000 years ago. States differ from hunter–gatherer bands in that <u>they</u> are not egalitarian, the society has a hierarchical structure, meaning <u>it</u> comprises strata; <u>they</u> are more complex than chiefdoms as <u>they</u> comprise several communities rather than just a few, and have a centralised government with power over religion, war, law and taxation; there is also heterarchical differentiation within each stratum as well as hierarchical distinctions. There are various characteristics of the state that can be recognised archaeologically which are outlined as a starting point; however, an important part of a state is the ideology which binds its people together, and <u>this</u> is harder to see in the archaeological record, particularly before people had written records. <u>This</u> makes it difficult to explain why societies became more complex and eventually formed states. This paper will look at the explanations advanced by Wittfogel, Carneiro, Marx and Flannery, as well as the more recent post-processualism theory.

that = ...

they = ...

it   = ...

they = ...

they = ...

this = ...

This = ...

 Answers online at: https://study.sagepub.com/hopkinsandreid

Be careful! When using pronouns to replace previously mentioned (noun) phrases, it is important that the meaning is not ambiguous. Sometimes *repetition* of the noun phrase is clearer.

YOUR TURN

Task 5

The following text is difficult to follow because it is not clear what the pronouns are referring to. Replace each underlined pronoun 'it' with the noun phrase it is referring to.

The standard deviation was used to work out the hazard bounds. Half of <u>it</u> .... was deducted from the soil guideline value to give the lower bound of the medium hazard, and half of <u>it</u> .... was added to <u>it</u> .... to give the upper bound of <u>it</u> ....

 **Answers online at: https://study.sagepub.com/hopkinsandreid**

Signpost words and phrases (connectors)

Another way to guide your reader is to use words/phrases such as 'however', 'therefore', 'in addition' to show *connections* between ideas and to indicate the kind of message that will follow.

These words are used to link ideas:

- within a sentence
- between sentences
- between paragraphs
- between different sections of academic writing.

YOUR TURN

Task 6

Analyse the extracts from academic writing below to see how the underlined connectors enhance the flow (which is explained in the right-hand column).

Samples	Effect of connector
1. From this analysis it is clear that all newspapers use techniques to persuade their readers towards particular views. <u>Therefore</u>, readers need to be cautious in their response to information reported through the media.	Indicates a reaction to information in the previous sentence
2. Anderson (2004) argues that lesser growth will prevent existing methods for reducing emissions from being mass-produced. <u>However</u>, economic growth is both a cause and a fixer of environmental damage.	Highlights a contrasting view between sentences
3. As engine speed climbed towards 9,500 rpm, the torque would rapidly drop, causing the car to 'stutter' and decelerate for the last stretch. <u>Similarly</u>, 'further' gearings failed to provide enough torque to beat the opposing car during the race.	Highlights another example of the same phenomenon

(Continued)

(Continued)

4. Figure 3 suggests that leaching from the refuse tip could be responsible for some of the river contamination. <u>In addition</u>, contaminants in groundwater from the heath itself are also evident in the river sediment.	Indicates additional support for the argument that will be given
....	
5. All of these will result in much greater levels of pollution, which in turn can lead to poor health of citizens. <u>In particular</u>, evidence suggests that those in major cities are at risk from chronic illnesses such as asthma and other respiratory conditions.	Indicates specific details will be given
....	
6. The data shows that there is a 1% average annual increase in energy efficiency. <u>While</u> this is a gradual improvement, it is not enough to provide the action necessary to reach the UK's climate targets.	Indicates a contrast between two clauses in the same sentence

Table 4.1 gives a list of useful signpost words and phrases and their meanings.

Table 4.1 Signpost words and phrases

Function	Signpost word or phrase	Examples
Showing sequence	Firstly, secondly, etc. Initially, Then … After this … Finally,	*This essay will firstly describe the different kinds of societies seen throughout history, and then go on to …* *Finally, the way societies have evolved into larger, more complex states will be discussed.*
Giving examples	For example, … such as … For instance,	*For example, one could assume that education and average income are related, since a higher level of education, could mean a higher average income.*
Adding or building on ideas	In addition, Moreover, As well as … Similarly, In the same way, Also… As well as …	*Similarly, Swain (1993) highlights the value of productive output which can be enhanced by noticing.*

Function	Signpost word or phrase	Examples
Showing contrast	However, Nevertheless, On the other hand, In contrast, Although … While …	*However, it has been suggested that smaller body size in the tropics is the result of poor nutrition in these areas, rather than an adaptation to temperature (Beall & Steegman, 2000).*
Showing logical connections: action or reaction to earlier information	Therefore, Thus, Hence,	*Biology can therefore be seen to contribute to gender differences in two ways.*
Showing cause	Because … As … Since … As a result … As a consequence …	*Since financial information is presented with the same use of language, investors are able to compare different investment opportunities.*
Showing condition	If … When … As long as … Provided that …	*As long as the organisation has succeeded in reducing inequality past the point where employees feel resentful, the method is still beneficial.*
Giving specific details	In particular, Specifically,	*Fires help to create a mosaic of diverse habitats for plants and animals, specifically red grouse in the UK peatlands.*
Generalising	In general, Generally, Usually, On the whole,	*An additional dimension of this partnership is the supportive involvement in trade unionism, which is usually discouraged in neoliberal models (Lewis, 1948).*
Emphasising a fact	Clearly, It is evident that … Of course,	*It is evident that the Partnership has made a real attempt to improve working conditions for employees.*
Giving clarification	In other words … Namely …	*In other words, a strong Prime Minister results in a less powerful Cabinet, and vice-versa.*
Signalling the end	In conclusion, To summarise, To conclude	*In conclusion, Homo sapiens as a species is well adapted to living in diverse environments.*

TIP

Using connectors helps guide your reader, but check you are using the correct punctuation (see Chapter 5).

YOUR TURN

Task 7

The text below from an archaeology student's essay is not easy to follow because there are no connectors. Improve the text's flow by adding words/phrases from the box below in appropriate places. The first one has been done as an example.

> although; also; as well as; finally; for example; generally; ~~since~~; whereas

In order to recognise a state, it is important to consider both the site, and the surrounding area as a whole; (1) .... Since a defining feature of the state is that it comprises many communities, the site hierarchy of an area must be taken into account, (2) .... the settlement pattern. A survey can be done to determine a site hierarchy of a particular area. A state society will (3) .... show a site hierarchy with hamlets, villages and small towns ranged around larger towns and one or two urban centres, (4) .... a band society will have a narrower range of variation in site size, and all sites will be relatively small (Renfrew & Bahn, 1996). (5) .... in Southwest Iran on the Susiana Plain, there is evidence of four different sizes of settlement, ranging from small villages of less than 0.9 hectares, through villages of 2.3 hectares and small centres of 5.3 hectares, to large centres of 14.8 hectares. (6) .... , there was Susa, which today might have been called a capital, which was around 25 hectares in size (Wright & Johnson, 1975). The settlement pattern can (7) .... be taken into account; the geographer Walter Christaller developed the Central Place Theory, which stated that in a uniform landscape, the spatial patterning of settlements would be perfectly regular; central places, i.e. towns or cities, would be equidistant and surrounded by satellite rings of smaller settlements. (8) .... a uniform landscape is rarely found in nature, in a state a ring of smaller settlements surround a ring of larger settlements, which in turn surround the major centre (Renfrew & Bahn, 1996).

 Answers online at: https://study.sagepub.com/hopkinsandreid

Ambiguous sentences

Be careful not to write sentences that may be interpreted in more than one way. You don't want to make your reader laugh at something you intended to be serious! Academic writing needs to be unambiguous. Ambiguous sentences may be unclear for the following reasons:

- The sentence structure has two meanings. For example:
  - *The study tested participants with new technology.* Is it (a) participants with new technology who were tested, or (b) new technology was used to carry out the test?

- Individual words in a sentence have two meanings. For example:
  - *Some of the results are outstanding.* Is it (a) the results are of a very high quality, or (b) some of the results are incomplete?
- Modifiers are not used clearly. For example:
  - *With a few small patches of deterioration, the researchers determined that the heath is generally of good-quality soil.* Is it (a) the researchers who have small patches of deterioration, or (b) the heath?

YOUR TURN

Task 8

Identify the ambiguity in the following sentences. Rewrite them to make them clearer (this may mean writing two separate sentences).

1. The researchers treated the subjects using drugs.

   ....

2. The situation affects university students and teachers.

   ....

3. The paper was published by a Chinese professor from Harvard University.

   ....

4. The marks were scored on the sheets of plastic.

   ....

➡️ **Answers online at: https://study.sagepub.com/hopkinsandreid**

Other ways to ensure clarity

Keep the subject close to the verb.

When a subject of a sentence is not close to the verb of the sentence, it can cause a strain to the reader. Look at this example, where the subject is underlined and the verb is in bold:

<u>A sentence</u> with phrases to describe nouns as well as long clauses which give more information about the subject **can be** difficult to follow.

Here there are 17 words between the subject and its verb. As a general rule, it is a good idea to try to maintain the distance between the subject and its verb as no more than seven or eight words. We can rewrite the example to be clearer like this:

<u>A sentence</u> **can be** difficult to follow when it has phrases to describe nouns as well as long clauses which give more information about the subject.

YOUR TURN

Task 9

Rewrite the following sentences to move the verb closer to the subject. Remember, try to avoid having a distance of more than eight words between the subject and the verb.

1. The argument that perpetual economic growth has a detrimental impact on employment and welfare, the environment, international aid, and public services will be explored.

   ....

   ....

2. The standard error, being very low, and suggesting that random error within the repeated measurements can be discounted, indicates that one of the control measurements is incorrect.

   ....

   ....

3. Questionnaires and answer sheets with questions relating to health and security as well as personal opinions on ethical issues were handed out to the participants.

   ....

   ....

4. Gender differences and inequalities, when gender is defined as the socially constructed roles taken on by males and females, and where inequalities are discussed in terms of status and roles, can be explained in two key ways.

   ....

   ....

 Answers online at: https://study.sagepub.com/hopkinsandreid

Avoid garden path sentences

Garden path sentences are sentences that send your reader the wrong way. Look at the following examples:

1. The doctor took the medicine the pharmacist had brought to the child.
2. They convinced her family are important at times like this.
3. The restaurant workers were boycotting was on London Street.

Now look at the clearer versions:

1. The doctor took the child the medicine which the pharmacist had brought.
2. They convinced her that family are important at times like this.
3. The restaurant which workers were boycotting was on London Street.

TIP

Proofread your work by reading it aloud. This will flag up ambiguity more clearly.

YOUR TURN

Task 10

Now identify the following six problems with clarity in the following sample from a student's reflective writing essay:

Problems with:

1. Flow of ideas between sentences.
2. Unclear use of pronoun reference.
3. Lack of signpost word to aid flow.
4. Repetition when pronoun reference would work better.
5. Ambiguity.
6. Too many words between the subject and the verb.

> Last summer I worked as a waitress in a large restaurant. The company were try-ing to increase the number of customers, and asked staff for ideas. We never gave any offers, I had noticed. For example, other restaurants would often do a '2 for 1' offer on a Monday evening. So I suggested the 2 for 1 offer idea to my colleague, but I did not say anything to my boss because I did not want to come across as too pushy and 'know-it-all'. The following week there was a meeting for all permanent

(Continued)

(Continued)

restaurant staff and other employees, where we were told that they had received some useful ideas and that there was going to be a prize for the best one. I was about to submit my idea when my colleague told me that she had 'acted on our conversation'. When the company selected the 2 for 1 idea as the winner and started promoting it straight away, I felt disappointed and angry that I had not had any recognition for the idea. I felt upset by my colleague's behaviour, and felt unable to talk to her initially, due to my feelings. I now realise that it was largely my fault. I had lacked the confidence to tell my boss my idea. I had assumed that the company would not pay attention to a temporary waitress, because I was not committed to a career with them. It was good (verified by being chosen as the winner), and I needed to have greater self-belief.

I no longer blame my colleague, as I made it clear that I was not going to talk to my boss. This experience of talking about something without actually doing anything about it, which is clearly not a good way to go about things, has taught me to act on my ideas instead.

....

....

....

....

....

....

➡ **Answers online at: https://study.sagepub.com/hopkinsandreid**

YOUR CHAPTER TAKEAWAY

Clarity Checklist

✓ (tick when completed)

Have I ...

- ( ) ensured my writing is clear and easy to follow?
- ( ) read my sentences aloud to ensure they make sense?
- ( ) checked my sentences aren't too long and confusing?
- ( ) made sure the main verb is close to the front of each sentence?
- ( ) considered the logical flow of ideas between my paragraphs?
- ( ) thought about the overall progression of ideas?
- ( ) included sufficient signposts, connectors and linking back and forward words?
- ( ) included a link sentence at the end of each paragraph?
- ( ) eliminated ambiguous sentences?
- ( ) checked for any garden path sentences?

Your one takeaway

....

....

YOUR PROGRESS

CHAPTER FIVE

Writing with Accuracy

YOUR PROGRESS

CHAPTER DASHBOARD

Your objectives list:

 Identify correct uses of grammar, spelling and punctuation in academic writing

 Produce written work that is free from grammar, spelling and punctuation errors

 Maintain consistently high professional standards in academic writing

min   max

'Fast is fine, but accuracy is everything'

– Wyatt Earp

My three accuracy goals:

1 ....

2 ....

3 ....

What your tutor is looking for

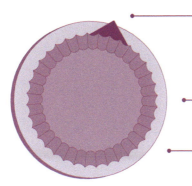

1. Accurate use of English grammar, spelling and punctuation

2. Accurate sentence structures

3. Accurate use of tenses

Accuracy

10

5

0

Core Skills

Style

10

5

0

Core Skills

Clarity

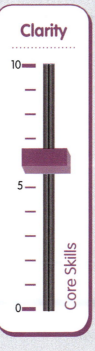

10

5

0

Core Skills

Being concise

10

5

0

Core Skills

Being informed

10

5

0

Core Skills

WATCH OUT FOR:

Write in complete sentences. Don't use run-ons and fragments

Diagnostic
How would you rate the accuracy of your writing?

In the paragraphs below, find and underline problems with accuracy. See if you can correct them too!

Humans like all animals need sleep, along with food, water and oxygen to survive. For humans sleep is a vital indicator of overall health and well being. We spend up to one third of our lives asleep, and the overall state of our sleep health remains an essential question throughout our lifespan. Most of us know that getting a good nights sleep is important, but too few of us actually make those eight or so hours between the sheet's a priority. For many of us with sleep debt, we've forgotten what being rested feels like.

To further complicate matters stimulants like coffee and energy drinks, alarm clocks, and external lights – including those from electronic devices – interferes with our circadian rhythm or natural sleep/wake cycle. Other factors such as lifestyle and stress can make us loose sleep. Sleep needs vary across ages, therefore, to determine how much sleep you need, its important to assess not only where you fall on the sleep needs spectrum, but also to examine what lifestyle factors are effecting the quality and quantity of your sleep.

Adapted from: http://sleepfoundation.org/how-sleep-works/how-much-sleep-do-we-really-need

How many problems did you find?

For feedback on your score, go online at:
https://study.sagepub.com/hopkinsandreid

Using correct grammar, spelling and punctuation in your formal writing is an essential life skill. Accuracy in writing tells the reader that you are a skilled and articulate writer and thinker. Accurate usage also demonstrates your knowledge and mastery of the language, and that you can write with focus, authority, and control.

Accuracy is the fundamental foundation of all good writing and your readers will judge you on your ability to produce meticulous and error-free work.

At university: The marking criteria of most assignments will assess the correct use of grammar, punctuation and spelling. Tutors will judge your ability to write effectively and appropriately, and your work will be penalised for inaccurate use of English (see Figure 5.1).

In the workplace: A lack of attention to detail and sloppy use of English reflects badly on both you as an employee and also your employer. Poor use of English may hinder your chances of employment, promotion and success in your career. In a recent survey of over 600 employers, 65% said that they would put an applicant's CV in the bin for inaccurate use of English.

This chapter will provide you with a range of skills to help you identify and address accuracy issues in your writing, and produce work of a high academic and professional standard.

FEATURES OF ACCURACY

Sentence breakdown

Knowledge of grammatical labels helps you to understand how to write clearly and accurately. If you can identify key components of a sentence you can:

- check that your sentences are accurate
- understand how to build more complex sentences
- understand how to link sentences correctly within paragraphs
- see how meanings are created through careful language choices.

What tutors say:

'Persistent grammar, spelling or punctuation errors will significantly reduce the credibility of your work.'

'Grammar or spelling mistakes are a lazy way of telling a tutor – "I just don't care about my writing."'

Figure 5.1 What tutors say

Parts of speech

YOUR TURN

Task 1

In the sample below match each underlined word or phrase to their parts of speech.

<u>Some</u> <u>people</u> find <u>it</u> easy to write <u>accurately</u> and clearly without thinking. Many of us, <u>however</u>, <u>may</u> have to work hard to ensure we <u>are</u> <u>writing</u> without errors and <u>in</u> <u>the</u> most <u>accessible</u> way. In order to check what we have <u>written</u> and to understand how to improve, we <u>need</u> to know a bit about English Grammar.

Noun ....

Main verb ....

Auxiliary verb ....

Modal auxiliary verb ....

Adjective ....

Adverb ....

Past participle ....

Present participle ....

Preposition ....

Pronoun ....

Article ....

Determiner (but not article) ....

Linking word ....

 Answers online at: https://study.sagepub.com/hopkinsandreid

Sentences: What are they?

- Sentences are groups of words that have a full grammatical meaning. They begin with a capital letter and end with a full stop.
- Sentences can be made up of one or several individual *clauses*.
- Clauses are the building blocks of sentences and they can be defined as the grammatical structure that includes at least one verb.
- Different parts of sentences have different purposes. The verb (usually) describes the activity, actions, states or events. A verb will have a subject, and it may have an object; in other words, **who** (subject) **does what** (verb) to **whom** (object).

YOUR TURN

Task 2

Label the subjects and objects in the following sentences. If there is no object, write 'NO' (no object).

1. This university has a music department.

   Subject .... Object ....

2. This practical introduces the fundamentals of neurobiology.

   Subject .... Object ....

3. This essay will discuss social conditions in the nineteenth century.

   Subject .... Object ....

4. My university is in London.

   Subject .... Object ....

➡ **Answers online at: https://study.sagepub.com/hopkinsandreid**

Clauses: What are they?

Every sentence has at least one clause.

- If a sentence has one clause only, that clause is an *independent* (or main) clause, which has (at least) a subject and a verb.
- When there is more than one clause, the other clauses may be independent clauses **or** dependent (subordinate) clauses.
- Dependent clauses depend on the independent clause to make grammatical sense, and cannot exist alone.

Look at the following sentences. Their clauses have been underlined.

1. <u>A lab report is a document</u>. (one independent clause)
2. <u>A lab report is a document</u> <u>which describes an experiment</u>. (two clauses, one independent, and one dependent (does not make grammatical sense alone))
3. <u>A lab report is a document</u> <u>which describes an experiment</u>, and <u>it is a short version of an academic paper</u>. (three clauses: one independent, one dependent, and another independent clause joined to the previous clause with the conjunction 'and')

YOUR TURN

Task 3

Which of the following are grammatically correct sentences? If they are correct, tick them ✓, but if they are incorrect, can you identify the problem?

☐ 1. Learning grammar is essential for good writing.

....

☐ 2. Because it is a complex thing to analyse.

....

☐ 3. By analysing the samples, a number of problems with the treatment.

....

☐ 4. Brown (2009) suggests different approaches to studying learning.

....

→ **Answers online at: https://study.sagepub.com/hopkinsandreid**

Punctuation

There are some punctuation errors that are very common. Correct use of punctuation is important because:

- it is punctuation that helps the reader make sense of language in longer sentences
- incorrect use (which may be underuse, overuse, or using one kind of punctuation when a different punctuation mark is needed) can cause a strain to the reader, or even confuse and mislead them.

Punctuation guide

There are some rules for using punctuation. The main things you need to know are included in the guide below.

Comma

Use commas:

- To show items in a list or a series. Although it is not usually necessary to include a comma before 'and' or 'or', it *can* aid clarity to do so when the items are made up of two or more words or short phrases. For example, notice how a comma would help to avoid ambiguity in the following example: *The research involved analysis of assignment types, marking criteria, samples of students' work and feedback.* It is not clear whether the feedback is grouped with the students' work or is a separate item. A comma before 'and' would clarify that it was a separate item.

Example 1: *The three main gases contributing to climate change are methane, carbon dioxide and nitrous oxide.*

Example 2: *The organisation needs to lobby on behalf of the business, put in place business processes and protocols that negate the need for more regulation, and influence relevant policy development.*

- To separate an initial dependent clause from the independent clause (but it is not necessary if your independent clause comes first).

  Example 1: *If there are changes in the way education is delivered, the profile of a typical student is likely to change.* (NB *The profile of a typical student is likely to change if there are changes in the way education is delivered.*)

  Example 2: *Whereas the burials during the Bronze and Iron ages were primarily of wealthy individuals, during the European Neolithic period some burial mounds and barrows were used communally.*

- To separate two independent clauses when a conjunction is used.

  Example 1: *There are likely to be changes in the way education is delivered, and this will lead to a change in the profile of a typical student.*
  Example 2: *A study of history can help us to understand certain behaviours, but it is not able to explain every conflict.*

- To show that a relative clause is providing extra description that is **not** essential for the reader.

  Example: *The methods used in this study were qualitative methods, which meant the responses were generally unstructured.* (The relative clause gives useful but not 'identifying' information.)

  Compare: *In my placement year I worked for a large company which provided parts to the automotive industry.* (Without the comma, the information is essential to the meaning and identifies the company.)

  NB Try to avoid using internal commas in the relative clause – it becomes confusing.

- Similar to above, extra descriptive information or explanation separated from the rest of the sentence.

  Example: *The funding for this research, initially problematic, has now been procured.*

- To separate an introductory phrase containing a verb from the rest of the sentence. Note that it is not usually necessary to use a comma if this phrase comes at the end of the sentence.

Example 1: *To succeed in this project, the company needs to involve all stakeholders.*

Example 2: *Built in the 1970s, the college is in need of an upgrade.*
If the introductory phrase is short and lacking a verb, it is not usually necessary to use a comma.

Example 3: *At the moment I'm working on the annual report.*

- After words that link the meaning between two sentences:

  Example: There is a general belief that natural foodstuffs are healthier than manufactured foods. However, some natural chemicals are more harmful than some synthetic chemicals, and it is important that this information is conveyed clearly.

Semi-colon

The semi-colon is frequently used incorrectly. If you're not sure, it's best to choose a different form of punctuation. Note that a capital letter is not used after a semi-colon.

Use semi-colons:

- To separate two independent clauses with related content, as an alternative to conjunctions such as *and, because, as,* or a full stop. An independent clause is a clause that makes sense without the other clauses. If one of the clauses cannot stand alone, a semi-colon cannot be used.

  Example: Correct use of punctuation isn't easy; misuse can cause communication problems.

- To separate one clause from the next one when using the linking words such as *however, therefore, thus, nevertheless,* etc. A full stop can be used here too (but not a comma).

  Example: The company assets have been frozen; therefore, no further payments can be made.

- Before expressions such as *for example (e.g.), as, that is (i.e.), namely,* used in a complete clause, or before a list of examples.

  Example: In the workplace you are constantly monitored in different ways; for example, through observation, meetings, and output assessment.

- To separate complex items in a list (for single words in a list, a comma is used – Example 2).

  Example 1: *At university you will be assessed in different ways: formally through essays and presentations; informally through group work, seminars and workshops; and most formally of all, through exams.*

Example 2: At university you are assessed in different ways: through essays, presentations, group work and exams.

Colon

A colon joins two sections of information together where the first part is introducing the second part. Use a colon to:

- Introduce a list of items.

  Example: *At university you are assessed in different ways: through essays, presentations, group work and exams.*

- Introduce a direct quotation.

  Example: *As Penrose notes: 'Left to their own desires and devices, nation-states will continue to pursue their own self-interests at the cost of enforcing international law' (Penrose, 2000, p. 371).*

- Although infrequently used, you may see a colon used to join two parts of a sentence when the second part is providing more information about the first.

  Example: *Plagiarism is an increasingly discussed issue: there is much debate over its exact definition.*

Brackets – round and square

Use round brackets to:

- Separate supplementary or clarifying information from the main information. This can also be achieved through commas and through dashes, with commas being the weakest, dashes being stronger, but more informal, and brackets being the strongest and most formal.

  Example 1: *Using dashes (sometimes referred to as 'hyphens') to separate out extra information is considered quite informal.*

  Note that this supplementary information can sometimes be an entire sentence (and in Example 2 the full stop needs to be inside the brackets).

  Example 2: *Stimulants are chemicals that speed up heart rate, and there are different kinds of these chemicals that operate in different ways. (There are also chemicals called depressants which slow down heart rate, but they are not the focus here.)*

- Add an in-text citation.

  Example: *A person's identity can change with time and with context (Burke, 2006).*

- Indicate a cross reference.

  Example: *Table 1 shows the summarised findings (see Appendix A for the raw data).*

- Indicate an abbreviation immediately after the full name has been given so that thereafter, the abbreviation can be used.

  Example: *Adenosine Triphosphate (ATP) is the main transporter of chemical energy within cells. The chemical energy stored in ATP is used to drive processes such as biosynthesis, and locomotion or transportation of molecules across cell membranes.*

Use square brackets to:

- Indicate when someone other than the original writer or speaker is inserting a comment or clarification.

  Example: *They [the French] have a big decision to make about the economy.*

- Indicate with ... to show that some of the text has been omitted. The square brackets can be omitted, and just ... used.

  Example: *This information cannot be used [...] as evidence.*

Quotation marks (or speech marks, or inverted commas)

Quotation marks are important in showing that you are citing another person's words. Forgetting to include them can lead to accusations of plagiarism.

Use quotation marks to:

- Indicate someone else's words (from written sources).

  Example: *Smith (2009, p. 89) suggested that 'society is rotten to the core'.*
  See Chapter 8 for more advice on citing sources.

- Show direct speech (i.e. spoken words).

- Highlight an unusual or controversial term.

  Example: *People working for large organisations frequently complain of the new 'Management Speak'.*

- Show titles of books, films, articles, etc.
  Example: *Conan Doyle introduced the world to Sherlock Holmes in 'A Study in Scarlet' which was published in 1887.*

Avoiding punctuation errors

Grammar checker

Turn on the grammar checker on your computer, *but* don't rely on it as it may not spot all errors (e.g. use of apostrophes).

Rule checker

Frequently review punctuation rules.

Friend checker

Ask a friend to check your work. A fresh pair of eyes will spot errors that you've missed.

Rest and revisit

If you can, step away from your work and leave it to rest overnight or for a few days so that you can review and edit it with a fresh pair of eyes.

Use and misuse

Commas: Overuse, underuse and misuse

Commas are used to separate ideas or items. Check your commas are doing this.

TIP

Commas

Try reading your work aloud. Where do you naturally pause? Is a comma needed here?

See the Punctuation Guide above for rules of use for commas – or try the following exercises first and then check the rules.

YOUR TURN

Task 4

Find and circle seven incorrectly used commas in the following sample from a student essay. (NB Not **all** commas are used incorrectly in this sample.)

This essay provides a focus on the importance of reflecting on practice, in order to improve skills. According to Brown and Studt, (2009), reflective behaviour leads to better outcomes, however, this is not supported by research done by Tynecroft (2015). Tynecroft suggests that although reflection is, clearly, useful in clarifying why there are successes and failures, it cannot guarantee an improvement in practice. There are three reasons for this, the reflection may be flawed, it may be insufficient, or, it may be correct but not lead to a corresponding change in behaviour.

YOUR TURN

Task 5

The following sample is hard to follow because it lacks any commas. Find eight places where commas would aid the reader's comprehension. Identify whether the comma is essential (E), or helpful but optional (O).

In this experiment Ohm's Law which states that current is directly proportional to the voltage across a resistor of constant resistance and current is inversely proportional to resistance at a constant voltage was tested and verified. As predicted by the law the experiment demonstrated that as voltage across a fixed resistor increases the current through it also increases. They are directly proportional. The current was measured through a number of different resistors whilst also varying the voltage across them. By varying the voltage or the resistance the current measured can be compared with the calculated value and in doing so the above relationship can be confirmed.

 Answers online at: https://study.sagepub.com/hopkinsandreid

Semi-colons: misuse

Semi-colons are used to separate two things which may be:

- independent clauses, or
- complex items in a list.

See the Punctuation Guide above for rules of use for semi-colons – or try the following exercises first and then check the rules.

YOUR TURN

Task 6

Decide if the semi-colons in the extracts below are correctly used (a) or incorrectly used (b).

1. An optical wedge is located between; the test-flash beam and the artificial pupil.   a / b

2. The subject must decide what criteria to use to determine when the test flash is at   a / b
   threshold visibility; they must then use these same criteria throughout the experiment.

3. Several theories have been proposed in the last 20 years and these include: a / b
   behaviourist conditioning theory; connectivist theory; social constructivist theory;
   and transformative theory.

4. Game theory is relevant to games in which one person's gains result in losses   a / b
   for the other participants; this theory is now often applied to a wide range of
   behavioural relations, and can be an umbrella term for any area related to the
   science of logical decision making.

5. Game theory can be an umbrella term for any area related to the science of   a / b
   logical decision making; however, the most common use of the theory is to model
   population growth.

 Answers online at: https://study.sagepub.com/hopkinsandreid

YOUR TURN

Task 7

The following sample does not use any semi-colons. Find one place where you could replace the existing punctuation with a semi-colon. Why is the semi-colon the better choice here?

> In the UK, government figures have shown that unemployment has risen and fallen in line with GDP growth (1)(2). Many economists argue that greater economic growth will create more jobs. This is because it is assumed that with a larger economy, the population will have more disposable income. They are expected to spend more money. Therefore, businesses would expand to cater to this greater demand, and consequently would need to employ a greater number of staff.

....

....

 Answers online at: https://study.sagepub.com/hopkinsandreid

Colons

Colons join two sections of information together where the first part is introducing the second part.

TIP

Colons

You can often test that you have used a colon correctly by replacing it with the word 'namely'. If it works, you have probably used the colon appropriately.

See the Punctuation Guide above for rules of use for colons – or try the following exercises first and then check the rules.

YOUR TURN

Task 8

Each of the four samples below includes a colon. However, only one is used correctly. Decide which one is correct and say why.

1. Ohm's Law is named after the German physicist Georg Ohm: he described measurements of voltage and current through simple electrical circuits containing various different lengths of wire.

2. Low blood pressure can be influenced by the following factors: the time of day; how stressed or relaxed a person is; how much exercise they do; temperature; if food has recently been eaten.

3. When researching human subjects it is important to be objective: therefore, information about thoughts or feelings should not be included, as these cannot be directly observed.

4. For example: fault in the immune system or genetic predisposition.

....

....

 Answers online at: https://study.sagepub.com/hopkinsandreid

YOUR TURN

Task 9

Replace existing punctuation with a colon in one place in the following sample.

The rules of punctuation have changed with time, and some marks are more commonly used than others; however, it is important to understand how to use the marks of punctuation to aid clarity and to ensure that the reader is guided through a text. Some rules are complex, and these include the following, use of colons, use of semi-colons, use of brackets, and use of commas.

Answers online at: https://study.sagepub.com/hopkinsandreid

Brackets – round and square

Brackets are used to separate supplementary or secondary information.

TIP

Brackets

- Have you used hyphens? These are generally too informal for academic or formal business contexts. Replace with round brackets.
- Check your punctuation. Full stops should only be inside brackets when the entire contents inside the brackets is a complete sentence.

See the Punctuation Guide above for rules of use for brackets – or try the following exercises first and then check the rules.

YOUR TURN

Task 10

Find and correct the mistakes with the use (or absence) of brackets in the following sample.

After WW2 (World War Two) the relationship between the USA and the USSR became very strained due to conflicting ideologies, the USA believing in Capitalism, and the USSR, Communism. This relationship became known as the Cold War, and lasted for over forty years. (There were many crises during the Cold War). For example,

(Continued)

(Continued)

the Cuban Missile Crisis, The Vietnam War, the building of the Berlin Wall. One of the most worrying aspects in the tension at this time was the build up of weapons of mass destruction, WMD, which include nuclear, chemical and biological weapons. (Gaddis, 2011).

 Answers online at: https://study.sagepub.com/hopkinsandreid

 **YOUR TURN**

Task 11

Insert brackets within the sentences below if they are appropriate.

1. Buildings with poor insulation are costly to heat, though they are cheaper to build, and are more likely to be inhabited by people on low incomes.

2. Functional theories of art suggest that something can be defined as 'art' if it was intended to produce aesthetic experiences. Nature cannot be considered art because it is not created in order to produce a response.

3. Electronics is widely used in the information processing industry, computer services, software, and data services, because the ability of electronic devices to act as switches makes digital information processing possible.

4. Brown, 2016, argues that fish in all parts of the world are under threat from excessive fishing as well as habitat destruction and decline.

 Answers online at: https://study.sagepub.com/hopkinsandreid

Apostrophe

Using apostrophes incorrectly can cause confusion and strain to the reader.

Use an apostrophe to:

- Show a possessive relationship. To show singular possessive nouns, place the apostrophe between the noun and the 's'. To show plural possessive nouns, place the apostrophe after the 's'.

Example 1: *This institution's mission statement indicates the principles that underpin the processes.* (singular noun)

Example 2: *The lecturer commented on the high quality of the students' assignments.* (plural noun)

- Show a contracted form. Be careful – in formal written texts, contractions should not be used.

  Example 1: *The students haven't received feedback on their work yet.*

  Example 2: *The recording mechanism wasn't working effectively during the lecture.*

NB Never use *It's* in your formal assignments and writing. *It's* is a contraction for *It is* or *it has.* The possessive does **not** have an apostrophe:

Example 1: *The project is finally coming to an end, but it's taken three years to reach this point.* (spoken, **not** formal written English)

Example 2: *Hosting the Olympics was considered a success, and it is hoped that its legacy will live on for many years.* (no apostrophe for possessive)

See the Punctuation Guide above for rules of use for apostrophes – or try the following exercises first and then check the rules.

YOUR TURN

Task 12

Decide if the apostrophes in the following sentences are correct (a) or incorrect (b). Correct them if they are incorrect.

1. It has long been recognised by fisheries' scientists that hatchery-reared fish have high death rates when released back into the wild.   a / b

2. A chemical bonds relative strength depends upon the level of attraction between atoms.   a / b

3. In order to maintain a balance between the energy from the sun and the energy that leaves the Earth, there is a constant adjustment in the Earth's climate system.   a / b

4. In the 1980's the numbers of fast-food restaurants, bank outlets and shopping malls increased significantly.   a / b

YOUR TURN

Task 13

General punctuation task

Identify and correct the errors in the sentences below. There may be: missing punctuation (MP), incorrect punctuation (IP), or use of punctuation when there should be no punctuation (UP). Some sentences may have more than one error.

1. The workers prior assumptions and their views on the importance of autonomy and innovation made them less willing to accept bureaucratic change. . . . .

2. In initial trials there were problems with sustainability, therefore the components were derived from a renewable source in order to improve the green credentials rating. . . . .

3. This example shows how in some situations, including the manufacturing industry, a bureaucracy may still be preferable and, can be linked with some characteristics of other organisational forms to establish a successful organisation. . . . .

4. The following organisations were involved in the decision to back the changes; UNICEF, Save the Children, Dr Barnados, and Care International. . . . .

5. The branded product market has shown remarkable resilience to the introduction onto the market of significant generic products which is a surprise. . . . .

6. Brown (2015) suggests that policy makers should consult interested parties to ensure there is a reason for new policy. Although it is important to remain unbiased at all times. . . . .

7. Research into climate change uses modelling techniques, which use existing data to project forward and make predictions. . . . .

8. The deposition of emperors by the army, became a common theme in the third century, as soldiers began to distrust their commanders and the emperors to whom they had sworn allegiance. . . . .

 Answers online at: https://study.sagepub.com/hopkinsandreid

Common spelling errors

Spelling is a perennial problem for many people, and making spelling mistakes is often habitual and difficult to eliminate.

Spelling errors can affect your grades at university, but they can also have a disastrous impact on your job prospects and career opportunities. So good spelling matters.

There are a number of things you can do to help reduce the risk of making spelling errors in your written work. Here are a few top tips.

Avoiding spelling errors

Spell checker

Turn on the spell checker on your computer, *but* don't rely on it as it may not spot all errors (e.g. easily confused words, US English spellings).

Rule checker

Frequently revise the rules of spelling.

Friend checker

Ask a friend to check your work. A fresh pair of eyes will spot errors that you've missed.

Rest and revisit

If you can, step away from your work and leave it to rest overnight or for a few days so that you can review and revise with a fresh pair of eyes.

Topsy turvy

Read your work from the bottom to the top of each page. This will help you avoid getting distracted by the narrative, so that you can focus on your spelling accuracy.

Brain game

Fool your brain into thinking you are reading a new piece of writing. You can do this by changing font size, text and/or background colours, printing out in large print, or reviewing on different platforms or devices such as a mobile phone.

YOUR TURN

Task 14

Find and correct the spelling error(s) in the following sentences (there may be more than one error in each sentence).

1. After a successful presentation, the research group acheived a distintion for their work on the project.

   ....

   ....

2. Some of the data was ommited as it was considered unreliable.

   ....

   ....

3. In the course of my studies, I developed a number of independant learning startegies that helped me meet targets and deadlines and succeed in my studies.

   ....

   ....

4. The study involved both qualatative and quantatative research, and reliability of results was improved through triangulation of results.

   ....

   ....

5. It is also interesting to note that fossil remains indicate the former occurence of therepods on this section of the Jurrassic coastline.

   ....

   ....

Answers online at: https://study.sagepub.com/hopkinsandreid

YOUR TURN

Task 15

Find and correct ten spelling errors in the following sample from a student's report.

Pertinant to our understanding of the current obesity epidemic is the role of effective communication between General Practitioners (GPs) and obese patients. Comparitive research has illustrated the health risks, which include hypertension and diabetes (Gray et al., 2011). As a result, GPs are considered to be a suitable medium for providing nutritional advice and information on suitable weight loss interventions (Malterud and Ulkriksen, 2010). However, literature has reported a reduction in comitment to weight loss interventions following GP consultations, highlighting a discontinuous relationship between communication and behaviour (Swift, Choi, Puhl & Glazebrook, 2012).

A fundimental determinent of bridging the communications gap capitalises on examining the impact of GPs' terminology on low self-esteem and self-blame when addressing an individual's weight status (Brochu & Esses, 2011; Gray et al., 2011). Augmenting the literature, Collier (2010) demonstrated noticable undesirability in obese patients, following GPs' adoption of the term 'obesity'. This implicated the importance of endorsing a sensitive language style when discussing obesity, alongside a need for accessibility to knowlege-sharing resources and effective proceedures. It also may call into question areas of competance within the medical profesion when it comes to dealing with patient care.

1	6 ....
2	7 ....
3	8 ....
4	9 ....
5	10 ....

 Answers online at: https://study.sagepub.com/hopkinsandreid

Easily confused words

Examine the following sentences. Which one contains a mistake?

I practiced three days a week until I was fluent.
I practised three days a week until I was fluent.

In UK English, **to practise** is a verb and **practice** can be a noun or adjective. Therefore, the second sentence is correct.

There are many words in English that look and sound very similar but their meanings can be quite different. You need to be able to spot any misuses when proofreading your work.

Easily confused words can be divided into different categories. These are explored in the following tasks.

Word-alikes

YOUR TURN

Task 16

Circle the correct word in the following sentences.

1. Smith (2010) goes **farther/further**, suggesting that the methodology is flawed.
2. The mechanism consisted of 18 **discrete/discreet** elements.
3. The **principal/principle** aim of the study was to determine the effects of UV light on the human skin.
4. The interview was conducted **verbally/orally**.
5. The heat loss was measured while the vehicle was **stationery/stationary**.
6. The report should be written **formerly/formally**.
7. This essay will examine the causes and **effects/affects** of global warming on the polar ice caps.
8. The software was **licensed/licenced** to the university.
9. **Less/Fewer** than five candidates were selected for interview.
10. The results of the study **infer/imply** that smoking causes cancer.

> **Answers online at: https://study.sagepub.com/hopkinsandreid**

Confusing verbs, problem pronouns and possessives

YOUR TURN

Task 17

Find and correct eight misused words in the following text from a PowerPoint slide.

- Composed of four sections: Background, Interview with CEO, Findings and recommendations

  Misused word: .... Correction: ....

- Focus on the board members of Brock Brothers Ltd and there wage increases between 2010–2015

  Misused word: .... Correction: ....

- Interview with Mr David Brock, who's position as CEO is under threat from stakeholders

  Misused word: .... Correction: ....

- Mr Brock justified his annual pay raise, stating, 'its reward for good management.'

  Misused word: .... Correction: ....

- Mr Brock claimed that shareholders were using there power to undermine his authority

  Misused word: .... Correction: ....

- The report concludes that Mr Bork should resign from the management board, and it's members should reconsider they're positions.

  Misused word: .... Correction: ....

 Answers online at: https://study.sagepub.com/hopkinsandreid

 **YOUR TURN**

Task 18

Now circle 12 misused words in the following sample from a student's job application letter.

During my degree, I developed and practiced many transferable skills that I believe compliment the roles, duties and skills required for the advertised post. For example, in my second year, I was appointed by the Student Union as a debt councillor. One of my roles was to provide advise and support to any one who's daily life may be effected by financial problems and difficulties, and to ensure that there personnel life did not adversely impact on there studies. The position also involved a number of administrative duties, which included the use of spreadsheets and general office tasks such as ordering stationary. I am confidant therefore that all together my skills match the profile that you're looking for and I am therefore an ideal candidate for your organization.

 Answers online at: https://study.sagepub.com/hopkinsandreid

Glossary of easily-confused words

Word-alikes

Accept (verb) – similar to receive or take:

Please accept my sincere condolences.

Except (preposition) – excluding:

I like everything on the menu except the curried lamb.

Advice (noun) – opinion about what could or should be done about a situation or problem:

My personal tutor offered me very sound and practical advice.

Advise (verb) – to offer advice, recommend, suggest, inform or notify:

My personal tutor advised me to develop an evidence-based appraisal of the case study.

Affect (verb) – to alter or influence:

The increase in moisture affected the overall result.

Effect (noun) – result, impact or power to produce a result:

The effect of prolonged exposure to the sun was measured each day for a week.

Also

Effect (verb) – to bring about or execute:

The appointment of a new senior tutor effected change within the department.

All together – all in one place, all at the same time:

The group should have discussed the problem all together rather than separately.

Altogether (adverb) – completely, on the whole, entirely, taking everything into consideration:

Muntzer (2001) rejected Lunt's interpretation altogether and devised a completely separate approach.

Amount of (used with uncountable nouns) – a quantity of something:

A large amount of money was lost during the banking crisis.

Number of (used with countable nouns):

The number of students.

Anyone (pronoun) – any person:

It is possible for anyone to learn how to use the software.

Any one (two-word phrase) – any singular member of a group (often followed by 'of'):

If any one of the presentation group is absent, the task will not be assessed.

Cite (verb) – to mention or quote:

Ten participants were asked to cite three times they experienced pain above the indicated threshold.

Laddal (1998; cited by Durkin, 1995) found that over time, cooperative children become increasingly popular among their classmates.

Site (noun) – refers to location (physical or virtual):

The East Building was selected as the most suitable site for the conference.

Complement (noun or verb) – something that contributes additional features to something else in a way that will enhance, improve or emphasise its quality.

verb: *The report was complemented by an excellent presentation that summarised the key findings.*

noun: *A new tablet was also offered as a complement to the cash prize.*

Compliment (noun or verb) – polite form of praise:

verb: *The director of studies complimented the group for their excellent presentation.*

noun: *Carter received many compliments for his ambitious and complex design.*

Continuous (adjective) – without a pause or interruption:

The strategy of the organisation was to focus on continuous improvement.

Continual (adjective) – something that happens repeatedly:

The CEO's continual involvement over the last ten years has ensured a highly functional management team.

It can also be used in a negative way to express annoyance:

The group failed to meet their deadline because of continual interruptions from the rival team.

Discreet (adjective) – to be careful to keep something a secret and avoid embarrassing someone:

The counsellor insisted that she would be completely discreet when dealing with problems.

Discrete (adjective) – separate of, distinct:

The post involved four discrete duties and responsibilities.

Dependent (adjective) – having to rely on someone for financial, emotional or other forms of support:

The success of the study was dependent on external funding.

Dependant (noun) – someone (often a child), who depends on another person for a home, bed, food and so on:

John is married and has three dependants: a boy and two girls.

Farther (adjective) – mainly used to describe physical distance:

The laboratory was much farther from the main campus than we expected.

Further (adjective) – generally used to describe figurative distance:

Shimmel (1994) goes further to suggest that cognition is a sociological construct.

Good (adjective) – someone, something, or some place having the required qualities; of a high standard:

The job was good until they changed my contract and increased my workload.

Good (noun) – benefit to someone or something:

The decision was made for the good of the company.

Well (adverb) – comments on how an action is performed:

The project went very well and we all received high marks.

Well (adjective) – 'in good health':

The employee reported that he was feeling well and was going to return to work on Monday.

Imply (verb) – similar in meaning to 'suggest':

Smith's views imply that she was not supportive of the theory.

Infer (verb) – used to deduce or conclude that something is true based on available information or evidence:

The research findings infer that the recruitment strategy of the organisation is flawed.

Led (verb) (past and past participle form) – took charge of, initiated, resulted in:

The project was led by Professor Johnson.

This change in policy has led to severe hardship and deprivation.

Lead (noun) – a position ahead of everyone else in a race or competition:

Group A is in the lead.

The lead was lost when Jones dropped the baton.

Lead (noun) – a metallic element:

The toxicity levels of lead were measured and the associated symptoms recorded.

Less (used with uncountable nouns) – to indicate 'a smaller amount of something':

We had less time for the meeting than anticipated.

Fewer (used with countable nouns) – to indicate 'a smaller number of something':

Fewer candidates than expected applied for the job.

Licence (noun) – a permit from an authority to own or use something:

The bar had a licence to sell alcohol.

License (verb) – to authorise the use of something, to permit (someone) to do something:

The student is licensed to drive the mini bus.

Lose (verb) – to misplace, be deprived of or fail to win something:

There was a possibility that the group would lose their place in the final round of presentations.

Loose (adjective) – not fastened or not tight fitting:

The garment should be worn loose so that there are no restrictions of movement.

Practice (noun) – the application or use of an idea, method or belief, as opposed to theories relating to it:

Japanese working practices have been adopted by companies throughout the western world.

Practice (noun) – habitual or expected procedures or ways of doing something:

Regular staff training is common practice throughout the company.

The practice (noun) – the business or premises of a doctor or lawyer:

The Solicitor's practice is located in Goldcrest Avenue.

In practice (adverb phrase) – in practical applications, in the real world:

While rules state that all students must attend revision sessions, in practice this rarely occurs.

Practise (verb) – perform an activity or exercise repeatedly or regularly in order to improve or maintain proficiency:

In the course of my studies, I practised and developed my writing skills.

Practise (verb) – carry out an activity, method or custom habitually or regularly:

Parts of the ceremony are still practised today.

Precede (verb) – 'to come before':

A full consultation often precedes any major structural review.

Proceed (verb) – 'to move forward':

The department must seek approval from the review board, before the project can proceed.

Also

Proceeds (noun) – money raised from an event or activity:

The company used the proceeds from the sale of their subsidiary to fund the takeover.

Principle (noun) – a rule or standard:

The Prime Minister agreed in principle to support the bill.

Principal (noun) – a person who holds a senior position or is very important:

The Principal stepped down from her post in January.

Principal (adjective) – chief, main or leading:

Non-attendance is often the principal reason for student failure on the programme.

Verbal (adjective) – things that are put into words and covers both oral and written communication:

The problem with the PowerPoint was visual rather than verbal.

Oral (adjective) – things that are spoken only:

They reached an oral agreement and then later signed the contract.

Confusing verbs

Lie (past tense = **lay**, past participle = **lain**) – to recline:

If you are suffering from back ache, lie down on a hard flat surface until the pain diminishes.

Lie (past tense = **lay**, past participle = **lain**) – to remain or be kept in a specified or certain state:

The cathedral has lain in ruins since the Second World War.

Lay (past tense = **laid**, past participle = **laid**) – to put somebody or something in a particular position, especially when it is done with care:

The samples were laid out in front of the participants.

Rise (past tense = **rose**, past participle = **risen**) – to come or go upwards; to reach a higher position or level:

Since the beginning of the century, the number of recorded cases has risen dramatically.

Raise (past tense = **raised**, past participle = **raised**) – to move or lift something to a higher level:

The election result raised speculation that the opposition leader would resign.

Raise (noun) – an increase in salary:

In light of all the additional work I have had to do, I would like to request a raise and three days holiday.

Consist of somebody/something – to be composed formed or made up of:

The soup consisted of a few vegetables and a tiny amount of chicken.

Comprise (more formal) – to be formed from the things or people mentioned:

The report comprised four sections and an extended appendix.

Be composed of somebody/something (formal) – to be formed from the things or people:

The product was composed of 75% water.

Problem pronouns and possessives

Its (the possessive form of it):

This is an example of healthcare practice at its very best.

It's (contracted form of it is) (NB Contractions are usually not used in most formal academic and professional written contexts):

It's too cold to go outside today.

Their (the possessive form of they):

Through increased awareness and changing structures within the government, women were able to challenge their position for the first time.

They're (they are): (NB Contractions are usually not used in most formal academic and professional written contexts):

I've just heard that the second group won't be able to make the meeting as they're running behind schedule.

There (noun) – an 'existential there', used to introduce information, usually followed by forms of the verb 'to be'.

However, Kline (2013), maintains that there are limits to Bhaskar's conception of naturalism.

Whose (possessive form of who):

These are the business leaders whose success inspires others, and provide role models for young people to copy.

Who's (who is) (NB Contractions are usually not used in most formal academic and professional written contexts):

Do you know who's chairing the meeting?

Your (possessive form of you):

Your assignment will not be marked if you fail to hand in on time.

You're (you are) (NB Contractions are usually not used in most formal academic and professional written contexts):

If you're the writer, then you should be the presenter.

YOUR CHAPTER TAKEAWAY

Accuracy Checklist
✓ (tick when completed)

Have I ...

- ( ) read each sentence carefully to check for grammar errors?

- ( ) checked my punctuation is accurate and appropriate?

- ( ) checked my tenses are correct?

- ( ) made sure my writing is free from spelling errors?

- ( ) made sure my sentences make sense grammatically?

- ( ) checked words that I know I sometimes spell wrongly?

Your one takeaway

....

....

YOUR PROGRESS

CHAPTER SIX

Being Concise

YOUR PROGRESS

CHAPTER DASHBOARD

Your objectives list:

 Write in a focused and succinct style

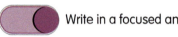 Eliminate wordiness and waffle

 Develop editing techniques to eliminate unnecessary words and phrases

min   max

'The road to hell is paved with adverbs.'

– Stephen King

My three editing skills goals:

1 ....

2 ....

3 ....

What your tutor is looking for

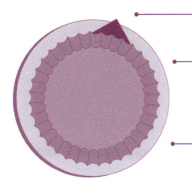

1. No unnecessary 'waffle' in your writing

2. Easy to understand message without more words than necessary

3. No unnecessary repetition of ideas

Accuracy

Core Skills

Style
Core Skills

Clarity
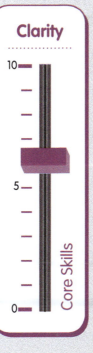
Core Skills

Being concise
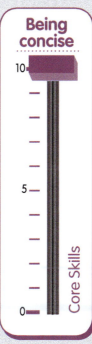
Core Skills

Being informed

Core Skills

WATCH OUT FOR:

Don't say it in ten words when six words will do. For every necessary word, there are at least three unnecessary ones

Diagnostic
How good are you at being succinct?

This wordy sample from a psychology lab report is 94 words. How many words can you cut it down to, while still retaining all essential information?

Each of the twenty participants were timed and were each given 20 seconds to fill in on a piece of paper the words they associated with the words in the list of words from the appropriate block from Blocks A or B. Once the test was complete, participants were given a different sheet of paper and were asked to write their voting choice from the available options. No names were taken to maintain anonymity and both the completed test form and piece of paper with the vote on were placed in an unmarked envelope.

My final word count

For feedback on your score, go online at:
https://study.sagepub.com/hopkinsandreid

We want our writing to be easy to follow, without taking up more of the reader's time and effort than necessary. This means we also want our writing to say what we want to say in as *few words* as possible.

It is not easy to write concisely. You need to allocate time to the process of hunting down and removing unnecessary words and phrases from your writing to ensure your ideas are succinctly expressed (see Figure 6.1). Writing concisely demonstrates to your reader that you have command and control over your ideas and the language you are using to express those ideas.

This chapter will equip you with the skills to say what you want to say concisely, and give you tips on how to recognise and eliminate unnecessary, repeated, or redundant words and phrases in your writing.

What tutors say:

'Writing concisely is a skill. It takes time to eradicate the waffle.'

'Why would I want to read more than necessary when I have so much to do.'

Figure 6.1   What tutors say about writing concisely

HOW CAN WE ACHIEVE CONCISE WRITING?

To achieve concise writing, essays and other academic writing need to:

- be clear and accurate
- use well-chosen language, with appropriate formality
- use the right words at the right time
- avoid meaningless words and phrases that do not add to the meaning
- avoid unnecessary repetition.

Being clear and accurate without excessive words

Sometimes we use more words than necessary and decide to edit our work to reduce the word count (for example, when we have gone over the allowed number of words for our essay). When cutting words, we need to be careful that we keep the intended meaning.

Task 1

Look at the pairs of sentences below. Does the rewritten, shorter version have the same meaning as the first, wordier version?

1a. A lot of research has been conducted to test the phenomenon of visual illusions, with results suggesting that horizontal stripes actually make a human figure look slimmer, contradicting the common assumption that vertical stripes make people look slimmer than they really are (Helmholtz, 1987; Thompson and Mikellidou, 2011). 42 words

1b. Results from several studies have suggested that horizontal stripes make a human figure look slimmer, contradicting the common assumption that it is vertical stripes that achieve this (Helmholtz, 1987; Thompson and Mikellidou, 2011). 27 words

....

....

2a. Also if this experiment was done again, other methods could be tried out to find a better method to estimate protein concentration such as the Lowry method, as it is a very widely used method and is seen as an acceptable alternative to absolute determination of concentration and is also a biuret method, so is still an optical method (Waterborg, 2009). 58 words

2b. Future experiments could use other methods, such as the Lowry method (also an optical method), which is better at estimating protein concentration and is seen as an acceptable alternative to absolute determination of concentration (Waterborg, 2009). 34 words

....

....

 Answers online at: https://study.sagepub.com/hopkinsandreid

Using well-chosen language, with appropriate formality

Formal language can be more concise than informal language (although not always!). Compare the two columns in Table 6.1.

Table 6.1 Formal vs informal versions

Formal version	Informal version
Verbs	**Verbs**
To repeat	To do again
To estimate	To work out
To consider	To think about
To analyse	To look into
To discuss	To talk about
To increase	To get/make bigger/to go up
To result in/to become	To end up
To cause/to create	To be the reason for
Words/phrases	**Words/phrases**
Many/much	A lot of
Some	Quite a lot of
Several	A few
No difference was observed/evident	There was not much difference
Because	All because
Due to	All down to
In addition,	On top of this,
Generally/overall/in general	On the whole

YOUR TURN

Task 2

Rewrite each sentence below to be more formal and more concise. We have suggested a target number of words you should aim for.

1. After mixing there was still quite a lot of residue left lying at the bottom of the flask. (18 words)

   Aim for 5 words:

   ....

   ....

2. On top of these stresses there is also the stress of ultraviolet radiation (UVR), which can give us sunburn and make the risk of skin cancer bigger. (28 words)

   Aim for 15 words:

   ....

   ....

(Continued)

(Continued)

3. The legalisation and spread of Christianity within the Roman Empire made internal tensions go up and was part of the reason for the circumstances in which the assassination of emperors ended up a viable option. (35 words)

   Aim for 28 words:

   ....

   ....

   ....

4. While economic growth can often get levels of unemployment to go down a bit, the belief that it is a means for a lot of jobs to be made could be thought to be a contradiction. (36 words)

   Aim for 28 words:

   ....

   ....

   ....

   ....

➡ **Answers online at: https://study.sagepub.com/hopkinsandreid**

Avoiding meaningless/wordy words and phrases

There are some phrases and expressions that do not add anything to your writing. When editing your work, look out for these kinds of expressions. Can they be deleted without losing any meaning?

Redundant words

These are (quite commonly used) pairs of words where each word in the pair means the same thing. One of the pair can usually go (Table 6.2).

Table 6.2 Redundant words

Don't say ...	Say
The end result	The result
The final outcome	The outcome
Each individual	Each

Don't say ...	Say
Separate individual	Separate
The alternative choice	The alternative
A brief summary	A summary
Connect together	Connect
Each and every one	Each
Remove completely	Remove
Reduce down	Reduce
Compete with each other	Compete
Exactly the same	The same
Merge together	Merge

Meaningless and/or wordy phrases

These are phrases that hold no meaning and can usually be removed entirely, or reduced in length (Table 6.3).

Table 6.3 Meaningless words

Don't say ...	Say
There is/are/was/were/have been	– (say nothing)
Due to the fact that	Because
Each of them	Each
Considered to be	Considered
Equally as	... as
In terms of	– (say nothing)
Of a xxx nature	– (say nothing)
Very/really/quite/completely	– (say nothing)
It is worth noting/mentioning/stating that	– (say nothing)
So as to	To

YOUR TURN

Task 3

Cross out the words and phrases that can be cut from the following extract from a psychology lab report.

There have been a number of studies which have established that men obtain significantly higher scores on the WAIS than women. However, each of the sub-tests has separate individual results. In the standardisation sample for the WAIS, men obtain higher scores on information, picture completion, arithmetic and block design. Women score better than men on similarities, digit symbol and vocabulary with exactly the same average scores on the rest of the WAIS subtests.

(Continued)

(Continued)

Previous studies have shown that on Raven's matrices, men do not outperform better than women, on the whole. Lynn et al. (2004) have shown that the Raven's matrices may measure at least three factors (perceptual, verbal analytic and visuo-spatial). It is worth noting that Raven's matrices do not test general intelligence, and it is on some of these factors that men outperform women due to the fact that because males and females have differently structured brains which they use in very different ways (Mackintosh and Bennett, 2005). (160 words including references)

 Answers online at: https://study.sagepub.com/hopkinsandreid

─── **TIP** ───

Being concise

When you proofread your first draft, look for the phrases from this section, and see if you can rewrite your sentence without them.

Transforming relative clauses

Sometimes we can reduce the length of sentences that contain relative clauses. We can do this in two main ways: by reducing the relative clause, or by using adjectives instead. Look at these examples:

1. The apparatus included a metal bucket ~~which was~~ positioned on a wooden surface.
2. Many plants ~~which are~~ growing in people's gardens can be used for medicinal purposes.
3. A species of bacteria which has been recently discovered appears to be able to consume metal. ⇨ A recently discovered species of bacteria appears to be able to consume metal.

YOUR TURN ───────────────

Task 4

Make these sentences containing relative clauses more concise.

1. The policies which related to health and education are considered to have been a success.

....

2. Electricity can be produced from heat which is emitted from industrial processes.

   ....

3. The patients who were taking the placebo showed no difference in their fitness levels at the end of the experiment.

   ....

4. Twenty participants who were regular sports players were studied over a period of ten weeks.

   ....

➡ **Answers online at: https://study.sagepub.com/hopkinsandreid**

Avoiding unnecessary repetition

We expect the abstract or summary to include information from the report, so here repetition is essential.

However, you need to ensure that you organise your longer pieces of writing so that you do not repeat the same ideas in different places. This is achieved through careful planning.

TIP

Avoiding repetition

Use the 'find' function in Word to look for key ideas throughout your essay. Check that each time you find a section talking about the idea, it is a *new* and *necessary* section and **not** repetition.

Using brackets

Sometimes information can be put inside brackets instead of being incorporated into the sentence. This can be a more concise way to give this information.

Compare these pairs of sentences:

The Raven's matrices measure the following three factors: perceptual, verbal analytic and spatial.

The Raven's matrices measure three factors (perceptual, verbal analytic and spatial).

A combination of physical capital, which is defined as a factor of production such as machinery, buildings, or equipment, the size of the labour force, the supply of materials and the supply of energy, provides the total productivity.

A combination of physical capital (e.g. machinery, buildings, equipment), the size of the labour force, the supply of materials and the supply of energy, provides information on the total productivity.

YOUR TURN

Task 5

Rewrite the following sentences using brackets to make the message more concise.

1. There are two conditions which need to be met for cartel success and these are stability within the cartel organisation and the potential for monopoly power.

   ....

   ....

2. Most recently the post-processualist school of thought has emerged, which is sometimes also referred to as interpretive archaeologies, which claims that we will never be able to understand the reasons for increasing social complexity, as much of human behaviour is illogical and the role of the individual is not necessarily represented in the archaeological record (Hodder, 1986).

   ....

   ....

3. Qualitatively, the results closely match the theory, which predicted that a linear relationship between applied load and deflection exists.

   ....

   ....

4. The fact that Hagelin did not appear to be acting out of greed, demonstrated by the fact that he asked for very little for the service he was providing, must be weighed against Hagelin's violations of his engineer's principles.

   ....

   ....

→ **Answers online at: https://study.sagepub.com/hopkinsandreid**

TASK 6

Edit the extract from an essay on economic growth to make it more concise. How many words can you reduce it to, taking care to *maintain the same meaning*?

It seems to be generally accepted that the richer a country is, the greater the number of jobs available and thus the greater the rates of employment. However, this belief is a contradiction. In order to maximise economic growth, a company needs to reach as high productivity as possible with as small an input and production cost as possible. This means a company has to become more streamlined so that fewer staff need to be paid, and fewer resources need to be purchased to make the same volume of product. The further labour is enhanced and mechanised, the smaller the production costs to product ratio.

....

....

....

....

....

....

....

→ **Answers online at: https://study.sagepub.com/hopkinsandreid**

YOUR CHAPTER TAKEAWAY

Concise writing Checklist

✓ (tick when completed)

Have I removed …

( ) waffle words?

( ) redundant words?

( ) meaningless phrases?

( ) two-word phrases?

( ) unnecessary pronouns from relative clauses?

( ) repetitive words and phrases?

Have I retained …

( ) clarity, understanding and meaning?

Your one takeaway

....

....

....

YOUR PROGRESS

CHAPTER SEVEN

Writing in Academic Style

CHAPTER DASHBOARD

YOUR PROGRESS

Your objectives list:

 Identify the key features of formal academic style

 Apply an appropriate and acceptable style in academic writing

 Remove informal words and phrases

min   max

'Style is the answer to everything.'

– Charles Bukowski

My three academic writing goals:

1 ....

2 ....

3 ....

What your tutor is looking for

1. A formal style
2. Use of academic style conventions
3. Caution and objectivity

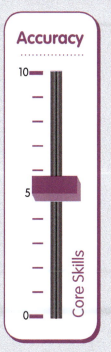

Accuracy

10
5
0
Core Skills

Style

10
5
0
Core Skills

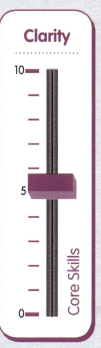

Clarity

10
5
0
Core Skills

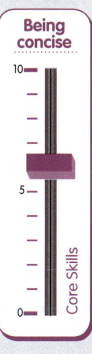

Being concise

10
5
0
Core Skills

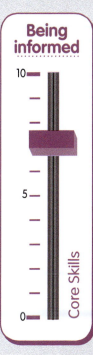

Being informed

10
5
0
Core Skills

WATCH OUT FOR:

Avoid over-formality. Good academic writing should be accessible and easy to read

Diagnostic
How confident are you with academic writing styles?

See if you can identify and underline all the academic style issues in this paragraph.

During my research, I discovered lots of studies that looked into the good and bad effects of feedback on learning. Hyland (2010) is really positive about the importance of feedback, saying that it helps push forward language development and consolidates learning. Furthermore, Brown (2009) is also inconsolable when he asserts that learning, and needless to say, the learning experience itself, is dependent on a tacit knowledge of results at a time when, and a place where such self same knowledge can be utilised in haste for corrective instruction. Jacob (2008) also sings the praises of feedback, and highlights two important elements of the process; the first he called informational, where data's provided to help students change and make their work better. And for the second, he coined the phrase 'hedonic', when feedback can help motivate students to take more risks, make further improvements and extend their abilities, etc.

What kind of problems could you see?

....

....

....

....

See if you can turn this paragraph into successful academic writing.

For feedback on your score, go online at:
https://study.sagepub.com/hopkinsandreid

Writing in academic style is a crucial feature of good academic writing. Your tutor will expect you to use a number of academic conventions in your written work, and if you fail to do this, your marks will suffer. These conventions may vary from subject to subject, but there are general rules that should be observed.

Academic style is generally formal (but not too formal), accessible and easy to understand. You need to make appropriate style choices such as when and how to use abbreviations, passive or active voice, cautious language, and so on.

This chapter will provide you with the tools to recognise, understand and apply effectively the conventions of academic writing, and produce work that is of a suitable academic style for the given genre. It will also help you identify and correct style issues in your own writing to ensure academic success.

A FORMAL APPROACH (BUT NOT TOO FORMAL)

Formality in your writing is important as it helps you to present an objective, reasoned and measured response to an assignment task.

However, it is also important that your writing is clear, concise and easy to read. It is not necessary therefore to adopt an over-formal and/or complex style.

How to avoid using an over-formal style – 'the Jane Austen effect'

There is a tendency for those unfamiliar with academic writing conventions to assume that academic writing requires a higher level of complexity, and use of over-formal vocabulary. However, this type of misuse and misunderstanding can often lead to meaningless or impenetrable structures and inappropriate style.

The following example illustrates the problem:

The arduous and challenging process of research may necessitate interrogation of one's tutor to elucidate advice and prescribe recommended readings, or a bibliographic list of empathetic authors who have critiqued similar topics.

The student has used archaic, over-formal and unnecessary vocabulary, and an overly long, complex sentence structure. The result is a rather stilted and old-fashioned style that reads like a Charles Dickens novel rather than an academic essay!

The sentence should look more like this:

The challenges of the research process can be mitigated by following tutor advice on recommended readings and also investigating other writers who have examined the topic.

YOUR TURN

Task 1

Underline the words that make the following sentences difficult to understand.

a. The essay is synonymous with academic writing which requires the diligent application of specific skills and techniques that many people believe or presume that they are not familiar with.

b. It has been duly noted by aforementioned critics that the plethora of roles and activities, endorsed and championed by the executive, and actioned under enforced duress by the workforce, has led to a profusion of confusion and a myriad of unquenchable challenges within the complexity of the company's labyrinthine structure.

Now compare with the improved versions.

a. Successful essay writing requires the application of a specific set of academic skills that some students may need to learn.

b. The highly complex structure of the organisation, imposed by the executive, has led to an expansion of roles and responsibilities and high levels of confusion among the workforce.

Have the words you underlined been replaced?   Yes ☐   No? ☐

STYLE CONVENTIONS – DO'S AND DON'TS

First person (I and we)

The first person is usually considered too subjective and informal to be used in academic writing. (For example, use 'This essay will …' instead of 'I will …'.) However, some types of written genres such as reflective writing, business reports and case studies, require its use. Also, there are variations in tolerance of first person use among the academic community, degree disciplines, and even assignment tasks. If in doubt, check with your tutor.

Contractions (they're, she's, it's)

You should ensure that full forms ('they are', 'she is', 'it is') are used at all times.

Never use 'it's'. This is the contraction for 'it is' or 'it has', so has no place in academic writing. If you are using a possessive adjective, there is *no* apostrophe:

The company was a victim of **its** own strategy.

Colloquialisms, slang expressions and informal language such as text speak

Avoid using expressions such as *stuff, a lot, lots of, and that, sort of, lol, things.*

Get

Don't use 'get' if there is a common but more formal replacement:

During the course of the experiment the sample size got bigger.

During the course of the experiment the sample size increased.

Clichés, generalisations and idioms

Clichés are phrases that have been over-used and their meaning has been lost over time. They may be common idioms or generalisations such as: 'the problem is a double-edged sword'; 'every cloud has a silver lining'; 'the modern world is a changing place'; 'it goes without saying that'; 'it boils down to'.

They should be avoided in academic writing because they tend to be vague, informal, simplistic, and risk being used as a replacement for more fully developed ideas.

Two-word verb phrases (e.g. put off, break off, end up, fall apart, grow up)

Two-word verb phrases are too informal to be used in academic writing:

This error meant that the sample ended up contaminated and had to be thrown away.

As a result of this error, the sample was contaminated and had to be discarded.

Asking questions (unless you are writing research questions)

Replace rhetorical questions with statements. For example:

Why did the financial crisis occur?

There are a number of reasons why the financial crisis occurred.

Using abbreviations and acronyms

You can use abbreviations and acronyms (etc., e.g., i.e., BBC) in your writing but there are some rules you need to follow.

General rule:

- The first time you mention a word or phrase that can be abbreviated, write the full form (usually with each word initial capital), followed by the abbreviation in brackets.
- Every time you refer to it after this, you can use the abbreviation. Example:

Heating Ventilation and Air Conditioning (HVAC) systems can be located in a central part of a building, or there can be individual units for smaller spaces within a building. HVAC systems are crucial to the successful design of buildings.

Common abbreviations

Common abbreviations include:

- e.g. and i.e.
- symbols for chemical elements, e.g. C, O_2, N.
- symbols for common chemical compounds, e.g. CO_2, H_2O. But be careful; if you are writing about a chemical compound in a non-specialist way, you may need to write the name in full. For example, compare:

Sulphuric acid is commonly used in school laboratories.

Several acids were used in the experiment, including H_2SO_4, HCl and HNO_3.

- symbols for temperature, e.g. °C:

A liquid-glass thermometer is not appropriate here for temperatures of up to about 200°C as they are fragile at high temperatures.

TIP

Common abbreviations

Don't use 'etc.' and 'NB' in your academic writing. They are informal style, and considered 'lazy' writing.

- Instead of etc., include more examples.
- Replace NB with a sentence that demonstrates the importance of the point: 'The participants gave permission for their names to be used in the report, which was an important ethical consideration.'

Meanings of e.g. and i.e.

- e.g. means 'for example' – it should be followed with a few examples.
- i.e. means 'that is' – it *explains or defines* something, and is similar to '='.
- do **not** use examples after i.e. – give the complete list or a definition.

Using e.g. and i.e.

You *can* use common abbreviations such as 'e.g.' and 'i.e.' in your writing, **but** only if you:

- use punctuation accurately
- know the difference in meaning between the two.

Punctuation with e.g. and i.e.

- Use **brackets** or **commas** either side of 'e.g. …':

For a paramagnetic material (e.g. air) we would expect to see a straight line for B–H plot.

For a paramagnetic material, e.g. air, we would expect to see a straight line for B–H plot.

- Do the same for i.e. …:

The Central Place Theory suggests that in a uniform landscape, central places (i.e. towns or cities) will be equidistant and surrounded by satellite rings of smaller settlements.

The Central Place Theory suggests that in a uniform landscape, central places, i.e. towns or cities, will be equidistant and surrounded by satellite rings of smaller settlements.

- Never start a sentence with the abbreviation 'e.g.'. Use the full words:

There are many performance-enhancing substances that have been banned by the World Anti-Doping Agency. For example, compounds such as anabolic androgenic steroids, diuretics and growth factors have been banned since 2000.

Abbreviations – other points

- Even common abbreviations may need to be written out in full, depending on the context and individual tutor's preferences.
- Individual subjects will have their own commonly accepted abbreviations.

TIP

Abbreviations

Always check with your tutor if you are unsure about what abbreviations are acceptable in your subject.

YOUR TURN

Task 2

Have the abbreviations been used correctly in the following sentences? Correct the sentences that have errors.

1. CO has no smell and is colourless.

   ....

2. The alternating current power supply was set to 50 Hz.

   ....

3. Research into climate change can receive funding from DECC (The Department of Energy and Climate Change).

   ....

4. Designers will generally use CAD to enhance their creation and ensure accuracy. Computer Aided Design is common in many disciplines, including architecture, mechanical engineering, and product design.

   ....

5. The freedom of information act (FOI) 2000 allows the public to access any recorded information held by public authorities.

   ....

6. The water was heated to 100 degrees centigrade (°C).

   ....

7. Many mammals nurture their young for long periods. E.g., leopard cubs stay with their mother for up to two years.

   ....

8. There was widespread panic buying, looting etc, following the collapse of the national currency.

   ....

→ **Answers online at: https://study.sagepub.com/hopkinsandreid**

Using cautious language (hedging)

In argument-based academic writing, ideas are rarely 100% certain, so we need to:

- avoid absolute terms (always, never, nothing, all, none) as these will close down and limit your ideas
- use cautious language such as may, might, could, likely, possible.

This will ensure your ideas remain objective, investigative, sceptical and flexible to develop and extend your analysis. Example:

Instead of:

A recession is always the consequence of high interest rates.

Use:

A recession may sometimes occur as a consequence of high interest rates.

YOUR TURN

Task 3

Using the words or phrases from cautious language guide (Table 7.1), re-write the following sentences to soften the meaning. One sentence should NOT be changed, as it is describing factual information.

1. The different body size of early hominins across these locations is an adaptation to temperature variation.

   ....

   ....

2. The spread of English around the world is responsible for the death of many other languages.

   ....

   ....

3. The extra signal conditioning introduced by the amplifier, and the additional balancing required by the Half Bridge introduced additional sources of error.

   ....

   ....

(Continued)

(Continued)

4. The additional complexity of the more advanced circuits is responsible for the unexpected results.

   ....

   ....

5. This proves that there is a significant difference between the male and female subjects' responses to the stimulus.

   ....

   ....

6. As temperatures warm, more water vapour evaporates from the surface into the atmosphere.

   ....

   ....

7. Human error needs to be taken into account.

   ....

   ....

8. The results were unexpected and this was because the equipment was not calibrated properly.

   ....

   ....

→ **Answers online at: https://study.sagepub.com/hopkinsandreid**

Cautious language guide

Table 7.1 Cautious language guide

Introductory (reporting) verbs	assume, believe, propose, tend, suggest, claim, support, deny, state, argue, contend, maintain, stipulate, infer, point out	Used to introduce or 'report' what a writer has said e.g. *Smith (2010) claims that …* Reporting verbs can be used to express strength of view and can distance you from the author's words (see also use of reporting verbs, in Chapter 10)
Modal verbs	may, might, can, could, should, would, will, must, appear	Auxiliary verbs that are used with a main verb to express degrees of possibility or probability e.g. *The adverse weather may have been the main cause of a surge in hospital admissions*

Modal adjectives	possible, probable, certain, uncertain, likely, unlikely, necessary, compulsory, essential, obligatory	An adjective that expresses likelihood. Often used in the phrase 'It is ...' e.g. *It is possible that the economy will improve this year*
Modal adverbs	possibly, probably, perhaps, certainly, essentially, necessarily, clearly, conceivably, unquestionably, apparently	An adverb that adds additional meaning or emphasis to verbs (modal verbs and/or main verbs) e.g. *This was clearly a difficult situation* NOTE: Don't over-use modal adverbs as they can be emotive
Modal nouns	possibility, probability, certainty, likelihood, assumption, chance, capacity, opportunity	A noun that expresses likelihood e.g. *There is a possibility of system failure*
Adverbs of frequency	sometimes, often, occasionally, never, seldom, rarely, frequently, continuously, constantly, regularly	Adverbs that qualify the main verb to describe how often something occurs e.g. *The task was completed regularly by the team*

Emotive language

Look at the following example:

Clearly, the most <u>alarming</u> aspect of this case is the <u>horrendous</u> treatment of the patient by <u>insensitive</u> medical staff who refused to listen to her <u>pleas</u> for help and support during her stay in hospital. The case also highlights the local authority's <u>arrogant</u> stance in ignoring the <u>barrage</u> of complaints they received over the years, and simply <u>brushing the problem under the carpet</u> for <u>the sake of</u> convenience and self-preservation. It must have been very difficult for the families to deal with such a <u>traumatic</u> and <u>wholly intolerable</u> situation.

The words and phrases underlined indicate the use of emotive language.

Emotive words should be avoided in academic writing because they present a subjective and one-sided point of view rather than a rational and evidence-based response to a topic or issue.

Maintaining an objective distance will help build a more measured and considered case, and strengthen your argument.

Choosing the passive or active voice

Knowing when and why to use the passive voice is part of being a good writer.

In order to understand reasons for choosing to use the passive, you first need to be able to recognise it.

YOUR TURN

Task 4

Underline all the passives in the following two texts (A and B) about chocolate.

Text A: The history of chocolate

Chocolate comes from the Cacao tree, or more specifically, from its beans. Cacao beans were first used to make a pleasurable drink in Mexico around 1400 BC, during the time of the Aztecs. After the Spanish conquest of the Aztecs in the 16th century, the chocolate drink made its way into Europe. The Spanish added honey and sugar to the drink, and then much later, in the nineteenth century, the Dutch chemist, Coenraad van Houten produced a less bitter, solid form of chocolate. This solid chocolate was further developed with the addition of milk, which gave it a better taste, and then, in 1879 its flavour and texture was improved still further by the invention of a mixing machine called a conch by Rodolphe Lindt. Many famous chocolate brands, such as Lindt, Nestlé, Fry, Cadbury, and Hershey, started manufacturing chocolate in the late 19th and early 20th century and still manufacture it today.

Text B: Method

First the beans were harvested from the pods, and allowed to naturally ferment over a period of two days to two weeks. The beans were then dried to preserve them. After this, the beans were roasted in an oven to develop the flavour. Next the nibs (inside of the bean) were separated from the shells using a centrifuge, and then put in a grinder to produce a fine powder. After more grinding the mixture became a paste, or liquor, due to the release of cocoa butter. This paste was then put in the conch (a machine that mixes the chocolate further and helps to remove the acidic taste). Finally, the chocolate was tempered by agitating it for a few minutes, in order to give it a glossy look.

 Answers online at: https://study.sagepub.com/hopkinsandreid

What is the passive?

- A form of a verb made with the auxiliary verb 'to be' (in an appropriate tense or form) + past participle. Example:

The sample <u>was analysed</u> using liquid chromatography. (past simple passive of 'analyse')

- A way of organising information in a sentence to highlight *what was done* rather than *who did it.*

YOUR TURN

Task 5

The passive is used for different reasons in the two texts in Task 4. Match Texts A and B to one of the reasons for using the passive below:

Reason 1: To aid coherence by making the topic at the end of one sentence the same topic at the beginning of the next.

Reason 2: To maintain the focus on the key topic and maintain an objective, impersonal style.

Answers online at: https://study.sagepub.com/hopkinsandreid

When should we choose to use the passive?

- When we are more interested in what was done than in the 'doer' of an action. For example, compare:

    a. The scientists **assembled** the equipment for the experiment. (active)
    b. The equipment **was assembled** for the experiment. (passive)

Sentence (a) is active and focuses on who assembled the equipment. Sentence (b) is passive and focuses instead on the equipment.

- When we want to maintain the flow of our ideas and keep the focus on a particular topic. Example:

As well as biological and physiological defences, humans also have behavioural adaptations to <u>extremes of temperature</u>. For example, <u>the impact of cold stress</u> **can be reduced** through the use of shelter, fire and clothing, as well as an efficient foraging strategy.

In the second sentence, we want to continue focusing on temperature ('the impact of cold stress'), and in order to do this here we need to use the passive. (See also Organising your ideas in Chapter 4.)

- When the 'doer' is not important and is already known. Example:

The bill **was passed** with a clear majority.

(We know that the politicians voted, but we do not need to state this.)

- When we do not know who (or what) the 'doer' is. Example:

The sample **had** clearly **been contaminated**, although the source of the contamination was not clear.

TIP

Style

Always check that you know *why* you are choosing the passive. Use the passive selectively and consciously.

The passive – other points

Academic writing is generally expected to be impersonal and objective. Do not, however, confuse being objective with using the passive.

YOUR TURN

Task 6

Compare the three sentence beginnings below. Which sentence beginning do you like best and why?

a. In this essay I will argue that …

....

b. In this essay it is argued that …

....

c. This essay will argue that …

....

Beginning (a) is not sufficiently academic in style – we usually avoid using personal pronouns.

Beginning (b) uses the passive and is impersonal, but feels too remote and wordy.

Beginning (c) is good style (despite the fact that an essay cannot literally 'argue') – it is active, direct and concise without being too personal.

TIP

Style

Overuse of the passive can make your writing less interesting to read. Ensure you use the passive to enhance your writing rather than weaken it.

The noun phrase: Making your writing 'nouny'

Compare these two samples. One is spoken and one is from an academic essay. Which is which and how do you know?

Sample A

I was pretty nervous when I had to write my first essay. I didn't know what they wanted and I didn't know where to start. Actually, I found the whole thing quite stressful and I was quite anxious about it.

Sample B

Writing a first essay at university can be a nerve-wracking experience. Students are often unsure of expectations and the whole process can cause feelings of anxiety and stress.

Sample A is spoken and B is from a piece of academic writing.

Features of spoken language shown here include:

- Use of personal pronouns (e.g. 'I')
- Use of contractions (e.g. 'didn't')
- Use of informal vocabulary (e.g. 'the whole thing'; 'pretty nervous'; 'quite stressful')
- Use of **verbs** to carry a lot of the meaning.

Features of academic writing shown here include:

- lack of personal pronouns
- no contractions
- use of formal vocabulary (e.g. 'nerve-wracking experience'; 'expectations'; 'process'; 'anxiety')
- use of **nouns** to carry the main meaning (e.g. 'Writing a first essay'; 'nerve-wracking experience'; 'students'; 'expectations'; 'process'; 'anxiety'; 'stress').

Using nouns as the main way of carrying meaning is a typical feature of formal academic writing.

YOUR TURN

Task 7

Look at samples A and B (above) again and underline the verbs in each sample.

Notice that sample B has fewer verbs and the noun phrases carry the meaning more than the verb phrases.

 Answers online at: https://study.sagepub.com/hopkinsandreid

Task 8

Look at the pairs of sentences below. Sentences (a) are from spoken English, and sentences (b) from academic writing. Complete the gap in sentences (b) with a noun made from the verb in sentences (a).

1a. When people write an academic essay they need to include more formal words.
1b. Formal vocabulary and style are key features of academic ....
2a. In self-report questionnaires, people answer the questions themselves and the researcher doesn't interfere.
2b. Self-report questionnaires are a type of survey involving the respondents selecting their responses without researcher ....
3a. It is okay to continue to use the land for leisure and sports activities.
3b. Current recreational .... of the land is considered appropriate.
4a. The workmen have to wear clothes to protect them when they remove the asbestos.
4b. Construction workers involved in the .... of asbestos should wear protective clothing.

 Answers online at: https://study.sagepub.com/hopkinsandreid

We make our writing 'nouny' because we can do more things with nouns than we can with verbs. Look at the following example of how we can add information to a noun to build up a long noun phrase.

We can:

- count: *two students*
- classify: *two politics students*
- describe: *two hard-working politics students.*

And we can add information *after* the noun using prepositional phrases (often with 'of' or 'with' or 'in' or 'on'), or participle phrases:

- two hard-working politics students from the University of Manchester
- two hard-working politics students from the University of Manchester currently studying for a Masters degree.

And here is the complete sentence, with the grammatical subject underlined:

<u>Two hard-working politics students from the University of Manchester currently studying for a Masters degree</u> have won the lottery.

YOUR TURN

Task 9

Use the information in the less academic sentences below (1a and 2a) to complete the alternative single sentence (1b and 2b). Make sure you pack the information tightly around the nouns.

1a. We need to do more research into how to use bamboo as a building material. Bamboo is more sustainable than conventional materials. If it is developed we may be able to use it instead of the materials we use in buildings at the moment.

1b. With increased .... and .... bamboo can serve as a .... to conventional structural materials.

2a. In our society, men and women are generally thought of as equal. We are not allowed to discriminate against women, but they are still more likely to be unemployed and to earn less than men.

2b. In our society, men and women are generally seen as equal and .... is illegal, yet the rate of .... and .... for women are lower than for men.

 Answers online at: https://study.sagepub.com/hopkinsandreid

COMMUNICATING WITH YOUR TUTOR

At some point in the course of your studies, you will have to communicate with your tutor through email. This may be to ask a question, discuss a problem you are having with an assignment, arrange an appointment, or ask for an extension!

You need to make sure that you use an acceptable style and follow appropriate conventions so that your message is received positively by your tutor. An inappropriate style can irritate your tutor, who will be marking your work, and this is something you want to avoid at all costs!

YOUR TURN

Task 10

Are the following statements about communicating with your tutor true or false?

1. If you are not sure about something relating to your assignment, you should email your tutor immediately.   true / false

2. At university it is customary to address your tutor by their first name.   true / false

3. Your tutor will expect you to use a chatty style in your emails.   true / false

4. You need to clarify who you are before you explain the purpose of your email. true / false

5. When you send an email to your tutor you can expect a reply within a day. true / false

Now check your answers:

1. If you are not sure about something relating to your assignment, you should email your tutor immediately.

   False. You should first try to find out through other means such as lecture notes, assignment briefs, your colleagues and your Virtual Learning Environment (VLE) (e.g. Moodle, Blackboard etc). If you still cannot find the answer, then you may have to email your tutor, but you should explain that you have been unable to find the information in these ways.

2. At university it is customary to address your tutor by their first name.

   False. You should not address your tutor by their first name unless they specifically tell you to.

3. Your tutor will expect you to use a chatty style in your emails.

   False. Even if you have a good relationship with your tutor, you should use a formal style in your emails to reflect the status of tutor and student.

4. You need to clarify who you are before you explain the purpose of your email.

   True. Write who you are (e.g. a student in your politics unit) so that the tutor understands the context before they read any further.

5. When you send an email your tutor you can expect a reply within a day.

   False: Your tutors are busy people, and you should not have any expectations about when they will be able to reply to an unsolicited email.

Email issues

YOUR TURN

Task 11

How many problems can you spot in the email in Figure 7.1? Circle the errors you find.

> **From:** CheesyChipolatas@yahoo.co.uk
> **Sent:** 16 October 2017 12:42
> **To:** Prof. Thomas Palmer
> **Subject:** [none]
>
> Hey Tom,
> How's it going?
>
> I'm ur student , and your PPT last week was very useful to me. But I can't find it anywhere online. Have u uploaded it somewhere yet? If not, could u please upload that asap?
> Cheers
> Dave ☺

Figure 7.1   Spot the problems in the email

Now check your answers.

Model email

A more appropriate and acceptable email should read like Figure 7.2.

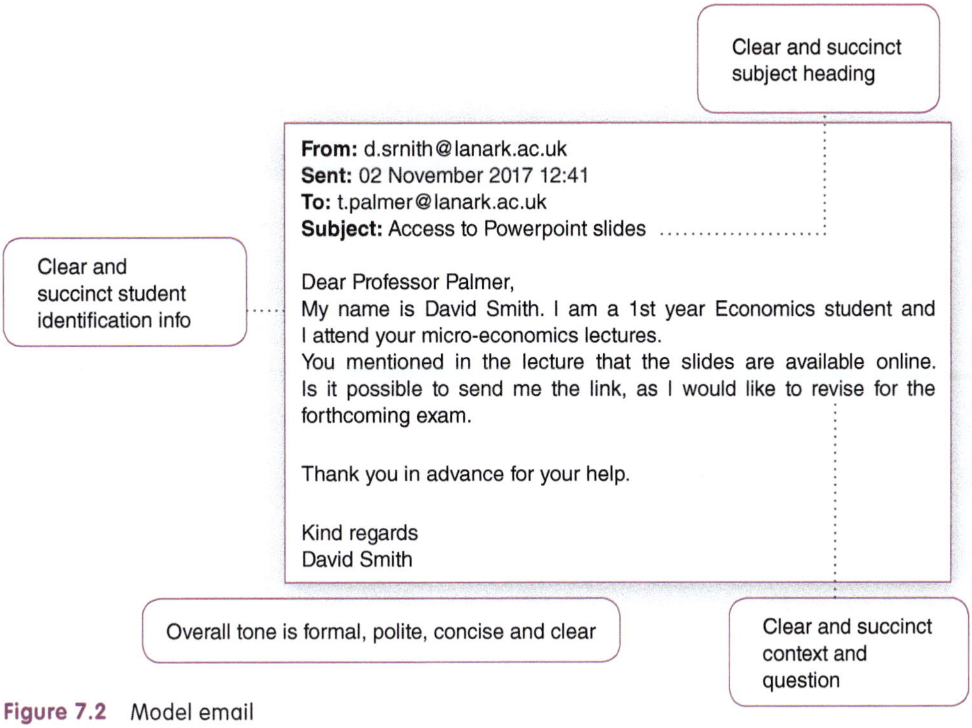

Clear and succinct subject heading

Clear and succinct student identification info

From: d.srnith@lanark.ac.uk
Sent: 02 November 2017 12:41
To: t.palmer@lanark.ac.uk
Subject: Access to Powerpoint slides

Dear Professor Palmer,
My name is David Smith. I am a 1st year Economics student and I attend your micro-economics lectures.
You mentioned in the lecture that the slides are available online. Is it possible to send me the link, as I would like to revise for the forthcoming exam.

Thank you in advance for your help.

Kind regards
David Smith

Overall tone is formal, polite, concise and clear

Clear and succinct context and question

Figure 7.2 Model email

Email communication checklist

Make sure you can answer 'yes' to these questions:

Do I **really need** to send the email – or can I find the answer elsewhere?	☐
Have I used my university email address?	☐
Have I used 'Dear' in my salutation?	☐
Have I used the title and surname of the tutor in my salutation?	☐
Have I provided clear personal identification info?	☐
Have I used a formal style?	☐
Have I used an effective subject line?	☐
Have I kept my message clear and concise?	☐
Have I given an explanation of why I have attached a document?	☐
Have I given my tutor a few days to respond?	☐
Have I included previous emails in any on-going conversations with my tutor, so that they can follow the thread?	☐

YOUR CHAPTER TAKEAWAY

Academic style Checklist
✓ (tick when completed)

Have I ...

○ used an appropriate formal style without being *overformal*?

○ been objective?

○ been rational, logical and informed?

○ demonstrated scepticism, caution and evaluation?

○ used abbreviations and acronyms appropriately and accurately?

○ checked that there are no informal, colloquial words and phrases?

○ checked that I haven't used any emotive or emotional language?

○ checked that I am not appearing over-dogmatic in what I say?

Your one takeaway

....

....

YOUR PROGRESS

CHAPTER EIGHT

Referencing with Accuracy

YOUR PROGRESS

CHAPTER DASHBOARD

Your objectives list:

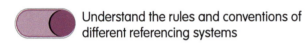 Understand the rules and conventions of different referencing systems

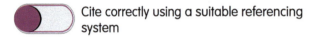 Cite correctly using a suitable referencing system

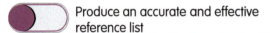 Produce an accurate and effective reference list

min   max

'Knowledge is of two kinds. We know a subject ourselves, or we know where we can find information on it.'

– Samuel Johnson

My three reference list goals:

1 ....

2 ....

3 ....

What your tutor is looking for

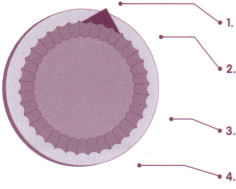

1. Accurate in-text citations of all sources

2. Suitable, recommended, or obligatory referencing system used

3. Consistent use of selected referencing system

4. Accurate reference list

Accuracy

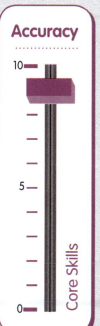

10
5
0

Core Skills

Style

10
5
0

Core Skills

Clarity

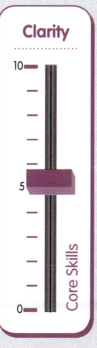

10
5
0

Core Skills

Being concise

10
5
0

Core Skills

Being informed

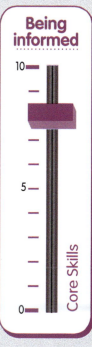

10
5
0

Core Skills

WATCH OUT FOR:

Referencing sources in your work is a mechanical process, but incorporating sources in your work requires critical thinking

Diagnostic
How well do you know the rules of referencing?

Highlight any errors with citations and referencing (based on Harvard style referencing) that you can identify in this extract.

There is significant evidence that poor housing with its accompanying lack of sufficient warmth can have a negative effect on health, Pevalin et al., 2008; Boomsma et al., 2017. Particular health issues related to cold housing are increased blood pressure, lower than average resistance to infections, as well as higher chances of influenza, asthma and heart attacks (Evans et al., 2000, Maidment et al., 2014). The effects of a cold house on health do not, however, end there. Other common problems associated with a poorly heated house include damp, condensation and mould and these carry their own risks to health. (Peat et al., 1998; Healy and Clinch, 2004; Sharpe et al., 2015) Research by Charpin and Vervloet has shown that dust mites thrive in damp, mouldy conditions. A strong association has been found between exposure to visible mould and dust mites and asthma and common colds (Lau, Illi, Sommerfeld, Niggemann, Bergmann, von Mutius, and Wahn, 2000), although a study by (Mendall et al., 2011), suggested that there was clear evidence for the association between damp conditions and asthma, the 'microbiologic agents in dust had limited suggestive associations' and therefore steps to improve health should focus on building design and energy efficiency (Mark J. Mendall et al., 2011). These findings indicate a clear rationale for ensuring that all housing in poorer areas is dry and warm, thus decreasing the possibility of the associated health effects of cold and damp conditions.

How many errors did you find?

O ne of the most important conventions in academic writing that you need to follow in your assignments is acknowledging where your information has come from. This is known as *citing your sources*, and we do this for three main reasons:

1. To give credit to the author or speaker whose information we are using. If we don't acknowledge that the information comes from somewhere else, we are suggesting that the ideas are our own!
2. So that your reader can find the original information in order to read in more depth or (particularly if they are your tutor) to check the information.
3. To give weight and credibility to our work.

This chapter will introduce the most popular referencing systems used in universities today, from Harvard and APA to numeric systems and the footnote method. It will show you how to incorporate and acknowledge sources in your writing as well as construct an accurate and consistent reference list at the end of your assignment.

CITING YOUR SOURCES

There are clear rules to follow for both the in-text citations and the list of references at the end, but these rules depend on what referencing system you are using. You will need to check with your tutor to find out what system they would like you to use. The most important thing is to be consistent and not mix conventions from two (or three) different referencing systems. The different systems are either **name and date** systems or **numeric** systems, but within these categories, there are several different styles.

Name and date systems include:

- Harvard, APA (American Psychological Association) and MLA (Modern Language Association) referencing systems: the references are listed in alphabetical order. Usually used in the Humanities, Social Sciences and Psychology.

Numeric systems include:

- RSC (Royal Society of Chemistry), Vancouver, IOP (Institute of Physics) and IEEE (Institute of Electrical and Electronics Engineers): the references are listed in the order the sources were cited. Usually used in Science and Engineering.

NB Footnotes use a mix of numeric (for each individual page of your essay) and name and date (for the list of references at the end of your essay) systems.

Always check with your tutors which referencing system they would like you to use.

THE NUTS AND BOLTS OF CITING YOUR SOURCES

Every piece of information that you use in your writing needs to be credited to the author(s). There are clear rules about how to do this in the different systems. You need to familiarise yourself with the conventions of the system you will be using.

The different systems of citation and referencing share similarities. You do not need to remember the details, but you will need to refer to one of the common referencing guides available online or through your university library to ensure that you are following the appropriate conventions. Your library will also be able to introduce you to the different versions of referencing software available.

Harvard in-text citations

The Harvard referencing system involves using names and dates of publication within the text, and then providing an alphabetical list of references at the end of the work. It is most commonly used in Humanities subjects, but it can be seen across the disciplines.

YOUR TURN

Task 1

Below are four rules for referencing based on the Harvard system. Match the rules to the appropriate citation (some may be used more than once).

1. One, two or three authors – write each surname in full.
2. More than three authors – write the first author's surname and then et al. (note the full stop followed by a comma then date).
3. Two publications from one author in the same year distinguished by date and 'a' or 'b', etc.
4. Author is part of the sentence, so put the date in brackets after the surname.

The relatively recent introduction of 'energy drinks' to the consumer market has been highlighted as a cause for concern (Reissig, Strain, and Griffiths, 2009).

Energy drinks are soft drinks that manufacturers claim boost performance and endurance with the main active ingredient being caffeine (McLellan and Lieberman, 2012). These products are often strategically marketed towards the young consumer (Reissig, Strain, and Griffiths, 2009), with 30–50% of adolescents and young adults now known to consume them (Seifert et al., 2011). Energy drinks have also been associated with behavioural problems (Richards et al., 2015), and a number of serious health complications (Reissig, Strain, and Griffiths, 2009).

A potential avenue by which energy drink use may negatively affect health is through their association with risk-taking behaviours as discussed by Arria et al., 2014. Miller (2008a), for instance, reported that the frequency of energy drink consumption in US undergraduates was positively associated with smoking, drinking, alcohol problems, use of illicit prescription drugs and marijuana, sexual risk-taking, fighting, seatbelt omission, and taking risks on a dare. However, it should be noted that such effects might also be explainable by personality characteristics of high users of energy drinks (Miller, 2008b), rather than necessarily to the products themselves.

➡️ **Answers online at: https://study.sagepub.com/hopkinsandreid**

Getting started with in-text citation in Harvard system

The following rules will help you get started. However, you may find you need more detailed information, in which case you should use one of the many online referencing guides to help you. In addition, look at the Answer Key to the Diagnostic and to Task 1.

Rules

1. Author's name as part of the sentence: provide the year of publication in brackets. Example:

Miller (2008) reported that the frequency of energy drink consumption in US undergraduates was positively associated with smoking.

2. Author's name is NOT part of the sentence: after the information, include the author(s) surname with year of publication inside brackets. Example:

… such effects might also be explainable by personality characteristics of high users of energy drinks (Miller, 2008).

3. Quoting from a source: include a page reference where possible. Example:

Mendall et al. (2011) suggested that although there was clear evidence for the association between damp conditions and asthma, the 'microbiologic agents in dust had limited suggestive associations' (Mendall et al., 2011, p. 1).

4. Source is a website: if there is an author and a date, you follow the same rules as in number (2). If there is no author, use the organisation or webpage name, and if there is no date, write 'n.d.' Example:

Recent concern over the increase in number of cases of Lyme disease, a bacterial infection spread by ticks ... (*New Scientist*, 2017).

Getting started with in-text citation in APA system

APA referencing system is a name and date system, like Harvard, but there are a few slight differences in conventions. It is commonly used in Social and Psychological sciences. For full information and details see The American Psychological Association referencing guidelines (2010) at: http://www.apastyle.org/learn/faqs/web-page-no-author.aspx

YOUR TURN

Task 2

Below are four rules for referencing based on the APA system. Match the rules to the appropriate sample.

1. One or two authors: write each author's name every time followed by year of publication.
2. Write 'and' when two or more authors' names are part of the sentence, but use '&' when you put the names inside brackets.
3. Three, four or five authors: cite all names the first time followed by year of publication, but use the first author and 'et al.' followed by year of publication thereafter.
4. Six or more authors: cite the first author's name followed by year of publication and 'et al.' every time.

Sample A

Sleep loss can have damaging effects on performance of tasks (Engle-Friedman et al., 2003).

Sample B

The relatively recent introduction of 'energy drinks' to the consumer market has been highlighted as a cause for concern (Reissig, Strain, & Griffiths, 2009). [...] These products are often strategically marketed towards the young consumer (Reissig et al., 2009).

Sample C

Anderson and Horne (2009) investigated the effects of ingestion of glucose on people who were already sleepy. Their findings suggest that energy drinks do not counteract sleepiness in these people (Anderson & Horne, 2009).

Sample D

According to Benton's findings (2002), sugar from soft drinks improves mental functions initially, but can lead to reduced function after a period of time. This suggests that users of soft drinks should consider the time frame for which they aim to have improved cognitive performance (Benton, 2002).

 Answers online at: https://study.sagepub.com/hopkinsandreid

Getting started with in-text citation in numeric systems

Numeric systems differ from the name and date systems by using a number to cite the sources in the order they are used. The number of the citation of a source remains the same every time you cite it in your writing. The difference with in-text citations between the various numeric systems are stylistic and often related to punctuation and effects such as superscript or square brackets.

YOUR TURN

Task 3

Use the text below to answer these questions:

1. Which information is supported by more than one reference?

   ....

2. Which references are used for more than one piece of information?

   ....

3. Which author's name is part of the sentence (rather than only a number)? What is the impact of this?

   ....

4. How are the full references at the end organised?

   ....

(Continued)

(Continued)

Demand for cross-laminated timber (CLT) products has grown strongly for the last decade. CLT components comprise layers of wooden boards, which are glued together crosswise to each other. Compared to reinforced concrete, a higher degree of prefabrication and less structural weight can be achieved with CLT.[1]

Alongside many advantages, however, noise insulation must be taken into account carefully. Unfortunately, the characteristics of CLT elements such as orthotropy of their basis material, differently directed layers, high shear deformations of transversely oriented layers, and biaxial load transfer mean that simple analytical models are not necessarily adequate to calculate their vibrational behaviour in the low-frequency range, unless only the first natural frequency is needed.[2] In order to calculate the deformations of CLT components, several dimensionally reduced models have been developed.[3–9] For example, the elastic compound theory[4] allows to calculate effective bending stiffnesses for homogeneous beams or plates from the properties of the layers. Shear deformations are neglected therein. A different approach is followed in the shear analogy method.[5] Here, a CLT component is represented by two coupled beams. One of them takes the shear flexibility of every layer into account, for example, in the form of a Timoshenko beam with an equivalent shear stiffness. Girder grids can be used to consider biaxial load transfer. In contrast, the higher order plate theory according to Murakami[8] takes shear deformations including changing slopes of shear warping into account by an extended deformation approach that contains not only degrees of freedom for translations and rotations but also for zig-zag-shaped in-plane displacements.[10]

References

1. Brandner R, Flatscher G, Ringhofer A, et al. Cross laminated timber (CLT): overview and development. *Eur J Wood Wood Prod* 2016; 74(3): 331–351.
2. Ussher E, Smith I. Predicting vibration behaviour of cross laminated timber floors. *IABSE Symp Rep* 2015; 104(19): 1–8.
3. Möhler K. Über das Tragverhalten von Biegeträgern und Druckstäben mit zusammengesetzten Querschnitten und nachgiebigen Verbindungsmitteln. Habilitation, Universität Karlsruhe, 1956.
4. Blass HJ, Goerlacher R. Brettsperrholz – Berechnungsgrundlagen. *Holzbau-Kalender* 2002; 2: 580–598.
5. Kreuzinger H. Flächentragwerke – Platten, Scheiben und Schalen – ein Berechnungsmodell für gängige Statikprogramme. *Bauen Holz* 1999; 101(1): 34–39.
6. Bogensperger T, Silly G. Zweiachsige Lastabtragung von Brettsperrholzplatten. *Bautechnik* 2014; 91(10): 742–752.
7. Chow TS. On the propagation of flexural waves in an orthotropic laminated plate and its response to an impulsive load. *J Compos Mater* 1971; 5(3): 306–319.
8. Murakami H. Laminated composite plate theory with improved in-plane responses. *J Appl Mech: T ASME* 1986; 53(3): 661–666.
9. Ren JG. A new theory of laminated plate. *Compos Sci Technol* 1986; 26(3): 225–239.
10. Stürzenbecher R, Hofstetter K, Eberhardsteiner J. Structural design of cross laminated timber (CLT) by advanced plate theories. *Compos Sci Technol* 2010; 70(9): 1368–1379.

Adapted from: Paolini, A., Kollmannsberger, S., Winter, C., Buchschmid, M., Müller, Andreas Rabold,M., Mecking, S., Schanda, U., and Rank, E. (2017). A high-order finite element model for vibration analysis of cross-laminated timber assemblies, *Building Acoustics*, Sage, Vol 24, Issue 3, 2017.

 Answers online at: https://study.sagepub.com/hopkinsandreid

Using footnotes

Some departments may ask you to use footnotes as your system of referencing. If this is the case, they are likely to give you a referencing guide explaining explicitly how to write them. However, as a general rule:

- Number your citations in your text using a superscript number after the full stop. Follow sequential numbering throughout the whole essay (in other words, do not start from 1 on each new page, but instead continue the numbering until the last citation). This is true even for repeated use of the same source.

Example:

The Ottoman Empire was not a majority Muslim empire until the 16th century when Syria and Egypt were conquered.[1]

Write the footnote (at the bottom of the page, under a separating line) to look like this:

[1]B. Braude, The Strange History of the Millet System, in K. Çiçek (ed.), *The Great Ottoman, Turkish Civilisation 2: Economy and Society* (Ankara, 2002), p.409.

Note that the name of the publisher is not necessary in your footnote.

If you use the same citation more than once, the first time you cite it you need to write the full footnote, but thereafter your footnote can be abbreviated. Example:

[15]Braude, The Millet System.

TIP

Citation

Create a table where you keep a list of all your sources, including page numbers and what part of your assignment they are relevant to. This will avoid any problems with citations that you later cannot find the full reference for.

Other points about in-text citations

Using quotations

We only choose to use quotations rather than using our own words in certain specific circumstances. Use a quotation when:

- it is a well-known word, phrase or sentence
- it is a controversial way of expressing something
- the specific words or phrases cannot reasonably be replaced or paraphrased.

If you do decide to include a quotation, ensure you are aware of the following rules:

- If it is a short quote, include it as part of the sentence and ensure it works grammatically. For example:

When considering some of the basic principles of the theories behind having continuous economic growth as a goal, it is significant to consider the value of labour and alongside the value of time. This was something that Churchill discussed when he stated that 'Time and money are largely interchangeable terms.' (Churchill, 1926).

- If the quotation is very long, you should start it on a new line (with a space above and below) and indent it (in other words, like an indented paragraph). You do not use quotation marks. Notice also that you can insert your own words into a quote (in order to make it clearer or work grammatically). Put these words inside square brackets. For example:

Many people believe that it was Winston Churchill who first coined the phrase 'The Iron Curtain', and he is certainly on record using it in his famous 'Sinews of Peace' speech in 1946:

> An iron curtain is drawn down upon their front. We do not know what is going on behind. There seems little doubt that the whole of the region Lubeck-Trieste-Corfu will soon be completely in their hands. [Following American withdrawal] a broad band of many hundreds of miles of Russian-occupied territory will isolate us from Poland. … it would be open to the Russians in a very short time to advance if they chose, to the waters of the North Sea and the Atlantic. (Churchill, 1946)

- If you want to miss out some words to make the quotation shorter, you can indicate that words are missing by using three dots. For example:

In the early days of the development of antibiotics, Alexander Fleming demonstrated that he was aware that microbes had the potential to become resistant to antibiotics when he stated:

It is not difficult to make microbes resistant to penicillin in the laboratory ... The time may come when penicillin can be bought by anyone in the shops. Then there is the danger that the ignorant man may easily underdose himself and by exposing his microbes to non-lethal quantities of the drug make them resistant. (Fleming, 1945)

TIP

Quotations

Always ensure that if you do use a quotation, it is relevant and it does not disrupt the flow of your message.

Using secondary sources

Sometimes we find information in a source that is taken from a different source. We should preferably find the original work and read that, but if this is not possible, we can mention it by using the phrase 'cited in', and giving the citation for your source, with the page number. For example:

Research into the rate at which speakers speak, to investigate whether it is a constant or can fluctuate, has been successful in identifying patterns (Brown, 1980, cited in Garrett, 2010, p. 90).

THE REFERENCE LIST

At the end of your assignment, you need to give full details of all the sources you have cited. The different systems have slight variations, but the main difference is that name and date systems list the references in alphabetical order (with the first author's surname first), and numeric systems list the references in sequential order (i.e. in the order they appear in the work).

TIP

Reference list

Don't confuse your reference list with a bibliography. Your list should include *every* primary source you cite in your work. A bibliography lists work that is cited *and* work that was consulted but not cited. It is more usual at university to have a reference list rather than a bibliography.

YOUR TURN

Task 4

Are the questions about the rules for writing reference lists below true or false for your preferred system of referencing? Use the relevant sample extract from a reference list (below the questions) to help you answer. You can use the same questions for Harvard, APA and numeric, but the answers may differ.

1. The title of a book is written in italics.   true / false

2. The title of a journal article is written in italics.   true / false

3. The full name of the author is included.   true / false

4. Authors' initials are followed by a full stop.   true / false

5. All authors' names are listed even if there are more than six.   true / false

6. If the source is a website with no author, the title of the site is written, and a   true / false
    phrase like 'Available from' followed by the URL or DOI is included. Information
    about the date accessed/retrieved is included.

7. For a book, place of publication is included at the very end of the reference.   true / false

8. The date is given after the title of the source.   true / false

9. The date of publication is inside brackets.   true / false

10. If it is a second edition (or later), the information is included.   true / false

11. The title of a journal article is in single quotation marks.   true / false

12. When listing journal articles page numbers are included.   true / false

13. If the information is from a website, square brackets around 'Online' are written.   true / false

14. For a book, the name of the publisher is given after the name of the town where   true / false
    it is based.

15. Page numbers are indicated by writing 'pp' before the numbers.   true / false

Harvard references

Frisancho, R. 1993. *Human Adaptation and Accommodation*. Michigan, University of Michigan Press.
Jablonski, N. 2006. *Skin: A Natural History*. London, University of California Press
Health Profile of England 2007. Department of Health. Available from: http://webarchive.nationalarchives.gov.uk/20130107105354/http://www.dh.gov.uk/prod_consum_dh/groups/dh_digitalassets/@dh/@en/documents/digitalasset/dh_079690.pdf [Accessed on 1 November 2017]

Hagandera, L.G., Midani, H.A., Kuskowski, M., and Parrya, G. 2000. 'Quantitative sensory testing: effect of site and skin temperature on thermal thresholds'. *Clinical Neurophysiology,* 111 (1), pp 17–22 [Online]. Available at: https://doi.org/10.1016/S1388-2457(99)00192-3 [Accessed on 1 November 2017]

Hallett, M., Di Iorio, R., Rossini, P.M., Park, J.E., Chen, R., Celnik, P., Strafella, A.P., Matsumoto, H., and Ugawa, Y. 2017. 'Contribution of transcranial magnetic stimulation to assessment of brain connectivity and networks'. *Clinical Neurophysiology,* 128 (11), pp 2125–2139 [Online]. Available at: https://doi.org/10.1016/j.clinph.2017.08.007 [Accessed on 1 November 2017]

Stinson, S., Bogin, B., and O'Rourke, D. (Eds), 2012. *Human Biology: An Evolutionary and Biocultural Perspective,* 2nd Edition. Oxford, Wiley Blackwell.

APA references

Anderson, C. A., Shibuya, A., Ihori, N., Swing, E. L., Bushman, B. J., Sakamoto, A., Rothstein, H. R., & Saleem, M. (2010). Violent Video Game Effects on Aggression, Empathy, and Prosocial Behavior in Eastern and Western Countries: A Meta-Analytic Review. *Psychological Bulletin, 136* (2), 151–173.

Archer, J. (2004). Sex Differences in Aggression in Real-World Settings: A Meta-Analytic Review. *Review of General Psychology, 8*(4), 291–322. Retrieved November 1, 2017 from: http://dx.doi.org/10.1037/1089-2680.8.4.291

Deselms, J.L., & Altman, J.D, (2003). Immediate and Prolonged Effects of Videogame Violence, *Journal of Applied Social Psychology, 33,* 1553–1563.

Health Profile of England (2007). Department of Health. Retrieved November 1, 2017 from: http://webarchive.nationalarchives.gov.uk/20130107105354/http://www.dh.gov.uk/prod_consum_dh/groups/dh_digitalassets/@dh/@en/documents/digitalasset/dh_079690.pdf

Holt, N. Bremner, A., Sutherland, E, Vilek, M., Passer, M.W., Smith, R. E. (2015). *Psychology: The Science of Mind and Behaviour* 3rd Edition. Maidenhead, McGraw-Hill.

Scutti, S. (2016). *Do video games lead to violence?* CNN. Retrieved November 1, 2017 from: http://edition.cnn.com/2016/07/25/health/video-games-and-violence/index.html

Sherry, J. L. (2001). The Effects of Violent Video Games on Aggression, *Human Communication Research*, 23, 409–431.

Numeric references

1   Kelly DP, Sharp RS. Time-optimal control of the race car: influence of a thermodynamic tyre model, *Vehicle System Dynamics* 2012; 50:4, 641–662.

2   ONS Digital. Are we ready to switch to electric cars? Office for National Statistics. 2017 [Accessed 29 Nov. 2017]. Available from: http://visual.ons.gov.uk/are-we-ready-to-switch-to-electric-cars/

3   Nice K. How four-wheel drive works. HowStuffWorks. 2001 [Accessed 6 Nov. 2017]. Available at: http://auto.howstuffworks.com/four-wheel-drive1.htm

4   Stone R. Introduction to Internal Combustion Engines, 4th Ed. Basingstoke: Palgrave Macmillan; 2012.

5   Hufenbach W, Langkamp A, Adam A, Krahl A, Hornig A, Zscheyge A et al. An integral design and manufacturing concept for crash resistant textile and long-fibre reinforced polypropylene structural components. *Procedia Engineering* 2011; 10: 2086–2091.

─── TIP ───

Referencing

Your university library will be able to show you citation software that will help you organise and store your references as you write. This can save you a lot of time and ensure your referencing follows appropriate conventions.

YOUR CHAPTER TAKEAWAY

Referencing with accuracy Checklist

✓ (tick when completed)

Have I ...

○ used the correct referencing system?

○ made accurate in-text citations throughout?

○ been consistent in my use of in-text citations throughout?

○ made sure that all sources are attributed?

○ made sure citation details are accurate?

○ all quotes given page numbers?

○ ensured my citations of secondary sources are accurate?

○ included an accurate reference list?

○ ensured all sources are attributed (only sources used in the assignment are included) in the reference list?

Your one takeaway

....

....

PART 2

READING AND CRITICAL ANALYSIS SKILLS

The big picture

Reading is a central part of all research activity. When you begin your university studies, the amount and types of reading you are expected to do can be daunting; from core reading texts to complex journal articles and beyond. You will be required to use your reading to inform all academic assignments and tasks. Your reading will help you develop a coherent, logical and informed critical response in your writing.

Research reading involves searching, investigating, identifying and incorporating key theories, ideas, quantitative data and, statistics, and qualitative views and arguments in your writing, to build an effective and appropriate critical response to an assignment question in such ways as to enhance your critical response.

At university level you need to be questioning everything you read, evaluating the reliability of information and ideas and identifying when something is an opinion. As a reader you should be able to assess the merits and deficiencies of a writer's stance (point of view) and how they fit with your own view and purpose relating to the tasks and assignments that you have to do. If you can do all of that, then you are an effective critical reader, and this will help you succeed in academic work.

Skills you'll learn

This Part will provide you with a practical, easy to use skills toolkit to help you get started with your reading and ensure that you are applying criticality at both the reading and the writing stages. By following this step-by-step approach you will be able to:

- identify and select appropriate sources
- develop an efficient strategy for reading and note-taking
- analyse and evaluate texts
- incorporate ideas of others with your own.

These skills will help you to elevate your work from secondary level (e.g. A level) to university level.

YOUR PROGRESS

CHAPTER NINE

Reading Skills

CHAPTER DASHBOARD

Your objectives list:

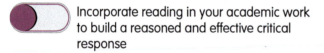 Take control of your reading

 Read selectively, strategically and for a purpose

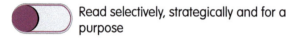 Incorporate reading in your academic work to build a reasoned and effective critical response

'Think before you speak. Read before you think.'

– Fran Lebowitz

My three critical reading goals:

1 ....

2 ....

3 ....

What your tutor is looking for

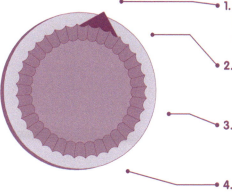

1. Demonstrated research knowledge beyond core reading materials

2. Use of a wide range of relevant and up-to-date texts in your academic work

3. Synthesis of texts in academic writing to develop an evidence-based response

4. Analysis and evaluation of sources used

Accuracy

10

5

0

Core Skills

Style

10

5

0

Core Skills

Clarity

10

5

0

Core Skills

Being concise

10

5

0

Core Skills

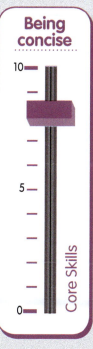

Being informed

10

5

0

Core Skills

WATCH OUT FOR:

Always read for a purpose, and your purpose is your assignment

Diagnostic

Which of the following best describes your approach to reading and note-taking?

Do any of the following describe your approach to reading and note-taking? Put a tick next to anything that applies to you.

I feel I should read as much as I can about a topic before I start my assignment	
I read every part of a text to make sure I understand everything	
I read the text over and over and try to memorise the key points to use later in my assignment	
I photocopy texts that might be suitable for my assignment and store them for later	
I copy out relevant sections of the text that I think I might use in my assignment	
I only read Wikipedia as this usually has most of the information I need	
If I don't understand the content, I stop reading	
I don't read much, as my views are the most important part of my assignments	
I borrow a large number of books from the library and then check to see if they can help me with my assignment	
I go through a book chapter by chapter until I find something I think might be useful for my assignment	
I collect together lots of notes and then work out how I can slot them into my assignment	

My score

For feedback on your score, go online at:
https://study.sagepub.com/hopkinsandreid

A t university, you will be required to read a range of texts and use what you learn from them in your writing. This can be quite daunting, and it is vital that you are able to manage the reading process to ensure that you do not read more than is necessary.

Reading provides you with the building bricks of knowledge and understanding to help you formulate reasoned, logical, persuasive, evidence-based arguments. From your reading you can find facts, figures and information to support and facilitate an understanding of ideas and activities. Reading is also a springboard for new theories, new ideas, new activities and helps you develop and extend your academic style and vocabulary.

This chapter will help you take control of your reading to become an efficient and effective critical reader. It will provide you with strategies for effective note-taking and show you how to use texts effectively to inform and enhance your written work to maximise your success.

TYPES OF TEXTS

In the course of your studies you will be required to read an often head-spinning variety of both academic and non-academic texts. Table 9.1 highlights some of the main text types.

Table 9.1 Types of text

Text type	Content and use
Academic books	Often core and supplementary textbooks recommended by your tutor
	Usually introductory and provide background to key theories, themes and topics on your course
	Offer links to further reading to help you drill down further into the topic
	May include end-of-chapter summaries and tasks to check your understanding and learning
	May include a companion website, with further information and tasks
Journal articles	Fundamental to your research reading
	Provide highly focused and up-to-date research in a specific topic area
	Often include literature reviews which offer gateways to further reading and research
	May also include a discussion section which provides an invaluable critique of findings and critical evaluation of previous research
	Journal databases accessed via your library catalogue
Critical reviews	Similar to literature reviews
	Offer critical analysis and evaluation of specific readings, books and/or journal articles
	Highlight key writers in the field
	Provide useful links to further reading and research

(Continued)

Table 9.1 (Continued)

Text type	Content and use
Case studies and field reports	Describe a real or hypothetical situation, activity, event that occurred in the workplace
	Used to help contextualise or test a theory or argument
	Demonstrate how the complexities of real life can influence decision-making
	Can highlight problems and solutions
	Provide examples that can be used to illustrate and evaluate theory in an applied real-world setting
Lecture notes, your notes, your classmates' notes	Your first steps towards understanding and knowledge-building
	May provide links to further reading and research
	Give you an insight and knowledge of your tutor's field of expertise, beliefs, ideas and position on specific topics
	Note-sharing can expand and enhance your understanding of a topic, resolve misunderstandings or misinterpretations and fill in any gaps missed during the lecture
Subject-specific and specialist magazines	Articles and features about specific topic areas
	May have a more journalistic style and be more accessible than some journal articles
	Good source of current and up-to-date information
	May be a little simplistic, inaccurate, editorial and/or unreliable as evidence of research
Newspapers	Broadsheet (quality) newspapers may provide information, comment and some basic analysis of topics
	Information may be biased and shaped by the political or editorial position of the newspaper
	Information can be unreliable and/or inaccurate
	Useful for background information or links to more in-depth research but generally should not be used as an academic source
	Tabloid newspapers should be avoided (unless your studies involve their use)
Theses and dissertations	Offer further insights and analysis of specific topics relevant to your studies
	Include useful and comprehensive reference lists that may help you open the door into your own research
	Provide useful literature reviews and critical analysis of specific topics, theories, research and current academic views
	Usually accessible via the library catalogue
Academic blogs	Provide useful, bite-sized posts on specific topics that may be relevant to your studies
	May be written by your tutor or other members of your department and so offer insights into their field of expertise and views
	May be presented in different formats to help with access and understanding of a specific topic (posts, podcasts, videos, etc.)
Wikipedia	Good for background information and further links
	May be unreliable and inaccurate as it is not peer-reviewed (academic)
	Should not be used or cited in your academic work
Websites	Good source of information and further links
	May be unreliable and inaccurate as may not be peer reviewed (academic)

TIP

Types of text

Use website articles with named authors to improve reliability.

BECOMING AN ACTIVE READER

Active reading involves:

- Being strategic:
  - prioritising your reading to fit with tasks and assignment deadlines.

- Being selective:
  - targeting parts of texts relevant to tasks and assignment questions (i.e. reading for a purpose).

- Being systematic:
  - organising your notes (quote, paraphrase, summary) to fit assignment content and structure.

Reading for a purpose

Before you start your research reading, you will need to rationalise your approach. This involves identifying your purpose for reading the text.

The purpose may include:

- a writing assignment task
- a presentation
- a seminar activity
- an individual or group project
- an exam.

Reading from the inside out (and not outside in)

Students often believe that before they begin an assignment, they should read as much as possible around the topic until they feel they have 'sufficient' knowledge to start writing. This is misguided as it is highly likely you will become overwhelmed by too many texts, too much information, and a muddled mess of ideas. You should always read for a specific purpose, and search for answers to the specific questions that you generated during the task and title analysis stage of the writing process (see Chapter 1, Getting started on your essay). In this way, you will be able to build up your knowledge and understanding of the topic piece-by-piece, like a jigsaw, and avoid information overload. This will allow you to:

- be able to make a confident start on tasks and assignments
- become an active reader, searching for the key pieces of your jigsaw puzzle.

And you will not:

- get bogged down and overwhelmed by the volume of complex theories, ideas, arguments and so on.

TIP

Reading for a purpose

You only need to read what you really need to know. Don't waste time reading irrelevant texts.

Figure 9.1 summarises the process and illustrates how your research reading should:

- begin with the focus of the task (thesis statement, research question, core aim of your presentation, purpose of the lab report, etc.), and work outwards

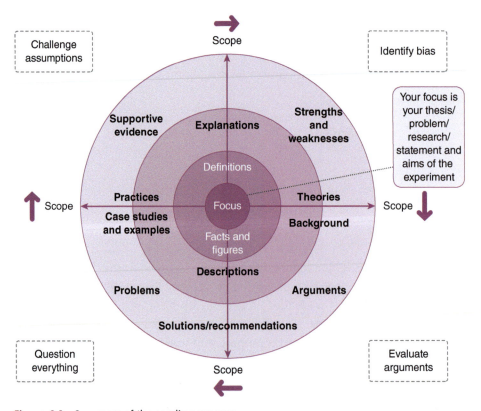

Figure 9.1 Summary of the reading process

- work through your list of questions (from simple definition types, to more detailed explanations and then on to critical analysis and evaluation), and locate sources that provide answers
- ensure you have identified the scope of your research (i.e. how far you should go, so you don't go beyond the limit and move off topic)
- think critically throughout – evaluate, challenge and question everything you read, including your own opinion /argument.

Quality versus quantity

Reading for a purpose will also help you to:

- rationalise the amount of reading you have to do and free up more time spent completing tasks and assignments
- target the most useful and relevant content, sources, studies, data, critics, examples, etc., for your research
- develop your summarising and synthesising skills by focusing on the most important parts of a text.

Searching for suitable texts

Your search begins with task/assignment analysis (see Chapter 1).

When you have identified your purpose for reading, you can then:

- start with the core reading material recommended by your tutor
- follow links and references to further readings
  - citations and sources used in the core text
  - sources uncovered in your library catalogue search
  - sources identified using key words and phrases and/or author searches online (Google Scholar).

TIP

Finding relevant texts

Google Scholar provides a 'related articles' button with links to sources similar to your search item. This can help you widen your search. It also generates a reference in various formats (APA, Harvard, Vancouver, Chicago, MLA) that can be linked to referencing apps and software.

THE READING AND NOTE-TAKING PROCESS

Stage 1: Searching for suitable texts

Let's assume you are working on the following essay assignment question:

Critically assess the relevance of Maslow's hierarchy of needs in the context of staff performance and motivation in business organisations today.

Firstly, have you have analysed the title/assignment question (see Chapter 1).

Subject: staff performance and motivation
Topic/focus: relevance of Maslow's hierarchy of needs
Scope (or limits): business organisations today
Instruction words: Critically assess

You have found answers to most of the simple questions (definitions and explanations). You are now looking for answers to the following question:

What are the strengths and weaknesses of Maslow's theory?

Step 1:

• Go to your lecture schedule and re-visit relevant sessions and associated readings (lectures may be recorded).

Step 2:

• Check your core texts – go to the indexes and search for key words 'Maslow', 'Hierarchy of needs' – to locate key sections.

Step 3:

• Search via Google Scholar or your library catalogue any writers and sources related to the topic cited in the core texts.

Step 4:

• Use key word search in Google Scholar and your library catalogue to search for books, journal articles and any other sources relevant to your reading task.

Stage 2: Choosing suitable texts

Before you consider using any text to support your academic work, you need take into account the process called **scholarly peer-review**.

Scholarly peer-review involves:

- subjecting an author's work, research, or ideas to the scrutiny of other experts in the same field, before the academic text is published
- checking the accuracy and validity of the research, arguments and so on, and challenging any shortfalls or inaccuracies before publication.

Therefore, you should aim to use peer-reviewed texts to support your academic work as they are considered more reliable and acceptable.

TIP

The importance of peer-review

Wikipedia can provide you with good background information but it is not peer-reviewed, and therefore should not be used as an academic source, as it is unreliable.

Argument versus opinion

When choosing sources to use in your work, it is important that the information is reliable and supported by sufficient evidence. Texts that present unsupported opinions are considered significantly less academic and tend to be avoided.

YOUR TURN

Task 1

Look at these two short texts giving similar information. The second text is a more appropriate source for you to use, but why?

There is evidence from many sources to suggest that these displaced people were peace loving and gentle prior to being displaced from their homeland. It is therefore clear that the forcible removal of these tribes to settlements created by the government is responsible for the violence and problems seen today.

According to Kidido et al. (2014) the people displaced for this industrial development were peaceful and gentle prior to being moved into purpose-built settlements. Once in their new environment, however, their previously well-ordered society appeared to break down, leading to some incidences of public disorder and violence (Kidido et al., 2014). This outcome, as a result of forcible displacement of whole communities, concurs with what Cernea (2006) identified as a common characteristic of displaced people, i.e. that they frequently fail to adapt to the new

(Continued)

(Continued)

environment, leading to tensions, unhappiness and often to violence both within and outside of the new community.

....

....

....

Answer

The first sample is opinionated and draws conclusions without using evidence to support them.

The second sample therefore is more likely to be a reliable source. It is balanced in its message, and shows that the information is based on and supported by external sources. Thus, the second sample is more academically acceptable.

Primary and secondary sources

A **primary source of information** is the original texts and evidence used for research purposes.

A **secondary source of information** is original texts and research presented by another writer – in other words, a second-hand account.

You should aim to use primary sources as much as possible in your academic work as the information is:

- likely to be a more accurate summary or account of the original text
- less likely to be distorted by bias or misinterpretation
- less likely to have drifted from the original meaning.

Now you have found a journal article, you need to decide if it is relevant/useful.

Follow the route map in Figure 9.2.

TIP

Reading process

Read the topic sentence(s) (the first one or two sentences of each paragraph) to help you identify the main theme of the paragraph.

If it looks relevant – READ ON!

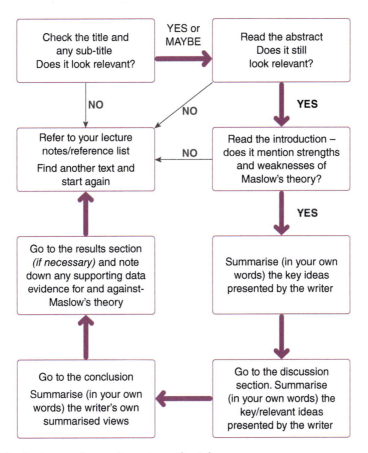

Figure 9.2 Route map for reading a journal article

Effective reading

Speed reading courses will often teach you how to eliminate and ignore 'unimportant' words in order to assimilate information quickly – to help you get through volumes of text. But academic reading is less about word counts and more about building a deep understanding of a topic. When you are reading for a purpose, it is more important to read and make notes on the 'right' information, or the parts of the text that are most relevant to your task, and will give you the answers to the questions on your list.

Here are some tips to help you identify quickly the relevance and usefulness of a text.

1. Use titles, chapter headings, and sub-headings to:
   - highlight possible relevant texts
   - look for key words that match or relate to your title/title analysis.

2. Read abstracts and introductions (journal articles) because:

   ○ abstracts offer a summary of everything contained in an academic report – read this to decide if the article is relevant

   ○ introductions give you more information about the topic, problem and (for journal articles) present the thesis or research aims of the paper.

3. Read topic sentences because they:

   ○ identify and establish the main idea of the paragraph

   ○ state the point the writer wishes to make about that topic

   ○ appear at the beginning of the paragraph and are usually the first or second sentence

   ○ allow you to skim through a text (or section of a text) to identify any relevant sections for your research.

4. Read the concluding sentence of each paragraph because it provides you with:

   ○ a quick summary of the preceding paragraph

   ○ the writer's views on the information contained in the paragraph

   ○ a linking idea to the next paragraph.

5. Look up your key words (identified during title/task analysis) in the index to:

   ○ find relevant chapters and sections of texts.

6. Skim selected paragraphs to:

   ○ find key words and phrases relevant to your assignment/task.

Stage 3: Reading and note-taking

Now that you have identified the texts you want to use, you need to develop effective strategies for noting down key information, relevant to your task.

YOUR TURN

Task 2

How do you take notes? (Choose the response that fits your method.)

1. I photocopy the page that I think contains the answer and file it for later.   yes / no

2. I copy the sentences with the answers to my research questions.   yes / no

3. I highlight or underline the key sentences or paragraphs in the library book, so that I can find it later, when I borrow it again.   yes / no

4. I read the entire section and try and memorise the meaning. yes / no

5. I go on Wikipedia for an easier explanation. yes / no

6. I note down the source details, including the author, date, publisher and page number. yes / no

7. I note down key words and phrases and then reconstruct the idea using my own words and sentences. yes / no

Answers

In the above quiz, only questions 6 and 7 represent good note-taking practice.

Question 5 may be a good idea, if you need an easier explanation. But remember, you can't cite Wikipedia in your academic work as it is not a reliable source of information.

Different note-taking methods

There are many different ways to take notes. You need to find an approach that works for you. Your chosen note-taking system may be similar to the type you use when taking notes in lectures (see Chapter 14, Getting the most out of lectures). However, reading and note-taking is different. It requires a more in-depth approach that incorporates critical analysis and evaluation, which can then be used in your writing.

In other words, your notes should include

- what the text says (description)
- what the text means (analysis)
- why it matters (evaluation).

For example, the Figure 9.3 shows an adapted Cornell template (see also Chapter 14, Getting the most out of your lectures), which now includes columns for description, analysis and evaluation.

Example

Imagine the following essay question has been set by your tutor.

Can money buy you happiness? Critically assess the psychological impact of spending on happiness and well-being.

So far your research has led you to the view that that money may not buy happiness. You are now in the process of searching for sources that support your view.

You have found a relevant text and you need to take notes (in your own words).

Author's name and initials: Year of publication: Title of article: Title of journal: volume and issue number: Page numbers: Full reference – as would be shown in a bibliography:	It is vital that you accurately record this information before you begin to take notes

Notes *(Description)*	Author(s) Who explains what it means? *(Analysis)*	Implications and your views and questions *(Evaluation)*
Use this column to take notes of key points relevant to your assignment What does the text say? Use bullets, abbreviations, symbols and shortcuts	Use this column to note down the writer's viewpoint/ position/ argument and the views of others (supporters and critics). What are they trying to say/argue? Explain in your own words	Use this column to note down any strengths and/or weaknesses of information/views expressed. What is the significance of the text and how/where/why does it relate to your assignment and what are your views (based on the evidence presented)?

Figure 9.3   Adapted Cornell template

Step 1: Select a section you wish to convert to note form

> **TIP**
>
> Note-taking tip – select short, manageable and relevant paragraphs and/or sections.

Above a low baseline, money is reported to have a surprisingly weak relationship with overall well-being (Diener & Biswas-Diener, 2002; Kahneman & Deaton, 2010). However, some researchers have begun to question this conclusion, arguing that if money does not buy happiness, it is because people 'probably aren't spending it right' (Dunn, Gilbert, & Wilson, 2011). These studies suggest that spending can indeed lead to increased well-being if it is directed at experiences rather than material goods (Carter & Gilovich, 2010; Howell & Hill, 2009; Van Boven & Gilovich, 2003), buying goods or services for other people as opposed to oneself (Dunn, Aknin, & Norton, 2013), and obtaining many small pleasures as opposed to a few large ones (Nelson & Meyvis, 2008).

However, recent research suggests that these relationships do not hold universally, as individual differences moderate at least some of them (Hill & Howell, 2014; Millar & Thomas, 2009; Zhang, Howell, Caprariello, & Guevarra, 2014). For example, while experiential purchases consistently result in greater happiness for experiential buyers, the effect is smaller or nonexistent for material buyers (Zhang et al., 2014).

Step 2: Highlight the key words/phrases/ideas

Above a low baseline, money is reported to have a surprisingly weak relationship with overall well-being (Diener & Biswas-Diener, 2002; Kahneman & Deaton, 2010).

However, some researchers have begun to <u>question this conclusion</u>, arguing that if <u>money does not buy happiness</u>, it is because people 'probably <u>aren't spending it right</u>' (Dunn, Gilbert, & Wilson, 2011). These studies suggest that <u>spending</u> can indeed lead to <u>increased well-being</u> if it is directed <u>at experiences rather than material goods</u> (Carter & Gilovich, 2010; Howell & Hill, 2009; Van Boven & Gilovich, 2003), <u>buying</u> goods or services <u>for other people</u> as opposed to oneself (Dunn, Aknin, & Norton, 2013), and obtaining many <u>small pleasures</u> <u>as opposed to a few large ones</u> (Nelson & Meyvis, 2008).

<u>However,</u> recent research suggests that these <u>relationships do not hold universally</u>, as <u>individual differences</u> <u>moderate</u> at least <u>some</u> of them (Hill & Howell, 2014; Millar & Thomas, 2009; Zhang, Howell, Caprariello, & Guevarra, 2014). For example, while <u>experiential purchases</u> consistently result in <u>greater happiness</u> for <u>experiential buyers</u>, the <u>effect</u> is <u>smaller</u> or <u>nonexistent</u> for <u>material buyers</u> (Zhang et al., 2014).

Step 3: Complete Cornell template as in Figure 9.4

- note down the bibliographic details of the source
- remove highlighted text from original source
- reduce and convert to notes, in your own words
- add sources linked to the key idea(s)/arguments
- include any comments or questions to help you develop your research.

When you have taken notes, you are now ready to convert them into summaries that you can incorporate into your essay. If you have followed the essay writing process (see Chapter 1, Getting started on your essay), you should have a good idea where your summary can be incorporated into your assignment.

The example below illustrates how your notes can be converted into summary form.

Summary

A number of writers including Diener & Biswas-Diener, 2002; Kahneman & Deaton, 2010 have **argued** that money and spending has a low correlation with happiness and well-being. However, this view has been **contested** by critics such as Carter & Gilovich, 2010; Howell & Hill, 2009 and Van Boven & Gilovich, 2003, who **assert** that happiness is present when spending is linked to experience rather than material gain.

In addition, purchasing for others rather than the self, and for small fulfilment rather than large-scale gratification may also lead to a greater sense of well-being and happiness (Dunn, Gilbert, & Wilson, 2011; Nelson & Meyvis, 2008). Zhang et al. 2014, go on to **maintain** that while experiential buyers may benefit from selfless purchases. Material buyers, on the other hand, find little or no pleasure in this activity.

You can see that the student has:

- summarised in her own words the key points made by the various writers
- incorporated sources as in-text citations

- used a range of referral verbs (in bold) to emphasise writers' opposing views on the topic.

When you incorporate sources in your work, it is essential that you use your own words, acknowledge the original text, and **do not** plagiarise the original work.

READING INTO WRITING

Incorporating sources: Plagiarism, summarising and paraphrasing

What is plagiarism?

Plagiarism is presenting the work and ideas of others as your own and using it in your work without acknowledgement. Plagiarism is considered as copyright theft, and is therefore a major disciplinary offence at UK universities. If you plagiarise,

---

Ref: Matz, S.C., Gladstone, J.J. and Stillwell, D., 2016. Money buys happiness when spending fits our personality. *Psychological science*, p.0956797616635200.

Notes (in your own words)	Analysis – who explains what it means?	Evaluation
Money has a low correlation with happiness and well-being	Diener & Biswas-Diener, 2002; Kahneman & Deaton, 2010 – **argument**	*But poverty is not good for health and well being.. ?*
But spending = well-being if connected to experiences rather than material things	Carter & Gilovich, 2010; Howell & Hill, 2009; Van Boven & Gilovich, 2003 – **counter-argument**	*What sort of experiences? Why? No explanation*
Buying for others rather than self & small fulfilments rather than looking for large-scale gratification	Dunn, Gilbert, & Wilson, 2011 – **further support for counter-argument**	What is a small fulfilment? Why does this work?
But depends on individual personality traits	Hill & Howell, 2014; Millar & Thomas, 2009; Zhang, Howell, Caprariello, & Guevarra, 2014 – **qualification of counter-argument with some more detail**	Why does it depend on this? What personality traits respond well to this .. and why?
e.g. experiential buyers find happiness in buying for experience and others but material buyers find little or no pleasure in this	Zhang et al., 2014 – **Evidence supporting counter-argument + my thesis**	This was a small-scale study and so is the generalisation justified? Is there more substantive evidence to support this point (and support my position)

Figure 9.4   Cornell template essay example Step 3

even unintentionally, your assignment marks will be disqualified and it is highly likely you will be dismissed from your degree course.

It is vital therefore that you understand what constitutes plagiarism, and develop effective paraphrasing techniques to help you use your sources effectively and with full acknowledgement.

Types of plagiarism

Word-for-word quotations (without acknowledgement of the original source)

You must clearly indicate using in-text citation where this information comes from.

Poor paraphrasing

When a few words are changed from the original text without acknowledgement of the original source. Here there are two issues: (1) the paraphrase is too close to the original and (2) the original idea has been stolen!

It may be better to summarise the author's ideas in your own words rather than play with language and vocabulary.

Cutting and pasting

This is the same as using word-for-word quotations without acknowledgement.

Collusion and failure to acknowledge assistance

Failure to disclose how much help you have received from your classmates or group members in a written assignment, and passing this off as your own is considered plagiarism.

Auto-plagiarism

Simultaneous submissions of the same work, or re-using whole or extracts of previous work in another assignment is considered auto-plagiarism. If the original work was published, you should acknowledge yourself.

Inaccurate citation

Failure to accurately reference or fully acknowledge sources in your writing also represents plagiarism. For example, using a secondary source as though it is primary, 'inventing' sources and page numbers, and so on.

YOUR TURN

Task 3

Plagiarism quiz

Read the extract below, taken from University of West of England, The History of Social housing (https://fet.uwe.ac.uk/conweb/house_ages/council_housing/print.htm).

Historically council housing is public housing that is rented to households who are unable to afford to rent from the private sector or buy their own home. It has been called council housing due to the role of district and borough councils managing the housing.

Now decide if the following six examples taken from students' assignments work represent plagiarism.

1. Traditionally, council housing can be defined as public housing that is rented to households who are unable to afford to rent from the private sector or buy their own home. This is called council housing due to the role of district and borough councils managing the housing.

2. UWE (2017) state that council housing is living accommodation in the public sector that is rented to people who cannot afford to rent from private landlords or purchase their own home. It is called council housing because district and borough councils own and maintain the properties.

3. Council housing can be defined as housing that can be rented by tenants who cannot afford to pay private rents. This type of housing is owned and managed by councils across the UK.

4. According to UWE, council housing is 'public housing that is rented to households who are unable to afford to rent from the private sector or buy their own home'. This type of housing is controlled by district and borough councils.

5. Council housing is a type of affordable rented property, owned and managed by district and borough councils, that is made available to tenants who are able to afford higher rents set by landlord in the private sector or purchase their own property (UWE, 2017).

6. Council housing refers to 'public housing that is rented to households who are unable to afford to rent from the private sector or buy their own home'. (UWE, p. 23). This type of rental accommodation is owned and maintained by local council authorities, hence the name, council housing.

→ **Answers online at: https://study.sagepub.com/hopkinsandreid**

Summarising and paraphrasing

Effective summarising and paraphrasing techniques will help you remove the risk of plagiarising the work of others.

TIP

Before you decide to summarise or paraphrase an original source, you should ask yourself; why do I need this and how does it fit into my assignment?

Summarising

Summarising is presenting a shortened version of an original source in your own words. A good summary will include only the essential information.

How to summarise

Here are two simple techniques:

1. Read the source and in your own words summarise the key points verbally. You could use a voice recorder on your phone to do this. Then write down what you said, and make minor alterations to your written summary.

   A spoken summary can help you focus on the ideas rather than written words. This will help you transform the original text into your own words, and ensure that the original meaning is preserved.

2. Read the source and write down the key words. Then using only your notes, reconstruct the main ideas in your own words.

   Focusing on key words only will help you identify the writer's main points and make it easier to change the original into your own summarised version.

Example (with key words highlighted)

From: Robock, A., 2008. 20 reasons why geoengineering may be a bad idea. *Bulletin of the Atomic Scientists, 64*(2), pp. 14–18.

Two strategies to reduce incoming solar radiation—stratospheric aerosol injection as proposed by Crutzen and **space-based sun shields** (i.e., mirrors or shades placed in orbit between the sun and Earth)—are among the most widely discussed geoengineering schemes in scientific circles. While these schemes (if they could be built) would **cool Earth**, they might also have **adverse consequences**. Several papers in the August 2006 Climatic Change discussed some of these issues, but here I present a fairly comprehensive list of reasons why geoengineering might be a bad idea, first written down during a two-day NASA-sponsored conference on Managing Solar Radiation (a rather audacious title) in November 2006.[4] These **concerns address unknowns in climate system response**; **effects on human quality of life**; and **the political, ethical, and moral issues raised**.

Summary:

Stratospheric injection and space-based sunshields are two methods that may be used to reduce solar radiation and cool the earth. However, Robock (2008) argues that these types of geoengineering projects may have negative consequences for the nature and quality of human life.

Note that the student has used her own words, and included an in-text citation to acknowledge where the idea comes from.

YOUR TURN

Task 4

Summarise the following paragraph in two or three sentences.

From: Flett, G.L. and Hewitt, P.L., 2005. The perils of perfectionism in sports and exercise. *Current Directions in Psychological Science, 14*(1), pp. 14–18.

> Research on perfectionism has increased exponentially over the past two decades. This increased attention has led to an enhanced understanding of the perfection-ism construct. For instance, it is now accepted generally that perfectionism is mul-tidimensional, and it is important, both conceptually and empirically, to distinguish the various dimensions of the construct. This multidimensional approach began with the initial work in our laboratory (see Hewitt & Flett, 1991) and in the labora-tory of Frost and his associates (Frost, Marten, Lahart, & Rosenblate, 1990). Our Multidimensional Perfectionism Scale (MPS; Hewitt & Flett, 1991) assesses three dimensions of the construct—self-oriented perfectionism (i.e., excessive striving and demanding absolute perfection from the self), other-oriented perfectionism (i.e., demanding perfection from other people), and socially prescribed perfectionism (i.e., the perception that other people demand perfection from oneself).

....

....

....

....

....

Answers online at: https://study.sagepub.com/hopkinsandreid

Paraphrasing

Paraphrasing can help you transform the original text into your own words.

Paraphrasing uses different words to represent an original source, in order to clarify meaning. Unlike summarising, paraphrases can be the same length or longer than the original text.

Paraphrasing is useful as it can enable you to clarify and interpret the meaning of original sources.

How to paraphrase

Here are a few techniques to help you paraphrase effectively.

Using synonyms

Find and replace original words and phrases with those of a similar meaning.
Example:

Original source:

The growth of council housing in this country has been largely determined by central government policies and legislation.

Paraphrase:

The increase in council housing in the UK is the result of UK Government Policies and laws (UWE, 2017).

But be careful! One of the problems of using synonyms is that they can alter the meaning of the original text, and so should always be used sparingly and with great care. Also, you need to be sure that your paraphrase is sufficiently changed into your own words, as it still may be considered plagiarism. The rough rule of thumb is that at least every third word should be your own and always acknowledge the original source.

Here is an example that illustrates how things can go wrong.

Original text:

Each objective has received priority from Government at different times over the years and their policies have influenced the amount of new building and the type and quality of construction.

Paraphrase:

Every target has been pivotal for the Government over many years and their activities have shaped the quantity, configuration and merit of new houses.

The student has over-used his thesaurus and the synonyms selected have altered the meaning of the original text.

Task 5

In the following sentences, circle the correct synonym to replace the underlined words.

a. Treating employees more <u>equitably</u> can help avoid deviant behaviour.

    equally   impartially   honestly   objectively   fairly

b. When designing structures, organisations must consider the <u>environment</u> in which it operates.

    atmosphere   ambience   climate   setting   circumstances

c. Questions of reliability therefore, remain <u>contentious</u> and unresolved.

    combative   antagonistic   controversial   destructive   dubious

d. Bipedalism <u>facilitates</u> life in diverse environments as it is a more energetically efficient mode of transport.

    expedites   speeds   promotes   simplifies   assists

 Answers online at: https://study.sagepub.com/hopkinsandreid

TIP

Paraphrasing

You should *always* focus on the ideas expressed rather than language when changing original sources into your own words.

Nominalisation:

This is the process of changing verb and verb phrases (actions or events) into nouns and noun phrases (things, ideas, people). Nominalisation is useful as it can help you:

- create variety in your writing and avoid repetition of the same verbs
- convey a more objective tone in your writing
- pack more ideas into your sentences.

Example 1:

Original text:

The Government responded first of all by repairing existing properties and rapidly building 'prefabs'.

Nominalised sentence:

The Government's initial response was a programme of short term repairs to existing properties and the rapid construction of 'prefabs'.

Example 2:

Original text:

The first prefabs were completed June 1945 only weeks after the war had ended.

Nominalised sentence:

Completion of the first prefabs was in June 1945, shortly after the end of the war.

YOUR TURN

Task 6

Choose a nominalised word to complete the table below.

Table X   Choose a nominated word

Verb	Noun
Deduce	....
Infer	....
Agree	....
Participate	....
Suggest	....
Assess	....

Adjective	Noun
Significant	....
Complex	....
Sceptical	....
Desirable	....
Intended	....
Frequent	....

 Answers online at: https://study.sagepub.com/hopkinsandreid

Task 7

Use nominalisation to transform the following sentences.

a. Heart rates increased in proportion to the levels of activity.

....

....

b. The researchers decided to widen their study, and this made the results more reliable.

....

....

c. The study examined the impact of greenhouse gases and showed that high levels of CO_2 can affect how quickly plants grow.

....

....

d. Direct and indirect approaches were compared and this highlighted the relative strengths and weaknesses of various types of indirect feedback.

....

....

→ **Answers online at: https://study.sagepub.com/hopkinsandreid**

COLLECTING AND ORGANISING YOUR NOTES

During your research, it is highly likely that you will accumulate a large number of relevant (and perhaps less relevant) texts.

It is important therefore to adopt an efficient and effective catalogue system.

Colour-coded notes

One method is to use coloured markers (on a photocopied section of text!)

Here is an example of how you could highlight different areas of importance:

Red = definitions
Yellow = descriptions and explanations
Blue = argument A
Green = argument B

Colour-coded notes will help you to:

- focus on only relevant sections of the text
- organise, categorise and rationalise information
- identify gaps or deficits in your research (i.e. few green highlights = more info on argument B required).

Referencing software

A wide range of online referencing apps are available to help you organise and collate your sources. They can be extremely useful and time-saving. A number of apps will generate reference lists based on the sources you use and others may even populate your assignment with in-text citations. You should check out what is available and choose the one that works for you.

You may be able to access a referencing app via your university library. The library may also offer training courses and workshops.

If you prefer a more traditional method, then make sure you develop an efficient and effective catalogue system.

YOUR CHAPTER TAKEAWAY

Reading skills Checklist

✓ (tick when completed)

Have I ...

- ( ) understood why I have selected this text?

- ( ) deemed the source relevant and necessary?

- ( ) ensured it fits my research question/thesis/problem statement?

- ( ) considered what will it add to my assignment?

- ( ) considered how and where the source will fit in my assignment?

- ( ) identified what each source will be used for in my work and where in my work I will use it?

- ( ) evaluated each source?

- ( ) made notes for each source?

- ( ) included information about the relevant pages from the source?

Your one takeaway

....

....

YOUR PROGRESS

CHAPTER TEN

Critical Thinking and Analysis

YOUR PROGRESS

CHAPTER DASHBOARD

Your objectives list:

 Understand what criticality means and how it is applied in academic work

 Develop critical thinking, analysis and evaluation skills

 Use sources to build and support your critical voice and stance

min   max

'It is the mark of an educated mind to be able to entertain a thought without accepting it.'

– Aristotle

My three critical thinking goals:

1 ....

2 ....

3 ....

What your tutor is looking for

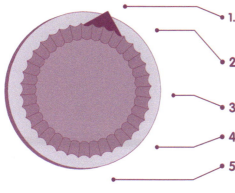

1. Objective, evidence-led critical response

2. Effective synthesis of sources to build argument and/or counter-argument

3. Analysis and evaluation of sources

4. Evaluation of your own position

5. Your voice and stance present throughout

Accuracy

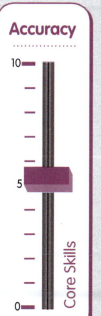

10

5

0

Core Skills

Style

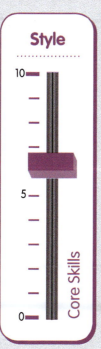

10

5

0

Core Skills

Clarity

10

5

0

Core Skills

Being concise

10

5

0

Core Skills

Being informed

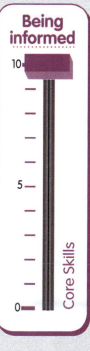

10

5

0

Core Skills

WATCH OUT FOR:

Criticality involves analysis AND evaluation

Diagnostic

How familiar are you with critical analysis?

The following short extract is descriptive, but does not include any criticality. Underline the problems, and suggest changes that would improve the text.

Deception is a behaviour that all people will be exposed to at some point in their lives. There are situations where it is important to know whether a person is telling the truth or not. One method to determine this is to use a lie detector. Lie detectors use changes in the skin's electrical activity (known as Electrodermal Activity or EDA) to ascertain whether someone is lying or being honest. Changes in EDA are related to an increase in sweat and people sweat more when they lie. This is a good system of detection as it is quick and easy to administer and also cheap.

What problems could you identify? Describe them here:

....

....

....

....

For feedback on your score, go online at:
https://study.sagepub.com/hopkinsandreid

C ritical thinking is at the heart of all scholarly activity. It is vital therefore that you develop and fine tune your critical and analytical skills, as these will affect the quality of your work and the level of your success.

Critical thinking can be defined simply as the objective analysis **and** evaluation of an issue in order to reach an informed and evidence-led judgement. In other words, it involves examining a topic or problem in detail, assessing the strengths and weaknesses of the ideas presented, and judging the merits and/or deficiencies of the ideas presented.

This chapter will provide you with the tools to develop and extend your critical and analytical skills. Using samples of students' work and tasks, we will show you how to apply a variety of analytical and evaluative approaches in your written work to build convincing and justified evidence-based arguments.

BECOMING A CRITICAL THINKER

Critical thinking and analysis involves questioning everything: what we read, assumptions and beliefs that are presented to us, facts and figures, and expert views and arguments. This can be difficult as you may have come from a learning environment where questioning voices of authority is not considered acceptable. At university, however, using logic and evidence to challenge assumptions and beliefs is a vital part of the research process, and academics will expect you to adopt this approach and reward you for it.

As a critical thinker you need to develop a habit of asking the following questions:

- What do I know and what do I need to know?
  - This will help you identify and address your goal and purpose, focus your research, and develop your thesis or problem statement.

- Is the information (evidence-supported) argument or opinion?
  - This will help you determine the accuracy or reliability of the information presented and whether you can trust it, as it may be one-sided and biased.

In all academic work, you are expected to apply criticality. This means when you read, you need to:

- assess the truth or merit of what the authors are saying.

And when we write, we need to:

- demonstrate that we have done this, and
- show our own judgement on the value of the information.

A critical approach means therefore that you have to use sources as evidence to support all of your ideas and arguments, in order to persuade your reader that your position is valid and justified.

The sample from student's essay in Figure 10.1 illustrates how criticality works.

Alongside a raft of conflicting results and conclusions regarding the relative efficacy of error feedback, Truscott (1996) argued that much of the evidence used to support the place and importance of feedback in the teaching curriculum was unreliable as many of the most influential studies, such as those by Lalande (1982) and Robb et al (1986), contained fundamental design flaws, and so called into question the empirical reliability of results and conclusions. Truscott's view was also supported by critics such as Ferris (1998) and Bitchener, Young and Cameron (2006), who maintain that the onus is on the supporters of corrective feedback to provide reliable evidence that feedback, via direct or indirect correction, improves learner abilities. Guenette's (2007) detailed analysis of a variety of key studies including those by Shepperd (1992), Fathman and Whalley (1990) and Fazlo (2001), detailed a range of **contradictory results**, and also concluded that **inadequate design** may be the cause of much of the apparent confusion. **However,** Ferris (2004 & 2006) has since **qualified** her previous position by pointing out that in a second language learning environment, ethical concerns may prevent the inclusion of a control group, as it may disadvantage one learner group over another. She adds that the inclusion of a control group is also inauthentic and false in that language courses are designed to improve linguistic ability through practice, repetition and error correction for the purposes of improvement. A zero feedback situation in written assignment work is therefore, highly unlikely (Ferris, 2004). Questions of reliability therefore, remain contentious and unresolved. **This somewhat confusing, contradictory and potentially unreliable body of research makes it very difficult for academic tutors to determine the most appropriate pedagogical choices to make when it comes to syllabus and course design, and the type of feedback that should be provided on students' written work.**

Paraphrased sources used to support (and justify) idea 1

Topic sentence sets up idea 1 (problems with reliability of studies into use of feedback in teaching)

Further analysis of idea 1, supported by paraphrased sources

A qualification of idea one – adding more analysis & a different perspective on the argument

Critical evaluation of evidence presented with writer's views clearly expressed

Figure 10.1 Criticality example from student essay

YOUR TURN

Task 1

Examine the two samples below and answer the following questions.

1. How does the writer use sources to present information?

....

2. Is there any evidence of evaluation of sources? If so, how does the writer demonstrate this?

....

3. Which sample is more effective? Why?

....

Sample A

Taylor viewed labour as a tool that 'could be engineered to achieve efficiency' (Koumparoulis & Solomos, 2012: p. 150). He identified the issue of systematic soldiering within groups, which is the organised restriction of output by workers to prevent their employers knowing how fast they could work, so they could pursue their own interests (Huczynski & Buchanan, 2013). He considered individualised work to be more advantageous to employers because it removes the risk of systematic soldiering, as well as 'group-think' which involves workers over-riding managerial direction and conforming to their team norms (Janis, 1972, cited by Locke, 1982). On the other hand, Lawrence (2010) and Marshall (1919, cited by Caldari, 2007) argue that the Taylorist approach to employee management does make for successful human beings.

Sample B

Taylor viewed labour as a tool that 'could be engineered to achieve efficiency' (Koumparoulis & Solomos, 2012: p. 150). He identified the issue of systematic soldiering within groups, which is the organised restriction of output by workers to prevent their employers knowing how fast they could work, so they could pursue their own interests (Huczynski & Buchanan, 2013). He considered individualised work to be more advantageous to employers because it removes the risk of systematic soldiering, as well as 'group-think' which involves workers over-riding managerial direction and conforming to their team norms (Janis, 1972, cited by Locke, 1982). However, Lawrence (2010) and Marshall (1919, cited by Caldari, 2007) argue that the Taylorist approach to employee management does make for successful human beings, as it severely inhibits aspiration and goal achievement. The writers go on to question the assumptions presented by Taylor and his advocates about employee attitudes to work, and state that much of the research in this area is biased and demonstrates a negative and distorted view of employee attitudes to work.

In Sample A, the writer has summarised a number of sources to compare two different views on Taylorism. The information is presented without comment or evaluation. This does not represent in-depth critical analysis.

In Sample B, the writer has provided a more in-depth summary of potential strengths and weaknesses of Taylorism. While the writer is moving towards a more critical approach, the writer is still absent as there is no evaluation of the ideas expressed in the sources.

DEVELOPING YOUR STANCE AND VOICE

When using sources to support your ideas or arguments, there is a risk that your own position and presence in your writing gets lost among the sources, ideas and voices of others.

There are two key elements that will help you avoid this happening.

The first is to make sure you **re-assert your position** or 'stance' throughout your assignment. This may be your research question, thesis statement or the problem you are focusing on. By doing this, you:

- maintain a logical and unified structure
- evaluate the ideas you are presenting
- remind the reader of your reason for writing the assignment, and how each new idea connects to this (see also Chapter 1, The academic essay).

The second is to assert and maintain your own presence or '**voice**' within your work. You can do this by using:

- Boosters – these are words and phrases that can help to emphasise your support for or criticism of the information in your sources. Boosters may include:
  - *clear/clearly* (use if you are certain it is clear)

    The study highlights a clear link between …

  - *substantial/substantive* (use only if the evidence is thorough and convincing)

    There is substantive body of evidence that supports the effectiveness of the current legislation.

  - *obviously*

    The study is obviously flawed.

  - *highly*

    It is highly likely that …

- Reporting verbs – when using in-text citations in your written work, you will need to use reporting verbs to present the information. For example, Smith (2015) **states** and Jones (2008) **claims** – and so on. There are many reporting verbs and which one you choose will depend on the type of information you are citing (facts, arguments, recommendations and so on).

Reporting verbs also provide a way for you to demonstrate to the reader that you understand the view the writer is putting forward.

Task 2

How does the writer assert her critical voice in sample C below?

....

....

....

Sample C

Taylor viewed labour as a tool that 'could be engineered to achieve efficiency' (Koumparoulis & Solomos, 2012: p. 150). He identified the issue of systematic sol-diering within groups, which is the organised restriction of output by workers to prevent their employers knowing how fast they could work, so they could pursue their own interests (Huczynski & Buchanan, 2013). He considered individualised work to be more advantageous to employers because it removes the risk of sys-tematic soldiering, as well as 'group-think' which involves workers over-riding man-agerial direction and conforming to their team norms (Janis, 1972, cited by Locke, 1982). However, Lawrence (2010) and Marshall (1919, cited by Caldari, 2007) argue that the Taylorist approach to employee management does not make for success-ful human beings, as it inhibits aspiration and goal achievement. The writers go on to question the **misguided** assumptions presented by Taylor and his advocates regarding employee attitudes to work. They **strongly** assert that much of the re-search in this area is biased and demonstrates a negative and **severely** distorted view of employee attitudes to work. Their substantive critique of Taylorism is sup-ported by a number of **well-respected** studies (Smith, 1988; Jones, 1994; Brown, 2001), which add **substantial** weight to the contention that **Taylorism is an out-of-date and redundant approach to managing people in modern organisations**.

In Sample C, alongside a comparison of two opposing views of Taylorist theory, the writer uses boosters (highlighted in bold) to emphasise her own presence or 'voice' in the essay and ensure that she is not lost among the voices of others. She also re-asserts her position or 'stance' at the end of the paragraph to re-connect with and remind the reader of her own position, and the evidence presented helps to convince and persuade the reader of the validity of her argument. Therefore, the writer has demonstrated in-depth critical analysis **and** evaluation.

The voice sandwich

Another technique you can use to assert and maintain your voice throughout your assignment is the voice sandwich.

YOUR TURN

Task 3

In the following sample, how does the writer combine her own ideas with her use of sources?

> One of the most significant traits that have evolved with the hominin lineage is bipedalism. Bipedalism facilitates life in diverse environments as it is a more energetically efficient mode of transport and allows a greater home range meaning that humans can travel further in search of suitable food (Wells & Stock, 2007). Bipedalism also allowed more efficient hunting which in turn increased meat consumption (Liebenberg, 2006). This is an example of niche construction as meat composition varies less than that of plant matter between ecosystems. Niche construction is achieved through technologically diverse and homogenised environments (Wells & Stock, 2007). This is a critical point as it allows humans to make their habitat more amenable and more likely to survive and flourish.

....

....

....

Answers online at: https://study.sagepub.com/hopkinsandreid

IMPROVING YOUR CRITICAL RESPONSE
The argument–counter-argument approach

Developing a critical response in your assignment involves carefully selecting and combining the voices of others to support your thesis (your argument, position or purpose), drive it forward, and convince the reader of the validity of your case.

These voices may include academic argument, empirical evidence such as data and statistics, theories, examples, case studies and so on.

The use of an argument–counter-argument approach in your writing can help you to:

- strengthen your argument or position by predicting and then counter-criticising opposing voices
- develop a more in-depth analysis and evaluation of an issue.

Here's how it works.

Stage 1

First, you need to consider and predict some of the arguments that may be pitched against your thesis (position). You need to unpack them and show how and why this evidence may be flawed. You can then present your counter-arguments or counter-evidence, using your academic 'soldiers' to counter-attack and strengthen your thesis. Thus, by predicting and counter-attacking your enemies' game plan with counter-evidence, you strengthen your own case.

Stage 2

Some of these arguments of course, may be directed towards the views or evidence presented by your academic supporters. The most effective critical responses in academic writing take this into account, and involve the evaluation of not only the evidence and arguments presented by critics of your thesis, but also the evidence and arguments of your own supporters.

So, if you spot a weakness in the evidence presented by one of your 'soldiers', then it is important to acknowledge and address this without undermining your thesis. You can do this by **finding further sources** that answer or refute these criticisms and so continue to support and further strengthen your thesis.

The argument–counter-argument approach therefore allows you to explore, analyse and evaluate all sides of the issues around your thesis. This approach also strengthens your argument as it shows that you have thought of every angle, whilst providing a compelling and convincing case.

Figure 10.2 illustrates how argument–counter-argument works in practice.

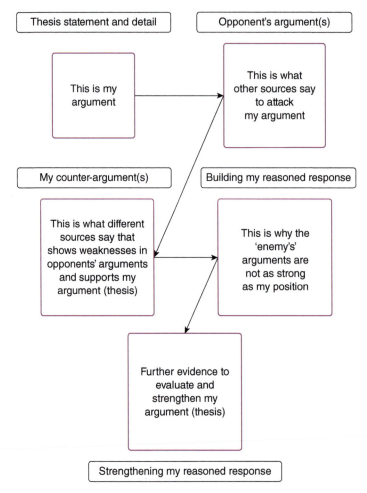

Figure 10.2 How argument–counter-argument works

YOUR TURN

Task 4

In the essay sample below, highlight where the student has used argument–counter-argument to strengthen her case and re-assert her stance (argument).

Enthusiasm for teamwork and groups stems from managers' expectations of productivity gains through the combination of individual knowledge and shared workloads.Psychological research has shown that acting in groups diminishes the pressure on individuals, as the impact is divided among members (Latane, Williams & Harkins, 1979). Smith (2010) highlights the benefits of teamworking for both individuals and employers, arguing that collective sharing of ideas can lead to effective problem solving and higher levels of motivation. However, Smith's somewhat limited study focused only on one particular area of the high-tech sector, where free-thinking, creativity and brainstorming are the norm. A number of more expansive studies, on the other hand, have revealed that by diminishing the pressure, and associated individual responsibilities, this can lead to lower productivity and thus representing a significant threat to organisations who employ the use of delegated teamworking, based on managers' misplaced expectations of success.

The phenomenon has been termed social loafing (Latane, Williams & Harkins, 1979) which has been described as a 'social disease' since the resultant reduction in human efficiency leads to lower profits and benefits for all. In the modern workplace, increasing globalisation is forcing organisations to explore different working arrangements for teams that span borders and time zones. The use of these new virtual teams (Jarvenpaa & Leidner, 1999) may potentially exacerbate the threats of social loafing. On top of the challenges virtual teams face such as the difficulties of communication and collaboration, the fact that members cannot actively see each other's work contributions poses a further threat to productivity and makes conflict susceptible. One of the potential reasons for social loafing is the belief other members are working less hard (Latane, Williams & Harkins, 1979), hence in a virtual team environment where there is a lack of transparency individuals may exert even less effort than in a traditional team. To solve this, managers must make sure there is excellent communication between team members, whilst simultaneously liaising between individual members themselves to be aware fully of any issues. Therefore, the use of a virtual team may result in the use of more resources with little to no gain in productivity, proving a great threat to organisations applying teamwork without careful consideration.

Answers online at: https://study.sagepub.com/hopkinsandreid

YOUR CHAPTER TAKEAWAY

Critical evaluation Checklist

✓(tick when completed)

Use the following checklist to critically evaluate a text or your own writing.

Have I ...

- ◯ deemed the source relevant and necessary?
- ◯ ensured it fits my research question/thesis/problem statement?
- ◯ considered what it will add to my assignment?
- ◯ ensured my sources are in the right place?
- ◯ considered how the source will fit with the overall paragraph and assignment structure?
- ◯ identified what each source will be used for in my work?
- ◯ evaluated each source?
- ◯ linked sources together logically and effectively?
- ◯ ensured the sources are collected together around themes or arguments, supporters and critics, to build a detailed response?
- ◯ asserted and maintained my stance and voice throughout?
- ◯ provided sufficient sources to support my ideas?
- ◯ evaluated the sources and identified strengths and limitations?
- ◯ provided sufficient evidence to support and justify my conclusions?
- ◯ provided a thorough, logical and evidence-based, critical response to the assignment question?

Your one takeaway

....

....

....

PART 3
PRESENTATIONS, SPEAKING AND LISTENING SKILLS

The big picture

During your studies, you are likely to be assessed on your spoken communication skills in a range of ways, including giving individual presentations, giving group presentations, and participating and contributing to seminars. The skills involved in being an effective spoken communicator, particularly through giving successful presentations, are not just useful during your time as a student. They are also valuable skills to have after you have completed your studies. Many employers select candidates through processes that may involve giving a short presentation.

Building confidence early on in your academic career will set you up for success in many future contexts. This Part will help you gain these skills and provide guidance on how to prepare, plan and write successful presentations and how to build your seminar skills.

Skills you'll learn

This Part will provide you with a practical, easy-to-use skills toolkit to help you get started with preparing for giving presentations and seminar contributions. By following this step-by-step approach you will be able to:

- plan and prepare for a presentation or seminar
- develop skills for delivering presentations successfully
- contribute effectively in seminars
- develop an efficient strategy for listening and note-taking.

These skills will help you to elevate your work from secondary level (e.g. A level) to university level.

YOUR PROGRESS

CHAPTER ELEVEN

Giving Effective Presentations

CHAPTER DASHBOARD

YOUR PROGRESS

Your objectives list:

 Follow a step-by-step process to successfully plan, structure and deliver a presentation

 Adopt effective presentation techniques and materials

 Improve your confidence during a presentation

min   max

'There are two types of speakers: those who get nervous and those who are liars.'

– Mark Twain

My three presentation skills goals:

1 ....

2 ....

3 ....

What your tutor is looking for

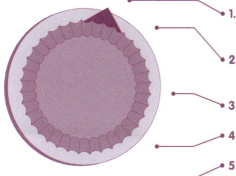

1. A confidently delivered, well-structured, and interesting presentation
2. Effective verbal communication of ideas
3. Appropriate style
4. Effective use of visuals (if appropriate)
5. Delivered within the allocated time

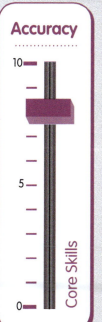

Accuracy

10

5

0

Core Skills

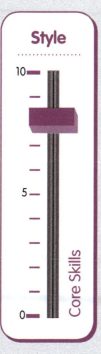

Style

10

5

0

Core Skills

Clarity

10

5

0

Core Skills

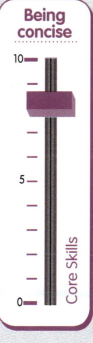

Being concise

10

5

0

Core Skills

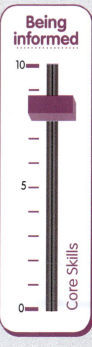

Being informed

10

5

0

Core Skills

WATCH OUT FOR:

Be prepared, practise and time your talk so that you are confident of both content and timing

Diagnostic
What makes a good presentation?

The best way to identify what makes a good presentation is to watch good presenters and analyse what makes them so good. Go online and have a look at the short video and answer the following questions:

1. Does the speaker provide an introduction?

2. How does he engage the audience at the outset?

3. How often does the speaker pause for a few seconds?

4. How often does the speaker refer to his notes? Does this detract from the success of the presentation?

5. What body language is used? Is it positive or negative in its effect?

For feedback on your score, go online at:
https://study.sagepub.com/hopkinsandreid

n the course of your studies, it is likely that you will be required to give presentations to your tutors and classmates. You may have to present on your own, or as
part of a group. They may form part of seminar activities or as stand-alone assessments. Giving a presentation can be a nerve-racking experience.

It is vital, therefore that you develop effective presentation skills; from preparation
through to delivery, to build your confidence, improve your competence, and
achieve high marks in your assignments.

This chapter will provide you with the tools to plan, prepare and deliver an effective, interesting and successful presentation. It will highlight key features and
conventions, and show you how to incorporate these in your talk, and offer strategies for dealing with nerves, building confidence, and what to do when things
don't go according to plan.

THE THREE STAGES OF A PRESENTATION

There are three key stages you need to go through to ensure your presentation is
as good as it can be: **preparation**, **delivery** and **reflection**. In other words, you need to
prepare your presentation *before* you give it, you need to ensure that during your
presentation you are effective, and you need to look back and learn from the experience *after* you have given it.

Stage 1: Before the presentation

Understanding the task: What does your tutor want you to do?

Before you begin preparation on your presentation it is vital to understand exactly
what your tutor wants you to do. This requires careful scrutiny of the instructions
and guidelines, and analysis of the task set.

Analysing assignment instructions and marking criteria

Assignment instructions are usually provided with a range of details to guide you.
Your tutor will often specify the topic of the presentation (although this may also
often be a subject of your choice). Other information that is useful to know includes:

- length of talk
- suggested presentation formats such as Prezi or PowerPoint
- number of slides
- marking criteria.

Table 11.1 is an example of the sort of marking criteria used for presentations by tutors
at UK universities.

Table 11.1 Example of presentation marking scheme

	F 0–19	P 20–39	S 40–49	G 50–59	VG 60–69	Ex 70–79	O 80–100
Content							
Information is clear, accurate and appropriate	☐	☐	☐	☐	☐	☐	☐
Topic is well-researched and where appropriate reference to literature is made	☐	☐	☐	☐	☐	☐	☐
Structure of presentation is logical	☐	☐	☐	☐	☐	☐	☐
The message is easy to follow and in the appropriate style	☐	☐	☐	☐	☐	☐	☐
Where appropriate clear description of findings is made	☐	☐	☐	☐	☐	☐	☐
Clear conclusions are drawn	☐	☐	☐	☐	☐	☐	☐
Delivery	F	P	S	G	VG	Ex	O
Presenter speaks clearly at a good pace	☐	☐	☐	☐	☐	☐	☐
Timing appropriate	☐	☐	☐	☐	☐	☐	☐
Varied tone of voice and pauses used effectively	☐	☐	☐	☐	☐	☐	☐
Body language used to good effect	☐	☐	☐	☐	☐	☐	☐
Eye contact made with the audience	☐	☐	☐	☐	☐	☐	☐
Slides and/or other visuals	F	P	S	G	VG	Ex	O
Attractive visuals	☐	☐	☐	☐	☐	☐	☐
Information on slides supports message appropriately	☐	☐	☐	☐	☐	☐	☐
Accurate information, easy to follow, with no errors	☐	☐	☐	☐	☐	☐	☐
Total mark	☐	☐	☐	☐	☐	☐	☐

Key: F = Fail; P = Poor; S = Satisfactory; G= Good; VG = Very Good; Ex = Excellent; O = Outstanding
Please note the weightings are **not** equal for different aspects of the work.

Researching your topic

You need to ensure that your presentation is well-informed and includes academic rigour, just as you do when you write an essay or other assignment. This means you need to read a lot, and only then consider what your main points will be.

Look at these notes made by a student preparing a presentation with the following title:

What impact does tourism have on the local economy of Bath?

Notes

1 **Key words for search:**

tourism AND economy

Bath AND tourism

2 **Sources found:**

Office for National Statistics (ONS)

WTTC Economic Impact of Tourism

www.tourismeconomics

The Economics of Tourism, M. Stabler, 2009

The Social Impacts of Tourism, A Case Study of Bath, UK, Haley, Snaith and Miller, 2004

3 **Key findings:**

Tourism – day, weekend or longer term?

Facilities required – hotels, restaurants, transport, things to do

Employment opportunities – hotels, restaurants, transport, things to do

Contribution to economy in general

The Bath story – how long has it been a tourist destination (Roman?, Georgians?, Victorians?, now?)

Statistics that show impact of tourism on local employment?

Statistics that show impact on local environment

i.e. good and bad issues relating to tourism in Bath.

Planning the content

Your presentation will not be very long – usually a presentation as part of an assessed course will be between 10 and 20 minutes long, and in a group presentation you may only have up to five minutes of the whole. This means you have to select the main, most important points you want to get across.

- Consider your audience. What do they already know? What do you want them to know at the end of the presentation?
- Think of your presentation as a tour on a sightseeing bus. There is a starting point and a finishing point, with key landmarks that help you understand the place you are visiting.
- You choose your tour dependent on how much time you have, with short tours only having time to visit the most significant sights.

Organisation and structure

A presentation is just like any other formal means of communication, and needs an introduction, a main body and a conclusion. It is, therefore, the same shape as the fishbone skeleton we saw earlier in Chapter 1.

You've identified the main points. These are the bones of the skeleton. You need to add the flesh. Then consider your introduction.

The introduction

The introduction is where you succeed (or fail) in getting your audience's attention. If you don't grab their attention in the first couple of minutes, you will find it hard to get their attention back!

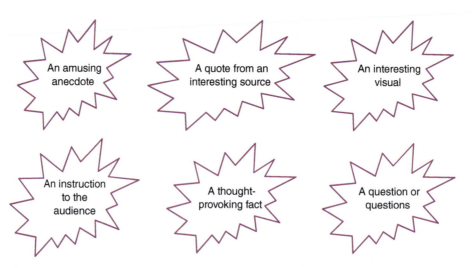

Figure 11.1   Grabbing the audience's attention

How to grab the audience's attention

There are several different techniques for engaging your audience at the outset as shown in Figure 11.1.

These act as a 'hook' to catch the attention of your audience.

Task 1

Read the following transcript of the introduction to a presentation given by a group of engineering students titled *New Materials in the Construction Industry*. What is the 'hook' and which of the above techniques is used to achieve the hook?

> Our presentation is on the topic of new materials in the construction industry, and we are going to focus our attention on one new material in particular. First, I want to show you something. (shows black and white photo of an old bamboo hut in Philippines) How old do you think this building is? (pauses) Well, this picture is over one hundred years old. However, despite bamboo being a very old construction material, we are going to demonstrate how it is now considered a cutting-edge material that architects and engineers are excited about. In this talk we will describe the history of the use of bamboo in construction, and then focus on the reasons for it becoming an important choice of construction material today. We hope to show you that something that has been used since ancient times has a very promising future as a modern construction material, due, amongst other things, to its versatility and strength. Our talk will last 15 minutes and we will invite questions at the end.

....

....

....

Answers online at: https://study.sagepub.com/hopkinsandreid

What else needs to be included in your introduction?

A good introduction that successfully engages your audience is likely to include information that fulfils the following functions:

- general introduction to the topic
- the hook, where the speaker engages the audience's attention and makes them 'sit up and listen'
- more detailed information on the topic
- an outline of the talk
- a reason why the audience should listen, i.e. the purpose of the talk.

YOUR TURN

Task 2

Using the same transcript of an introduction as in Task 1, highlight which sentences are used to achieve the five functions given above. (NB They may not appear in the same order as that given above.) You have already identified the hook!

> *Our* presentation is on the topic of new materials in the construction industry, and we are going to focus our attention on one new material in particular. First I want to show you something. (shows black and white photo of an old bamboo hut in Philippines) How old do you think this building is? (pauses) Well, this picture is over one hundred years old. However, despite bamboo being a very old construction material, we are going to demonstrate how it is now considered a cutting-edge material that architects and engineers are excited about. In this talk we will describe the history of the use of bamboo in construction, and then focus on the reasons for it becoming an important choice of construction material today. We hope to show you that something that has been used since ancient times has a very promising future as a modern construction material, due, amongst other things, to its versatility and strength. Our talk will last 15 minutes and we will invite questions at the end.

1 ....

2 ....

3 ....

4 ....

5 ....

→ **Answers online at: https://study.sagepub.com/hopkinsandreid**

TIP

Timing

Your introduction should generally be no longer than 10–15% of the total time of your talk (so for a 15 minute talk, your introduction should take up no more than two minutes).

The body of the talk

Just as you have done in your essays, your talk needs to be organised into sections that are logically ordered and link clearly with each other. The number of separate sections you have will depend on:

- the topic
- the length of the talk
- your overall purpose.

For the talk introduced in Tasks 1 and 2, the group included the following sections:

1. The history of bamboo use in the construction industry.
2. Characteristics and qualities of bamboo.
3. How it is being used today and why.
4. Conclusion.

The conclusion

Your conclusion is very important. It is the last thing the audience hear so you want it to have an impact. A conclusion usually includes the following stages:

- A signal to the audience that you are concluding the talk. For example, with signpost words and phrases such as: *To conclude …, In conclusion …, So, as a summary …, We have talked about …, We have shown …*
- A summary of the main points.
- A final thought/point/question to leave the audience thinking and interested.

YOUR TURN

Task 3

Identify the three parts to the conclusion to the talk about bamboo.

So, to conclude, we can see that bamboo is a versatile and flexible building material that has many advantages over more recent commonly-used materials such as steel and wood. It is cheap, can be used in an incredible variety of ways, and due to its fast growth, is sustainable. We wonder if this material will be the 'go to' building material in the future. We are not trying to bamboozle you – we are telling the truth about bamboo!

1 ....

2 ....

3 ....

Answers online at: https://study.sagepub.com/hopkinsandreid

TIP

Timing

Your conclusion should generally be no longer than 5–10% of the total time of your talk (so for a 15 minute talk, your conclusion should take up no more than 1.5 minutes).

Preparing visual content

Most presentations include some sort of visual support, usually in the form of slides (for example, PowerPoint or Prezi). Visual support can be useful for providing the audience with the main points you are making, for providing a variety of focus for the audience (i.e. they can look at the slides instead of only looking at you), and for helping to engage the audience. However, poorly used visuals can have a negative effect on your talk, so it is important that you prepare them carefully and wisely. Here are some useful rules to follow:

- Make sure all visuals follow a uniform style (e.g. logos or design are the same for each slide or other visual).
- Include 'white space' – in other words keep the information on your slides clear and to a minimum.
- Data should be large enough for the audience to see (about 22 pt with a clear font such as Arial).
- Consider how to make your slides attractive – avoid clashing colours.
- Avoid colour-blind combinations such as red and green or different shades of the same colour (e.g. dark blue and light blue).
- State your aims on a slide at the outset.
- Proofread for errors (typos, grammar …).
- Make sure bullet points are consistent in style (e.g. capital letter at the beginning of each bullet or not, punctuation or not, etc.).

YOUR TURN

Task 4

Identify problems with each of the following slides (Figures 11.2–11.4).

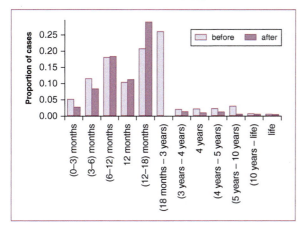

Figure 11.2 Identify the problems – slide 1

1 ....
2 ....

Initial comparison of the bands of custodial sentence lengths reveal no change in severity from the pre- to post-riots period. As shown in Figure 1, the proportion of sentences longer than three years went down in the post-riots period, however, so did sentences shorter than six months, with only the bands encompassing more than six months to three years going up. Hence, it is difficult to identify a net effect attributable to the riots.

Figure 11.3 Identify the problems – slide 2

1 ....
2 ....

Bruglary rates

Key points:

- The custodial rate, for cases of robbary remains stable across 2011

- the custodial rates for offence of commercial burglary is higher after august than before.

- An aggregate increase in sentence severity following the riots.

Figure 11.4 Identify the problems – slide 3

1 ....
2 ....

Source of information for all slides: http://journals.sagepub.com.ezproxy1.bath.ac.uk/doi/full/10.1177/1748895816671167

 Answers online at: https://study.sagepub.com/hopkinsandreid

Preparing notes, cue cards or memory aids

You may see some advice that suggests that you should memorise the first couple of sentences of your talk, as this will help you get off to a confident start. Whilst getting off to a confident start is exactly what you should be aiming for, memorising the words may not be the best way. More important is to be absolutely clear about what you want to say, and practise and practise. This way, you will probably say the opening sentences in the same way each time you practise, but you will not sound as if you are reciting a memorised talk.

Most people feel more confident if they have notes to use as prompts. Notes can be written on numbered cards to move through as you speak. Using paper is fine, but if you are nervous, paper can give away shaking hands! Alternatively, print out your slides and add written cues to remind you of what you want to say.

Many skilful speakers use notes. It is not a problem to pause and look at these to aid your memory. However, what *is* a problem is if you *read* from your notes. Reading from written notes will make your voice sound unnatural, encourages a monotone, and is likely to send your audience to sleep!

Figure 11.5 shows a possible process you can go through to prepare your notes.

Giving a group presentation

At university, you are often asked to do your presentation in groups. This has the advantage of shared responsibility, so it may be a little less nerve-wracking. However, it has its challenges too. Your tutor will be checking to see that you have worked together well as a team, and that you are all contributing equally. They do not want to see any 'lone wolves' (i.e. people that have clearly prepared their part of the presentation without consulting the rest of the group), or any 'free riders' (i.e. people who just present the work the rest of the group have done). Your final

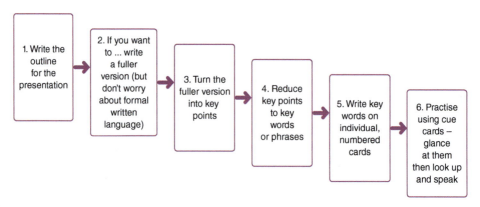

Figure 11.5 Flow chart for the presentation process

1. Meet to discuss the task. Decide what to do before you meet again. For example, all of you should probably do some preliminary research to get an overview of the topic.

2. Meet again (physically or through social media) now that you all have some understanding of the topic. Divide the talk into 'chunks' or sections and allocate roles (who will focus on what section).

3. Do your research. Write notes of main points you identify that will need to be included in your talk.

4. Meet again. Run through the ideas identified by each team member. Agree a structure, order of information and who will be starting and ending the talk, etc.

5. Prepare your notes, practise your part, prepare visuals.

6. Meet again to practise. Ensure everyone's section flows smoothly from the previous section, and the slides are uniform. Review content, reflect and adapt. Practise again. And again!

The coiled spring analogy – the longer the spring is and the more coils it has, the more energetic and full of bounce it is. So for you, the more preparation and practice you do, the more full of energy and 'ready to go' you will be.

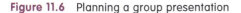

Figure 11.6 Planning a group presentation

mark may be a combination of a group mark and an individual mark, with the group mark usually being for the content of the whole presentation, and the individual mark for your own presentation style.

To maximise your group's chances of a high mark, you need to discuss the instructions together and make a plan of how you will proceed. Starting early is the key! Figure 11.6 gives a possible route.

Stage 2: During the presentation

By the time you come to deliver your presentation you will have practised it many times. You will know what it is you want your audience to learn, and you will have prepared how you will get this to happen. You now need to concentrate on the delivery. For an effective delivery, you need to consider:

- the language you use
- your body language
- pace and timing
- your voice
- how to deal with nerves
- how to deal with questions
- what to do if things go wrong.

The language you use

Your delivery needs to be clear, and this means using language that everyone understands.

YOUR TURN

Task 5

Look at the short sample from a presentation. What is wrong with the language used?

When a Central Bank generates new money electronically so that liquid assets such as government bonds, and stocks can be purchased, it is called Quantitative Easing. Quantitative Easing is an unconventional financial policy which is implemented when the government desires to escalate the quantity of money spent by the private sector in the economy so that inflation is restored to the level that is required.

....

....

....

Now compare with a more natural version

> Quantitative Easing (or QE) is something Central Banks do when they want to return inflation to a more normal rate during times of economic crisis. They will have tried more conventional things to stabilise prices and maintain economic growth, but if these fail, they need to do something a bit unconventional, and this is where QE comes in. So, the Central Bank creates new money, usually electronically, and then this money is used to buy assets such as government bonds. By doing this, they hope to encourage spending in the private sector, so that the inflation rate returns to the desired rate.

Answers online at: https://study.sagepub.com/hopkinsandreid

Notice how this is longer than the previous, more written-like version. Natural spoken language is less 'dense' than written language, using more words to say the same thing, and often including repetition of ideas. It should also include words that a general audience can understand. In a presentation this is important because:

- it allows the listener more time to process the key information
- it does not overload the listener.

Be careful with jargon. Only use jargon that you know the entire audience will understand. The best presentations are usually low on jargon, and include clear definitions of important terms.

Avoiding waffle

When we are nervous, we sometimes find ourselves speaking too much and including unnecessary or meaningless information. In other words, nerves can make us waffle. This is a distraction for the listener and can make your talk boring, so you need to try to avoid it. First you need to be able to identify it.

Task 6

What waffle can be cut from this transcript of a sample from a presentation? Cross out any sections that you think can be removed.

There have been real changes to the English language since the advent of mobile and other electronic devices. There are so many of these nowadays. People may have a mobile phone, a lap top, a tablet and a desktop computer, to name just a few. I have all of those things and so do most of my friends. Anyway, since we started using these devices to communicate, corresponding adaptations to our language have developed. Things that we call 'textspeak', and that were originally only used in text messages have

(Continued)

(Continued)

recently joined the language as spoken forms. I'm talking about things like lol, and omg, and other less polite forms. I use these all the time, and I think my parents find it quite annoying, but that's just a generation thing, I guess. So, the question linguists ask is, is this new vocabulary that evolved to help with written, real time communication, enhancing the language or is it having a negative effect?

Answers online at: https://study.sagepub.com/hopkinsandreid

In order to reduce the amount of waffle in your talk, you need to first be aware that you are doing it. To do this you need to *listen* to yourself. Try recording yourself when you practise. If you find that you are prone to waffle, you now need to take action to reduce it. Try the following things:

- Actively listen and monitor what you are saying.
- When you notice that you have started to waffle, stop.
- Restate the point you were making, concisely.
- Look at your notes for the next key point you need to make and continue with your talk.

Don't say things like 'Oh, I'm sorry, I'm waffling', as you don't want to draw attention to it!

Signposting language

When you write, your reader is guided through the different sections by features such as headings, sub-headings and paragraphs. In a presentation, you need to signpost the sections verbally.

YOUR TURN

Task 7

For each sample from four different presentations below, identify the signpost words or phrases, and state which section of the talk they are likely to be from.

1. In this presentation, we are going to discuss the Michelson Morley experiment of 1887, and we hope to show how this experiment paved the way for Einstein to make his theory of relativity.

2. I will start by defining what is meant by the commonly used term, psychopath, then Alex will discuss some well-known examples. Laura will then go on to talk about how this personality disorder correlates with offending and criminal activity.

3. As Erin has just said, there are several reasons for these figures to be questioned.

4. To sum up, we have explained how we designed our balsa wood bridge and what we have learnt from this experiment to help us understand forces.

···

···

···

···

 Answers online at: https://study.sagepub.com/hopkinsandreid

Table 11.2 includes a range of different words and expressions that can be used to signpost different parts of your talk.

Table 11.2 Signposting words and expressions

Function of signposting language	Examples
Providing an overview in your introduction	*In this talk, I am/we are going to discuss …*
	Today, I want to discuss …
	This presentation will provide information about …
Previewing/sequencing main points in your introduction	*First I/we will talk about …, I/we will then go on to … and then finally I/we will demonstrate …*
	The first thing I/we want to talk about is…, and then …, finishing with …
	I'm/we're going to talk about … as well as … and show that…
Indicating a change in topic	*First, I/we want to explain …*
	Now I/we will look at …
	This leads us on to the next point…
	So, we have seen that …
	The next thing I/we want to talk about is …
	Moving on from this, …
	I want to turn now to …
Transitioning between speakers	*Thank you, Amy. Now, I'm going to …*
	As we have just heard in Paulo's section…
	As Zhou has just described …
	Maisie is now going to tell you about …
	I'll hand over to Jack now to talk about …
Using examples	*So let's have a look at an example, …*
	Here's an example to show you what I mean …
	For instance, …
	To understand this better, we need an example, such as …

(Continued)

Table 11.2 (Continued)

Function of signposting language	Examples
Indicating visual support	*This slide shows us …*
	You can see from this graph that …
	If you have a look here at this data table, you can see …
	I'm going to show you an image/a diagram/a figure to help clarify what I'm saying.
	Here's a graph that will help to explain …
Restating something in other words for clarity	*So, what I mean by that is …*
	I mean …
	In other words, …
	That is to say …
	So what this means is …
Bringing to a conclusion	*To conclude, …*
	To sum up, …
	In conclusion, …
	As a summary, …
	So, we have shown/demonstrated that …
Asking for questions	*We are happy to answer any questions.*
	So, does anyone have any questions?
	And we have now got time for some questions.
	Any questions?

Your body language

As we have seen, a presentation is not just a spoken version of a written paper. There are several things that contribute to the differences between a presentation and a written piece of academic work. One of these is the fact that you are present, communicating your ideas in real time, in front of an audience. This means that the audience will be looking at you, so you need to ensure that your body language is being used to enhance your message rather than distract from it.

Appropriate body language and facial expressions play an important role in contributing to a successful presentation. They help you to:

- engage your audience
- support the information you are giving
- emphasise a point
- appear believable and reliable as a source of information.

But, body language can also have a negative effect. Table 11.3 shows some clear do's and don'ts for body language.

Table 11.3 Body language do's and don'ts

Do's	Don'ts
• Use open body language, such as open arms, head up	• Don't use closed body language such as crossed arms or legs, or your head looking down
• Use gestures to support or emphasise a point (e.g. hand gestures to show that something is important)	• Don't use distracting gestures such as playing with your hair, or pulling your sleeves up and then down again, or waving your arms around too much
• Smile in appropriate places – this will help to engage your audience	• Don't look miserable, even if you feel it! If you look miserable, your audience will feel miserable too
• Make eye contact with the audience (if you find this hard, focus on the person's forehead – they won't know you are not looking in their eyes)	• Don't look down or to the side for long periods
• Move around if you want, but use your movements to enhance your message (not distract from it)	• Don't move around inappropriately. In other words, don't fidget

Pace and timing

The timing of your talk is important and you will be assessed on how well you keep to the time limit. To ensure that you do this, you will need to practise your talk many times, timing it each time.

When we are nervous, waffle is not the only hazard. Nerves can also make us talk too fast. If we talk too fast, we may leave our audience behind, as they will need time to process the new information.

If you think you are talking too fast, there are some things you can do:

- At the end of the sentence, stop, count to three in your head, and then start speaking again.
- Build pauses into your talk at the practice stage and write the places where a pause is useful on your cue cards or notes.
- Repeat a point that you think you made too quickly. Say something like: *in other words, ...* or *What I mean is ...* and then restate using different words.

Your voice

A presentation is a performance and this means, that just like an actor in a play, you have to use your voice to communicate effectively. Audiences respond best to a speaker who is engaging, both in terms of their body language *and* their tone of voice. Your voice needs to be varied in tone, rather than monotone. A speaker whose voice is unvarying in tone is likely to send the audience to sleep! A speaker who sounds enthusiastic about the subject is likely to gain the audience's attention.

What you need to do:

- Project your voice so that the audience can hear. The audience will soon give up if they can't actually hear what you are saying.
- Vary the pitch by beginning new information at a higher tone than the end of the previous sentence.
- Stress important words and phrases by raising the pitch slightly and increasing the volume.
- Pause for effect at key points.
- Practise with someone you trust, who can give you feedback.
- Keep reminding yourself that you are telling the audience something interesting – this will help to make you sound enthusiastic.

What you mustn't do:

- Never read aloud from written notes. This encourages a monotonous and unnatural delivery.
- Don't memorise big chunks, as this will not sound natural and it will be obvious if you suddenly go blank.
- Never talk into your shoes. You need to be audible!
- Don't sound bored and look as if you lack confidence. If you appear bored, your audience will be bored too!

Dealing with nerves

Look at the quote from Mark Twain at the beginning of this chapter. Everyone is nervous before they give a presentation. The important thing is to pretend that you are not! Remember your audience want you to succeed and are on your side.

Here are some top terrors and some tips for dealing with them.

Terror 1

I feel terrified before I start a presentation and want to run away.

Tip: Before you start, imagine you are feeling confident. Visualise the talk with you as a successful speaker, and imagine your audience being positive and responsive. This technique is called 'visualisation' and is used by coaches with athletes and other sports performers. Also practise breathing deeply and focus on your breathing to calm you down.

Terror 2

I shake when I stand in front of an audience.

Tip: This will not be noticeable to the audience unless you are holding something. If you have cue cards, make sure they are made of card not paper.

Terror 3

I find it hard to make eye contact with people in the audience.

Tip: Look just above the eyes, at the forehead. It is not noticeable that you are not actually looking at their eyes, but it's not as unnerving for you.

Terror 4

I get nervous when talking to big audiences.

Tip: Look at the audience and find one or two friendly nodding, smiling faces. Keep looking back at them to help you feel positive.

Terror 5

I worry I will forget what I want to say.

Tip: Follow the guidelines earlier in this chapter for writing cue cards or notes. Refer to your notes and then look up and speak. Many very experienced speakers refer to notes during their talks.

Terror 6

I'm worried that I'll talk too fast.

Tip: Pause at the end of key points, and at the end of sentences, and count to three in your head before starting again.

Dealing with questions

Most presentations include a time for questions (usually at the end). Your tutor and other members of the audience are likely to ask you something. This is something you need to plan for in your preparation stage. Here are some techniques you can use to help you prepare:

1. Predict what you expect to be asked and prepare answers.
2. Ask a friend to listen to your talk (and give you feedback on all aspects) and to ask questions at the end.
3. Ensure you are familiar with information relating to your topic that is not actually covered in your talk.
4. Find some sources that you could direct the audience to that cover the topic in depth.

If someone asks a question you cannot answer it is best to admit that you don't know. However, you can then direct them to a source that may give them the information they seek. This demonstrates that you know *where* to find the information, even if you do not have it at your fingertips.

Table 11.4 Common presentation problems and what to do

Common problem	What you can do
Your PowerPoint presentation won't open	• Make sure that you have printed out the slides before your talk. With a small group you can display the paper copies for essential visuals
	• With a larger group, you may be able to draw figures and graphs on the board, and write key points up
	• Anticipate this problem beforehand, and think of ways to get the information across without the visuals
	• Prepare a handout for the audience that includes key images
	• Check the room beforehand to ensure the equipment is working and find out in advance who to contact if you need help
One member of your group does not turn up	• Ensure at the planning stage that you all know what each person is going to say
	• Explain the situation to your tutor, and tell the audience that you will be talking on behalf of someone else (the audience will be on your side)
One member of your group talks about the information you had planned to talk about	• This should not happen, as you should have worked together to agree who says what. However, if it does happen, you can reiterate the importance of the information and say something like:
	• *Paul has just told you about ..., and because it is such an important part of our presentation, I'm going to tell you some more about it ...*
One member of your group does not say something that is essential for you to follow on from	• Introduce the missing information before you start your part of the talk
You realise that you only have five minutes left but you have a lot to say	• Make 'timing decisions' on the spot. What is essential information and what can be cut? You may need to skip a couple of key points, but keep the ones that are crucial to your argument
	Say something like:
	I haven't got much time left, so I'll just focus on the most important points
Someone asks a question but you don't understand what they mean	• You can ask them to repeat it, but this is only possible once. If you still don't understand, you may need to cover it up by saying something like:
	If I've understood your question correctly, I think ...
	You can then talk about something you know about! The audience will not notice

When things go wrong

Sometimes things go wrong. A good presenter will have strategies for dealing with disaster!

Table 11.4 gives common problems and what to do about them.

Remember that every good presenter has had bad experiences in the past. They are how we learn and what makes us better presenters in the end!

Presentation of a poster

A poster presentation is a bit different from other kinds of presentations. They usually involve a number of posters displayed in a large open space. You usually stand next to your poster and the audience wander around stopping to look at posters they have an interest in.

Your role is to be able to answer any questions the readers of your poster may have.

You should prepare for this presentation by ensuring that you are familiar with all the information you have included in the poster, and the details that you have *not* included. People generally want to know more about the subject than is given in the poster.

This is usually quite easy, as a poster is often a presentation of your own research, or your own experiences. You are the expert and the audience is interested.

Stage 3: After the presentation
Revisit, review, revise and reflect

Once you have delivered your presentation and recovered from the experience, it is important to learn from it. This means you need to reflect on what went well and why, and what went less well and why.

If you have to give the same presentation again you may wish to make some changes to the content. However, the most important thing is to review the whole process you have been through and consider how you can improve things for next time.

Ask yourself the following questions and make notes to inform your next presentation.

1. What did I like about my presentation?
2. Why was it successful?
3. What was less successful and why?
4. What do I want to do differently next time?
5. What do I need to do to achieve this?

YOUR TURN

Task 8

Read one student's reflection on her performance. What advice would you give her for next time?

> My presentation didn't go very well. I wasn't as nervous as I thought I was going to be, but when I came to talk, I seemed to forget everything I wanted to say and it all came out a bit garbled. I seemed to get through everything really quickly – much quicker than I expected. When I looked at the audience, they seemed bored, and that really put me off and affected my confidence.

....

....

....

This reflection indicates that the student had not prepared sufficiently. She should now plan how to improve next time by ensuring she plans her talk, practises her talk, times her talk, prepares cue cards to act as prompts, and practises appearing enthusiastic and confident.

Peer learning and support

Reflection can also involve analysing and evaluating our peers' performances. We learn from others as well as from ourselves.

As you watch your peers give their presentations think about what you can learn from them. What makes them successful? What are they doing that is less successful? How would you advise them?

TIP

Peer learning

Practising your presentations with a group of friends you trust is a good way to develop confidence and learn from each other. Give each other feedback on delivery, content and visual materials. Evaluating our friends' presentations helps develop our awareness of what contributes to successful presentations.

YOUR CHAPTER TAKEAWAY

Presentations process Checklist

✓ (tick when completed)

Have I ...

- ( ) planned my presentation and researched the topic?

- ( ) understood the topic sufficiently?

- ( ) identified the key points?

- ( ) written notes using key words only?

- ( ) practised many times?

- ( ) ensured that I can say my part without needing to read from notes, but instead referring to cue cards?

- ( ) considered my body language?

- ( ) timed it?

Your one takeaway

....

....

YOUR PROGRESS

CHAPTER TWELVE

Communicating in Seminars

CHAPTER DASHBOARD

YOUR PROGRESS

Your objectives list:

 Understand the purpose of seminars, and types of activities to expect

 Develop skills to participate and contribute effectively in seminars

 Build confidence

min   max

'Don't raise your voice, improve your argument.'

– Desmond Tutu

My three seminar goals:

1. ....

2. ....

3. ....

What your tutor is looking for

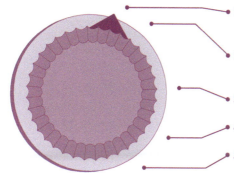

1. Engagement with pre-seminar tasks and reading

2. Participation and meaningful contributions

3. Open-minded approach

4. Rational and measured discussion

5. Use of non-judgemental language when talking about your peers and their opinions

Accuracy

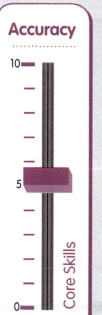

10

5

0

Core Skills

Style

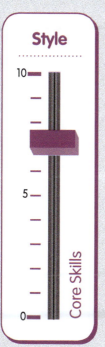

10

5

0

Core Skills

Clarity

10

5

0

Core Skills

Being concise

10

5

0

Core Skills

Being informed

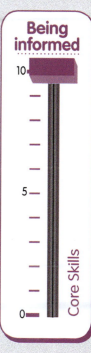

10

5

0

Core Skills

WATCH OUT FOR:

The keys to successful seminars are preparation and participation. Make sure that you engage fully with tasks, your colleagues and your tutor

Diagnostic
Are you ready for a seminar?

On a scale of 1–5, where 1 = not confident and 5 = very confident, rate your responses to the following statements.

How confident are you...

Speaking in a group

Starting a sentence with 'I think' or 'in my opinion'

Beginning a sentence with 'I disagree'

Asking a question of the lecturer

Being in a debate

Giving a short presentation to open a discussion

Discussing a topic in a pair

Sharing your opinion with a whole seminar group

Sharing the floor with other speakers

Asking questions of other students

Giving constructive criticism to your peers

Actively listening to other students

Including other students in your discussion

Using inclusive, collaborative language

How did you score?

For feedback on your score, go online at:
https://study.sagepub.com/hopkinsandreid

L earning on your university course takes a variety of forms. A large amount of time is spent in independent study, but the taught element is usually provided through lectures, seminars, workshops and labs. You may be assessed on how well you participate and communicate in seminar activities.

A seminar is small group learning. You work with a tutor and a small group of your peers to investigate and explore a topic in depth. It can involve pre- and post-seminar tasks and activities such as pre-readings, and follow-up assignments and assessments.

This chapter will help you get the most out of your seminars. It will highlight the key features of typical seminar scenarios and tasks, so that you understand clearly what your tutor expects you to do. It will help you to plan and prepare for your seminars, so that you are able to contribute effectively with confidence and authority.

WHAT IS A SEMINAR FOR?

The main purpose of a seminar is to encourage critical discussion and argument between students and members of academic staff in order to:

- increase understanding of a topic or concept (often presented in a lecture)
- develop communication skills in an academic context (including *active, supportive listening*)
- develop problem-solving skills
- encourage peer learning and support (not only in terms of content, but also in terms of skills)
- increase confidence in small group discussions.

In addition, by participating in seminars and having to *talk about* content from your course, information becomes more memorable, and learning is enhanced.

Seminars may or may not be assessed. Your tutors are looking for evidence of understanding and collaborative learning. Unlike lectures, in a seminar it is a requirement for each student to contribute in some way.

We saw that presentations require planning and preparation, and this is true for seminars too. Also, like presentations, you will become more skilled at participating effectively with practice and with reflection.

PREPARING FOR A SEMINAR

Whatever the format of your seminar, you are likely to be set pre-seminar work. This may involve a set of questions that you need to investigate, a specific paper you need to read, or a topic that you are asked to research. As we saw above, you may need to prepare a presentation on the topic.

Preparation for your seminar will be similar to preparation for an essay, although now you are preparing in order to:

- answer specific and focused questions
- be ready to *talk about* specific issues
- find out what you don't understand so that you can ask for clarification from your tutor
- work as a group to understand issues in more depth.

The process in Figure 12.1 should be helpful.

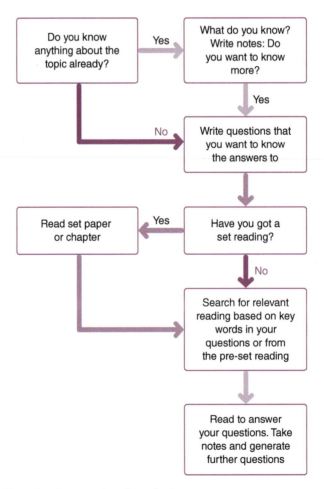

Figure 12.1 Preparing for a seminar flow chart

In this preparation stage, you need to ensure that you do the following:

- Understand the pre-seminar tasks and goals by analysis of the instructions and aims.
- Follow the process outlined in Figure 12.1 to ensure that you have read sufficiently.
- Identify problems and issues.
- Consider all sides of an argument.
- Develop your position.
- Support your position with evidence (so you need to move beyond your opinion, and find evidence in the literature that supports your ideas).

You will now feel confident that you can contribute to the seminar effectively.

DURING THE SEMINAR

Participating fully in a seminar can be difficult the first time. You will probably not know all of the other participants or the tutor very well, you may not have done anything like this before, and you may feel worried that you will make a fool of yourself. All of these feelings are completely normal, but if you go into the seminar well prepared, both on the topic, and on *how* to interact and communicate effectively, you will feel more confident and you are likely to be more successful.

YOUR TURN

Task 1

Read the transcript from a seminar (below) and answer the following questions.

1. Who starts the seminar off and how?

....

....

2. Do you think the language the students use when talking to each other is threatening or non-threatening?

....

....

(Continued)

(Continued)

3. Find and circle examples of language that is collaborative or inclusive.

....

....

Seminar transcript

Tutor	OK, so now that we've all introduced ourselves, let's get started. Let me remind you of the instructions for this seminar: I asked you to read this paper by Cheung and research answers to the questions on this slide. In small groups of four I'd like you to discuss your answers to these questions for about five to ten minutes and then we'll share key ideas as a whole group.
	...
Student A	Shall I start us off? I don't know if anyone else found this, but I found the paper quite hard to follow in a few places, and I wasn't sure about question 1 and how to relate what I read to what Dr Lee said in the lecture. So, that said, my initial thoughts about Scott's research on the issue of shy performativity are that it seems quite obvious in a way, if you know what I mean. I mean, the research didn't seem to throw up anything particularly exciting. Do you know what I mean? Did anyone else think this, or is it just me? (laughs)
Student B	I think I get what you mean. I wrote down a few questions when I was reading the paper, because I didn't think I could really find the answer to the question of what the real purpose of the research was. I mean, it's interesting that performers sometimes self identify as 'shy', when most people would be surprised to hear that, but I wasn't sure exactly what the author was trying to find out, and even after reading the whole paper I still wasn't clear. What do you all think about it? What did she actually gain from the research?
Student C	I guess you are both saying something really interesting that I hadn't even thought about actually. I really enjoyed the paper – it was easy to relate to the ideas, especially because she talked about famous performers who say they are shy. I thought the findings were interesting in that different participants had different views of which part of their 'self' was the authentic 'them', and I liked the way the author used the terms 'I' and 'me' to distinguish the two personas. I did have some questions, however, about the research methods, so I suppose I'm going on to question 2 here. Shall we move on to question 2 now, or does anyone want to talk about question 1 a bit more?
Student D	Oh, can I just say something about question 1 and the point of the study? I just wanted to say that I didn't really notice the 'obviousness' of the research when I was reading it, but now that you say that, I can see what you mean. Mind you, I think sometimes it is useful to find out more about something without necessarily having to have an outcome, if you know what I mean. But I think you have made some really good points and I want to reconsider how I felt about the paper now. I do, though, think it was interesting to read about this research having heard Dr Lee talk about Goffman's research into self from way back in 1959. We probably ought to consider this study in the context of Goffman's book. Anyway, sorry, what was it you wanted to say about question 2 and the research methods?
Student C	Well, yeah, I just thought that the sample itself was a bit unreliable – I know this was acknowledged, and I thought it was odd to choose face-to-face interviews as the first way to communicate with people who have identified themselves as shy.

Student B	Yes, I agree about that, but wasn't this discussed by Scott when she talked about the two participants who used email? Don't you think?
Student C	Yes, I know, but I was just surprised that this was the first choice of method. Anyway, I guess it's a minor point. What do you think about the findings – shall we go on to number 3?

Discussion based on the following paper: S. Scott, 'Transitions and transcendence of the self: stage fright and the paradox of shy performativity' *Sociology*, 51(4): 715–31.

 Answers online at: https://study.sagepub.com/hopkinsandreid

THE LANGUAGE FOR SEMINARS

As we have seen, a good seminar discussion involves all participants making a contribution. In order to get the most out of the discussion you need to be an active participant. This means:

- Sharing your ideas: *I don't know if anyone else found this, but I found …; I thought that the sample size was unreliable; I was just surprised that this was the first choice of method.*
- Asking others for their ideas: *Do you know what I mean? Did anyone else think this, or is it just me?; What do you all think about it? What did she actually gain from the research?; Don't you think?*
- Agreeing with others: *I think I get what you mean; Yes, I agree about that…*
- Indicating that you don't have the same view: *I can see what you mean. Mind you, I think sometimes it is useful to find out more about something without necessarily having to have an outcome, if you know what I mean.*
- Accepting someone else's different view: *Yes, I know, but I was just surprised that this was the first choice of method. Anyway, I guess it's a minor point.*
- Showing appreciation of someone's ideas (but not necessarily agreeing!): *I guess you are both saying something really interesting that I hadn't even thought about actually.*
- Asking for clarification when something is not clear: *Anyway, sorry, what was it you wanted to say about question 2 and the research methods?*
- Showing that you are listening, even when you are not directly contributing: do this by nodding and saying 'yes' and 'uhuh' and other noises that show you are listening.

In order to allow for a balanced and successful seminar, it is important not to use negative and judgemental language in response to comments from your peers (although it may be acceptable to use judgemental language about the source/ideas being discussed).

Say: *That's an interesting idea*. Don't say: *That's a stupid idea*.

Use hedging language rather than absolute language to soften your stance:

Say: *I wonder if that's exactly what the author meant*. Don't say: *That's not what the author meant*.

SEMINAR ETIQUETTE

A discussion involves agreement and disagreement. It is not easy to disagree with your peers, and it's important to remember that you are disagreeing with the information they are putting forward rather than with them personally. It is important to be respectful and use positive, constructive language.

A good way to disagree with someone is to use the 'praise sandwich'. In other words, say something positive, state your disagreement, then say something positive again. Compare the following two different ways of disagreeing and the effect that each would have on the speaker:

a. *I don't really agree with that idea.*
b. *I think there are some really valid points in what you say. However, I suppose I think that … I suppose this is similar to the thing you said earlier about …*

Other ways to show disagreement include using questions such as: *Don't you think that may not be as effective as …?*; *Do you think there may be another way to look at it?* But remember to place these questions within a praise sandwich!

Sometimes you may have a very strong view on something and find yourself getting angry with other people in the group. It is important that a seminar does not become a battlefield! In these situations, you should remain quiet and breathe deeply, and *think* before you speak. If you want to challenge what someone has said, consider carefully how to do so without sounding confrontational.

YOUR TURN

Task 2

The following contributions are unacceptable and are likely to lead to conflict in the seminar. Rephrase the contributions to be more appropriate.

1. I really don't think that's true. I think you have got the wrong end of the stick completely.

....

2. That kind of view is exactly what I have come to expect from you.

....

3. How can you possibly say such a thing?

....

4. None of the rest of us agree with what you have just said.

....

→ **Answers online at: https://study.sagepub.com/hopkinsandreid**

INTERCULTURAL AWARENESS

Universities are international places and you will very likely be sharing your seminars with people from a wide range of cultural backgrounds. How we communicate with others can be influenced by our culture and this can lead to differences in the way we interact. If we want to benefit from the knowledge, expertise and experience of our peers, we will need to appreciate these differences. In order to appreciate them, however, we need to recognise them.

 **YOUR TURN**

Task 3

Look at the three following interactions which include some kind of misunderstanding caused by cultural differences. What is the underlying misunderstanding?

1. Student A: Shopping habits have changed so much recently, and most people do a lot of their shopping online. Interestingly, people still seem to like the Argos approach though.

   Student B: Oh, was there some kind of special way that the ancient Greeks bought their goods?

   ....
   ....

2. I have done all the talking. Why doesn't anyone else say anything?

   ....
   ....

(Continued)

(Continued)

3. Student A: I understand what you mean about that, but don't you think it might be possible to look at it a different way?

   Student B: Oh, no I don't.

....

....

 Answers online at: https://study.sagepub.com/hopkinsandreid

By noticing differences, and accepting them, we will be more successful in our interactions.

AFTER YOUR SEMINAR

Take time to reflect on what you have learnt in your seminar. You may want to:

- add or make changes to notes from your lectures as a result of the seminar
- think about how to help others in the group feel more comfortable next time
- think about how to participate more next time
- prepare more thoroughly next time.

Remember, seminars are there for you to increase your understanding of a topic, and it is a great opportunity for you to clarify and extend your knowledge.

YOUR CHAPTER TAKEAWAY

Seminar process Checklist

✓ (tick when completed)

Have I ...

○ researched the question(s) set?

○ considered my stance on the problem or topic?

○ prepared key things I want to say?

○ considered what sort of language to use in a seminar?

○ ensured I'm able to be collaborative in my language use?

○ considered how to disagree with someone's view without appearing judgemental or confrontational?

Your one takeaway

....

....

YOUR PROGRESS

CHAPTER THIRTEEN

Working in Groups

YOUR PROGRESS

CHAPTER DASHBOARD

Your objectives list:

 Develop effective group and team-working strategies to build group cohesion

 Produce high-quality group assignments

 Adopt effective methods of dealing with group conflict and issues

min   max

'Talent wins games, but teamwork and intelligence wins championships.'

– Michael Jordan

My three goals for group work:

1 ....

2 ....

3 ....

What your tutor is looking for

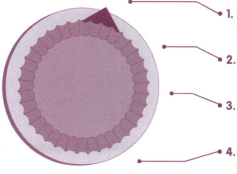

1. Participation of all group members

2. A cohesive, well-organised team

3. Evidence of collaboration in course work

4. A coherent, unified product (report, presentation, etc.)

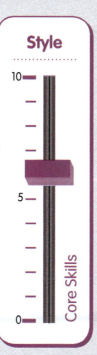

Accuracy

10

5

0

Core Skills

Style

10

5

0

Core Skills

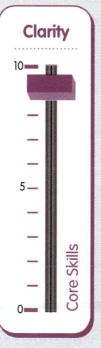

Clarity

10

5

0

Core Skills

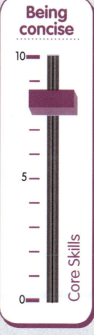

Being concise

10

5

0

Core Skills

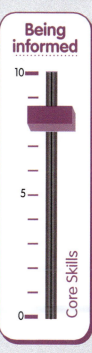

Being informed

10

5

0

Core Skills

WATCH OUT FOR:

Group work often carries one final mark, shared by the group. It is vital therefore that you build a strong and motivated team from the start

Diagnostic
How comfortable are you working in a group?

Write down some of the advantages and challenges of working in groups.

Advantages	Challenges

Group and team working is a core activity at university. Group activities and assignments may include presentations, group report writing, and problem-solving tasks and challenges. Sometimes you will be able to choose your own groups, but your tutor may set the groups. So you will often be working with people you don't know. There are many advantages to working, sharing and learning with and from others, but it also presents a number of challenges.

Group assignment marks may be shared equally amongst your team, so it is vital that you work as a cohesive and fully functioning unit to ensure optimal results and success in the task or assignment.

This chapter will show you how to make a positive contribution to group work. It will provide you with strategies to help you establish and maintain effective group cohesion when working on group tasks and assignments. It will also provide you with tips on how to avoid inter-group conflict and issues.

THE FIVE STEPS TO EFFECTIVE GROUP WORKING

Step 1: Get to know each other

There is a tendency for newly formed groups to jump straight into the task. However, before you start to think about your task or project, you need to work on inter-personal dynamics and group cohesion.

Find out about each other's interests, strengths and preferences when it comes to academic work. For example, one member might be an enthusiastic researcher with a finely tuned critical eye, and another may be a highly skilled writer and editor. You will need to make sure that members are doing the right tasks, so that you can draw on these individual strengths for the project or task.

Step 2: Establish ground rules

Before you begin your group task, you need to agree on an open and fair set of group rules, which set clear guidelines on what is expected of each member and shared obligations and responsibilities.

This is important as it can help to minimise future conflict and ensure every member pulls their weight and contributes equally.

Below is a checklist of key areas to consider. You can use this to formulate your own set of ground rules. You may even wish to draw up a ground rules agreement (see Figure 13.1).

Group Members:	Signature:	Date:

We, the above group members, agree to abide by the following ground rules

We agree to …

1.

2.

3.

4.

5.

6.

7.

8.

9.

10.

Figure 13.1   Ground rules agreement template

Effective group working guidelines

Share your shared goals:

- Identify and respect the shared goals of the group.
- Help each other understand and adhere to the shared goals.

Respect the views of others:

- Everyone's opinions count.
- Give people time to consider and respond.
- Listen before you speak.
- Be honest.
- Be fair and respectful.
- Discuss don't argue – ideas should be supported and justified with reasons.
- Try to reach agreement rather than agree to differ.
- Stay calm at all times.
- Be open to 'out of the box' ideas.

Share responsibilities and workloads:

- All tasks should be shared equally.
- Foster an 'all for one' attitude.
- Don't take over or sit back and let others do all the work.
- Establish a contingency backup for sick or absent members, and be ready to step up.
- Be ready to switch roles and task allocations if necessary.
- Be flexible.
- If you need help, ask for it, don't be proud or ashamed!

Be prepared for meetings:

- All members must ensure that they are prepared and ready for meetings (e.g. bring content updates, suggestions and ideas, and prepare some troubleshooting questions and/or answers).

Cooperate and compromise:

- Be willing to cooperate and support each other's ideas.
- Be ready to compromise your own ideas for the benefit of the group.
- Be willing to admit mistakes and that you may be wrong.
- Vote on any disagreements to ensure fairness.
- Be ready to help when a member is struggling.
- Be generous and inspiring – it is not an internal competition!

Meet deadlines and keep records:

- Set clear and attainable interim targets and deadlines – and stick to them.
- Meet regularly to check progress and troubleshoot issues.
- Appoint a task manager to check everyone is working to target.
- Everyone should attend meetings on time.
- Everyone should complete tasks (within the agreed timescale.)
- Limit non-group talk.
- Nominate a chairperson – to manage meetings and ensure fairness.
- Nominate a group 'administrator' who will email the group, maintain agendas and take notes on group decisions, etc.

And finally …

Respect the ground rules agreement:

- Decide and agree together on your ground rules and stick to them.
- Set clear guidelines on what to do if a member breaks the rules set by the group.

Step 3: Allocate roles and tasks

Identify the strengths and personal preferences of group members and set roles and tasks accordingly. This will ensure that you are working to maximum efficiency and effectiveness. But you should also be prepared to switch roles and tasks if the project is floundering. Group working is also an opportunity to develop new skills, and you may find that you discover talents and abilities you didn't think you had. So be open-minded and ready to try new things.

Roles may include:

- Team leader/task manager
  - Level of power can be set by the group – the group leader may be responsible for final decisions, ensuring group cohesion, rules are adhered to, targets are met by everyone, and the group is motivated.

- Chairperson
  - Ensures meetings run smoothly and to time, that everyone has a voice, and that discussions don't escalate into conflict. The Chair can also summarise decisions taken for accurate records and set the agenda for the next meeting.

- Editor
  - Collects and collates project materials from group members; for example, different sections of a report, or presentation slides. The editor may check the continuity of work, ensure a unified style and approach, look for gaps and issues, check the length and edit if necessary, and proofread for spelling and grammar mistakes.

- Researcher
  - Investigates and finds relevant and appropriate materials – academic texts, examples, cases, statistics and other evidence to support the project.
- Administrator
  - Maintains accurate records of meetings: agendas, minutes, actions and decisions, progress checks, etc. They are also responsible for communicating all important information to the group.

Step 4: Plan your project and set interim targets

When planning your group project or task, unpack activities and break each down into a number of manageable sub-tasks with **achievable** interim targets. Each team member should have individual targets that they should meet within an agreed deadline. It is vital that your targets are measured and achievable. Be realistic and don't under-estimate how long or how difficult tasks can be.

This logical and practical approach will help your group stay focused and motivated, and reduce inter-group conflict, as progress will be measurable, the submission deadline attainable, and the project will seem less daunting and stressful.

Step 5: Meet regularly to check progress and unity of the project

Regular meetings will ensure that group cohesion is maintained, and everyone is up-to-date and on track. Meetings provide opportunities to share ideas, solve problems, support each other and help curb worries and anxieties.

You should also meet regularly to practise group presentations and provide verbal feedback on written assignments.

TIP

Group working

Email messages can be easily misinterpreted and misunderstood, and this can quickly escalate into full blown conflict. Avoid long discussions, negotiations or decision-making on email. Such things should always be done face-to-face.

GROUP WORKING SCENARIOS

YOUR TURN

Task 1

What would you do to resolve the issue(s) in the following group working scenarios?

Scenario A

One member of your group seems to be dominating group discussions and not allowing anyone else to express their opinions or suggestions about the assignment. What do you do?

....

....

Scenario B

Two members of your group have fallen out over a personal issue, and as a consequence, the project is running behind schedule and you may fail to submit on time. What do you do?

....

....

Scenario C

Everyone in your group seems to have different ideas about how to answer the assignment question, and as a consequence, you haven't reached any decisions about how to proceed. The project is now running behind schedule and you may fail to submit on time. What do you do?

....

....

Scenario D

One member of your group is not contributing his share of work to the project and his non-participation has led to delays. As a consequence, you may fail to submit on time or submit sub-standard work. What do you do?

....

....

Scenario E

One of your team is ill and is unlikely to recover in time to contribute to the project. To add to your problems, she was working on the main part of the project and it is difficult to ask her for the work she has done so far. What do you do?

....

....

Scenario F

You seem to be the only member of the group who is working on the project, and your team mates are contributing very little or nothing to the assignment. What do you do?

....

....

Scenario G

Three out of four of the group members are from the same country. During meetings, they discuss the project in their own language and you don't understand what they're saying. What do you do?

....

....

→ **Answers online at: https://study.sagepub.com/hopkinsandreid**

YOUR CHAPTER TAKEAWAY

Effective group working <u>Checklist</u>

✓ (tick when completed)

Have I ...

○ considered how to ensure the group understands and agrees on shared goals?

○ thought how to use language that is inclusive and co-operative?

○ checked that the group has shared the tasks equally or logically?

○ understood how to foster a team-working atmosphere?

○ understood how to avoid conflict and ensure we all work together well?

○ considered how to disagree with someone's view without appearing judgemental or confrontational?

○ ensured that I am ready to be flexible if necessary?

○ considered how to compromise for the sake of the group's co-operation?

Your one takeaway

YOUR PROGRESS

CHAPTER FOURTEEN

Getting the Most Out of Lectures

CHAPTER DASHBOARD

YOUR PROGRESS

Your objectives list:

 Develop effective listening and note-taking methods in lectures

 Practise active listening and participate fully in the lecture experience

 Prioritise and target the most relevant content and ideas during lectures

 Use lectures as a springboard for further research

min　　　max

'There's a lot of difference between listening and hearing.'

– G.K. Chesterton

My three goals:

1 ....

2 ....

3 ....

What your tutor is looking for

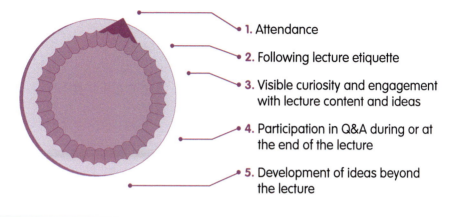

1. Attendance
2. Following lecture etiquette
3. Visible curiosity and engagement with lecture content and ideas
4. Participation in Q&A during or at the end of the lecture
5. Development of ideas beyond the lecture

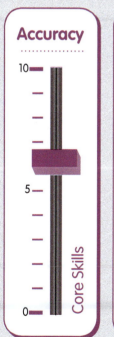

Accuracy

10

5

0

Core Skills

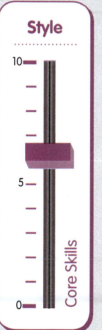

Style

10

5

0

Core Skills

Clarity

10

5

0

Core Skills

Being concise

10

5

0

Core Skills

Being informed

10

5

0

Core Skills

WATCH OUT FOR:

Write down questions as you listen, to keep your brain awake and alert, and follow up in Q&A or post-lecture

Diagnostic
Can you get the most out of lectures?

Go online and listen to the extract from a lecture, titled 'What English Do You Speak?', and take notes on the key ideas.

....

....

....

....

Did you find this task difficult? Why?

....

....

....

....

For feedback on your score, go online at:
https://study.sagepub.com/hopkinsandreid

L ectures and talks form a central part of most academic degrees. The lecture format is normally approximately one hour in length, though longer lectures, sometimes up to three hours (with breaks!) are becoming increasingly common.

Listening and taking notes in lectures presents a number of challenges; for example, how to take notes effectively, maintaining focus and attention over an extended period, deciding which parts of the lecture are useful and important. It is vital, therefore that you develop efficient and effective methods of dealing with the lectures in order to make the most of the experience.

This chapter will provide you with an essential toolkit for effective listening and note-taking in lectures. We will introduce different note-taking styles and systems to help you choose and/or adapt your own preferred method. We will also include strategies for prioritising your listening and dealing with the challenges presented by the lecture experience, and show you how to build your knowledge beyond the lecture.

STYLES OF LECTURES

In UK universities, there are essentially three styles of lecture.

- Public speaker style
  - In this style, the lecturer reads from a script or sounds as though she/he is reading from a script.

- Interactive style
  - The lecturer uses informal conversational language, may use some brief notes and encourages a workshop-style approach in the lecture with lots of interaction and 'audience participation'.

- Presentation style
  - The lecturer uses visual technology such as PowerPoint or videos to support the content. The lecturer may provide notes and there may be opportunities for some interaction during or at the end of the presentation. In other words, sometimes you may have to sit and listen intensely for long periods, or be prepared to take part and get involved in hands-on discussion and activities with your classmates and lecturers.

ACTIVE LISTENING

Trying to concentrate and listen for a long period of time is difficult. It is easy for your brain to switch off and drift away into distracting thoughts or (waking) sleep. It is crucial, therefore that you develop strategies to keep your brain awake, attentive and active.

Listening for a purpose

The first thing you need to do, before you do anything else, is establish your purpose for listening. What is it you need or want from the lecture and for what specific reasons are you listening? This will help you to establish and maintain an active approach throughout.

Your purpose may include:

- to develop a critical understanding of the topic
- to help you ask critical questions about the topic
- to kick start your research
- to help you understand related reading materials
- to help you pass your examinations.

Above all, your purpose for listening should *always* be aimed at helping you complete your assignments and improve your scores, and you need to prioritise this when preparing for your lectures.

TIP

Active listening

Some research on the lecturer may also reveal their views and position on a number of key issues. This may help you shape the topics, focus, and your critical response in assignments which deal directly with her/his area of interest, which can help you achieve a higher mark.

BEFORE THE LECTURE

Predicting lecture content

When preparing for a lecture, you need to predict content and generate pre-lecture research questions.

Start by looking for:

- The lecturer profile
  - You can find this either in your course handbook or on the university website. This will give you vital information about the lecturer's area of expertise and their publishing record.

- Lecture content
  - Titles and brief synopses of lectures are usually found in your course handbook. This may provide you with some key terms as well as the main focus of the lecture.

- Course reading lists: (a) essential and (b) further/recommended
  - Again, this is usually included in your handbook. There may also be specific pre-reading tasks listed for each lecture.

YOUR TURN

Task 1

Examine the following lecture title and synopsis and generate six to eight pre-lecture research questions.

Lecture 2: Segmentation, targeting and positioning

When attempting to meet customer needs and demands, marketers often focus on three strategies: segmentation, targeting and positioning. This lecture will outline the methods and processes used by marketers to incorporate each of the three strategies into a marketing plan, and explore the benefits and drawbacks of this approach, using some up-to-date examples from the business world.

Essential reading

Jones, T.R. (1987) Discovering product differentiation and market segmentation in the marketing strategies of modern business enterprises. *Marketing Now*, 20(2), pp. 12–16.

Questions:

1 ....

2 ....

3 ....

4 ....

5 ....

6 ....

Your questions should look something like these:

1. What is segmentation, targeting and positioning?
2. Are they important? Why/why not?
3. Do these strategies help companies meet the needs of their customers? Why/why not?
4. How do these strategies work?
5. Which companies have used or are using these strategies?
6. Who is Jones and why do I have to read this article? (Why is it so old?)
7. What is product differentiation?
8. Are there any other, alternative approaches?

Reading for a purpose (see also Chapter 9, Reading skills)

You can now use these questions to explore and investigate the topic in more detail. Start with the essential reading and then using key words check out related texts on your course reading lists, Google Scholar, etc.

TIP

Research reading

It is likely that your research will initiate more questions for further research and/or to take with you to the lecture.

Developing your listening and note-taking skills

Before you start to attend lectures, you will find it useful to practise listening and note-taking skills. By exploring different methods and techniques, you will be able to develop your own style of note-taking, and improve the speed and efficiency of your approach. There is a wealth of recorded lecture material available online to help you prepare for your first lecture.

Here are a few suggestions:

Ted.com	hbr.org	bbc.co.uk/learningzone
Tedx.com	youtube.com	bath.ac.uk/podcasts
podcasts.ox.ac.uk	sms.cam.ac.uk	lse.ac.uk/iq

DURING THE LECTURE

Choosing a suitable note-taking method

There are various methods you can use to take notes in lectures. Which type you choose will depend on a number of factors including your learning style and personal preference, and the content and style of the lecture. You may find that you like to stick to the same method, or you prefer to mix and match from lecture to lecture, or even within the same session.

Linear (or classic)

In this approach, information is organised chronologically with headings, key words/simplified notes and vocabulary listed vertically on the page. Bullets, abbreviations, symbols and language shortcuts can be used to simplify the note-taking process.

Example

Figure 14.1 gives an example.

27/9

Module: Ted   Title: 4 Ways That Sound   J. Treasure
                    Affects Us

Intro: MOST SOUND = Accidental

                  ∴ We Suppress Sounds

                  Unconscions Relationship.

How Sound Affects Us

1. Physiological

            → Hormones

                – E.g. Fight Or Flight

                – Hairs Rise On The Back Of Neck

            → Breathing

                – Soothing & Horror Music

            → Heart Rate   ↑?

                – Bird Song

            → Brain Waves

                – Affect Elec Signals

2. Psychological

            → Emotional → Sad Or Scary Music

3. Cognitive

            → Small Bandwidth= Limited Processing?

                Eg. Open Plan Office = 1/3 ↓ Productive

4. Behaviour

            → Move Away From Horrible Sounds

                +Towards Pleasant Sounds   ↑↓

Four GOLDEN Rules Of Commercial Sound

1. Make It Congruent?

2. "   Appropriate   [?]

3. "   Valuable

4. Test It

Figure 14.1 An example of the linear note-taking method

Pros

- Information is arranged logically and sequentially, so it should capture most of the key information which should be easy to review post-lecture.

Cons

- There is a risk that you try to note down everything that the lecturer says without thinking about the relevance of the information. Consequently, your brain could move from active to passive mode as you work through your list.

Dynamic

The dynamic method is a simplified version of the classic method. Here, key words are listed and details such as definitions, explanations, etc., are added alongside or beneath.

Example

Key Word Heading 1:

Detail

Key Word Heading 2:

Detail

Key Word Heading 3:

Detail

Pros

- This method may help you to focus on the most important elements of the lecture and note down relevant detail.
- It is easier to filter and organise information around key words rather than trying to list everything in order.

Cons

- You may get bogged down in the detail and write too much.

Lecture details in here	
Module: **Title:**	**Lecturer:** **Date:**
AFTER THE LECTURE	**DURING THE LECTURE**
Use this column to highlight:	Use this column to take notes of:
• Key vocabulary/terms	• Main points
• Main ideas	• Diagrams, charts
• Key people	• Lecturer comments
• Equations/formulae	Use bullets, abbreviations, symbols and shortcuts
• Questions about the lecture	**Cornell Method Tip:** You can use the side column to help you recall your notes and revise for examinations – fold the paper and use key words and questions as revision cues.
• Any references and sources mentioned	
AFTER THE LECTURE:	
Summary: Use this box to summarise (in 3–5 sentences) the key points of the lecture. This is helpful for review and revision	

Figure 14.2 Cornell lecture details template

- You may not understand the key words and concepts and find yourself lost very quickly.
- You may focus on the wrong 'key words'.
- Your notes may become a long list of disconnected key words and detail, and you miss the inter-relationships between ideas.
- It is repetitive, so your brain may switch off and you become a passive listener.

Cornell

Information is divided into four sections on the page (Figures 14.2 and 14.3).

Module:	Title:	Lecturer:	Date:

Figure 14.3 Blank Cornell template

Example

Module: TED Title: The 4 Ways Sound Affects Us Lecturer: J. TREASURE Date: 27-9

Unconscious	Intro: Most Sound = Accidental
Relationships	∴ We Suppress Sounds ➡ Become Unconscious Relationship?
What Does This Mean?	How Sound Affects Us
	1 Physiological
Physiological	• Hormones - eg Fight Or Flight
What Happens To Our Hormones?	• Breathing - Soothing Or Horror Music
	• Heart Rate - Bird Song
Why?	• Brain Waves - Affect Elec Signals
Physiological	2 Physiological
	• Emotional Response - Sad Or Scary Music
Examples?	-Industrial Noise
Cognitive	3 Cognitive - Small Bandwidth?
What Does Small Bandwidth Mean?	To Process Info
	E.g. Open Plan Office = 1/3 Less Productive
	4 Behaviour
What Does These Mean?	• Move Away From Horrible Sounds
	• Run Faster (Jogging Music)
⬇	4 Golden Rules Of Commercial Sound
	1 Make It Congruent?
Congruent	2. Make It Appropriate
Appropriate	3. Make It Valuable
Valuable	4. Test It, Test It
Test It	

The 4 Ways Sound Affects Us Are:
Psychologically Physiologically, Cognitively & Behaviourly'
These effects can be used to improve retail exp.

Figure 14.4 Lecture details example

Figure 14.4 gives an example.

Pros

- Information is arranged logically and compartmentalised to help with review and recall.
- The layout makes it easy to categorise ideas.
- You can use your questions to research the topic in more depth after the lecture.
- It can be adapted to incorporate critical analysis and evaluation in your notes (see also Chapter 9, Reading skills).

Cons

- You may feel that there are too many sections to complete, and find this confusing. If so, try simplifying the layout with one column instead of two.
- It may be difficult to recall or extract the most important key words or ideas from your original notes after the lecture. You may find that you can add information to the left and right columns during the lecture as you go along, and supplement this when you review later.
- It is difficult to use this method if you are taking notes on a laptop or tablet.

Slide notes

Your tutor may provide you with her/his lecture slides as handouts before the session. You can use these to take notes alongside each slide (Figure 14.5).

Pros

- Information is ordered around each slide and you can supplement it with additional detail/questions, etc.
- Good for review and revision.

Cons

- Your lecturer may not provide slide handouts so you can't rely on this method. (She may upload them to your course Virtual Learning Environment after the lecture but that won't help you on the day.)
- You may miss key points in the talk by focusing too much on the PowerPoint slides.
- As you work slowly through the slides your brain may start to switch off and you become a passive listener.

Spidergrams and mind maps

These are visual methods of organising notes, using circles and lines to connect main ideas and important details (Figure 14.6). Drawings, doodles and colour coding can also be included to help organise key ideas.

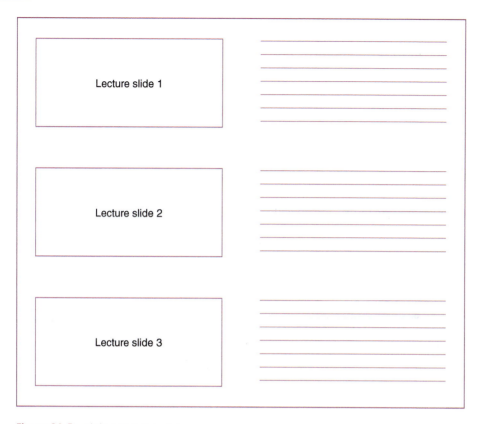

Figure 14.5   Slide notes template

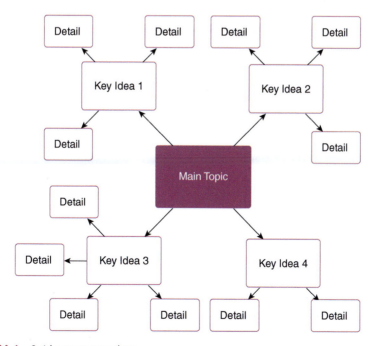

Figure 14.6   Spidergram template

Example

Figure 14.7 gives an example.

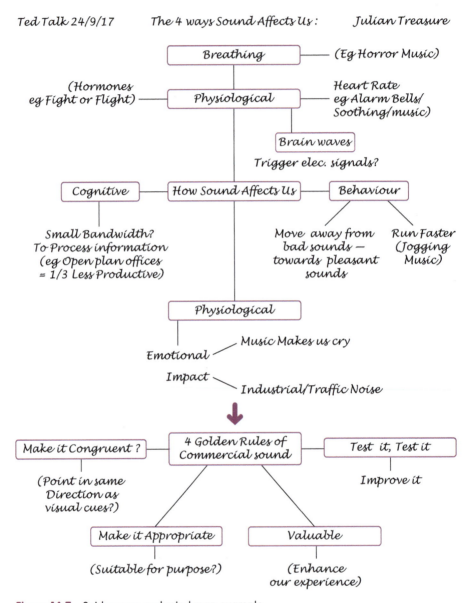

Figure 14.7 Spidergram and mind map example

Pros

- Helpful for visual thinkers/learners.
- Pinpoints and organises most important information.
- Good for exam revision.

Cons

- May not suit non-visual learners.
- Can be difficult to produce during the lecture – information may not be presented in a format that can be easily represented in this format.

Using laptops and tablets

Some tutors allow students to use laptops or tablets to take notes during lectures. But while these devices have some advantages over a conventional pen and paper, there are also some major pitfalls.

Pros

- Typing can be faster than writing by hand, so it may be easier to capture information.
- Files and folders provide a ready-made filing system to organise your notes.
- A variety of apps can provide different note-taking systems that may be suited to your learning style.
- Note-taking apps and software can be used to improve your notes.

& or +	and/in addition
$\therefore$	therefore
$\because$	because
c.	approximately/about/around
→	leads to
↓	decreasing/going down/falling
↑	increasing/rising
=	equal to/the same as
≠	not equal to/not the same as
info	information
>	greater than
<	less than

Figure 14.8 Conventional abbreviations and symbols

Cons

- Some lecturers ban all technology from their lectures – they don't like to speak to a sea of laptop lids!
- As you type, your brain may disengage from the content and you become a passive note-taker.
- As typing is faster, you may write too much or include irrelevant information.
- It may not suit visual learners.
- There are too many distractions – it may be too tempting to check your email or social media.

Using abbreviations, symbols, bullets and codes

Replacing words and phrases with a code system will improve the efficiency of your note-taking. You can use conventional abbreviations (Figure 14.8) or develop your own system – *but don't forget what they mean!*

Signposts and cue words

Signpost cues can help you identify key information, such as:

- The structure and different sections of the lecture – 'So let's start ...' 'Now, that brings me to ...'
- Definitions –'This can be defined as ...'
- Processes – 'The first step ... the second ...'
- Summaries and conclusions – 'So to wrap up ...' 'The key points of my lecture today are ...'
- Examples and evidence – 'One example of this ...' 'You can see from the diagram that ...'
- Connectors linking ideas – 'Therefore ...' 'and this shows that ...' 'It can be seen that ...'
- References – 'I would recommend you read ...' Your lecturer may point to core and additional readings to help you dig deeper into the topic and answer some of the questions you may have.
- Key information – 'This is an important/critical/crucial/essential point ...'
- Stress and repetition – can indicate an important point.
- Moving on or drilling down – 'So let's now consider ...' 'Another aspect of this is ...'

Recording the lecture

You could use your phone or a voice recorder to record the lecture. Most lectures are now recorded either in audio or video format, but you should never rely on this. Sit near the front so that the microphone will record the lecturer and not your classmates!

BUT

If you decide to record lectures you **MUST** seek permission from every lecturer that you wish to record. Otherwise, you are stealing their thoughts and ideas!

Pros

- This a a fail-safe option if the lecture is not recorded by your department.
- It will give you the opportunity to review after the lecture and fill in the gaps in your notes.
- You will have a record of the lecture that you can return to again and again.

Cons

- You need permission from all lecturers – some may say no!
- You might over-rely on the recorder and your brain switches off – never replace notes with recordings!
- The technology may fail.
- The lecture may be recorded anyway (always check with your tutor).

AFTER THE LECTURE
Re-visit, review and reflect

It is important to read through your notes **as soon as possible** after the lecture. If you leave it for more than two or three days, you may not understand your notes and/or lose the thread of the lecture.

Ask yourself:

- Can I read my notes (and understand my shorthand!)?
- Have I noted down all the main (or relevant) points, and key words/concepts?
- Have I noted down important sources and recommended readings?
- Do I need to add more information to ensure I'll understand at a later date?
- Which parts are relevant to up and coming assignment(s)?
- How do ideas link together?
- Is there anything I still don't understand?
- What questions still need to be answered?
- Do I have any more questions?
- How does this lecture link to the next lecture?
- Can I summarise the key points in three or four sentences?

Post-lecture reading

Further reading will help you fill in the gaps in your understanding of the topic and provide answers to some (or all) of the questions you still need to answer. It will also help you build on the knowledge foundation that the lecture has given you.

Sharing your notes and exchanging ideas

Work together with your classmates to fill in any gaps, find answers to questions, and share questions, thoughts and ideas about the lecture. You could also test each other on how much you can remember and explain. This is particularly useful for exam revision.

Reviewing the lecture recording

Many lectures are now recorded (as audio or video format – with or without accompanying slides), which are made available shortly after the lecture. You can use the recorded version to:

- fill in any gaps
- help answer your list of questions
- re-visit difficult concepts and ideas
- check the accuracy of any references that you noted down
- Re-visit any tasks or activities you worked through during the lecture.

REMEMBER: The lecture recording is an **aid** to your note-taking and should **never** replace it. **Live** lectures will always give you so much more than the recorded version.

THE TEN GOLDEN RULES OF LECTURE ETIQUETTE

And finally …

There are a few simple rules of lecture etiquette that your tutors will expect you to follow during their lectures.

Remember: your lecturers will be marking your assignments and helping you with course work, so it is always best to avoid antagonising them!

Here are our top ten:

1. Arrive on time – don't interrupt the lecture.
2. Don't speak while the lecturer is speaking (unless she/he asks you to).
3. Don't eat or drink during the lecture.
4. Don't fall asleep (your lecturer can see you!).

5. Don't check your phone/social media or send texts or emails during the lecture (some lecturers will ask you to switch off your mobiles).
6. Don't leave half way through.
7. Don't interrupt the lecturer – unless she/he gives you permission to do this.
8. Ask for permission to record the lecture.
9. Check that laptop and tablet use is OK (some lecturers don't mind, but many hate it!).
10. Don't start packing up your books before the end of the lecture.

YOUR CHAPTER TAKEAWAY

Listening and note-taking in lectures
✓ Checklist
(tick when completed)

Before

Have I ...

- ◯ researched the lecture topic?
- ◯ completed pre-lecture tasks and reading?
- ◯ predicted content, key terms and vocabulary?
- ◯ devised questions to investigate during the lecture?
- ◯ selected a preferred note-taking method?
- ◯ practised note-taking?

During

- ◯ considered what abbreviations I will use?
- ◯ answered any of my questions?

- ◯ written any more questions?
- ◯ focused on the most relevant and useful content and ideas?

After

- ◯ reviewed, revised and developed my notes as soon as possible?
- ◯ filled in gaps and omissions?
- ◯ asked more questions – extended my research reading beyond the lecture?
- ◯ shared notes and ideas with colleagues?
- ◯ made further links to course work and assignments?
- ◯ developed an effective catalogue system to retrieve notes quickly and easily?

Your one takeaway

....

....

INDEX